God's Plan for the Ages

The Mature Wisdom of the Cross

By Trevor Maddison

Title: God's Plan for the Ages
Format eBook-ePub
ISBN: 978-0-9931711-3-0

Published By Trevor Maddison Publishing

Copyright © Trevor Maddison

Contact: trevor.maddison@revcad.com

Synopsis

God's Plan for the Ages is a book of reasoned theology of the Christian faith, written largely without theological language, exploring God's plan and purpose for the world and for the ages, including the whole reason, purpose and wisdom of the cross of Christ.

The apostle Paul speaks of treasures of wisdom and knowledge that can greatly enrich our spiritual life. This explores the whole purpose of this world, written from the heart of a mature Christian who was just compelled to share his riches with those with whom he shares a common destiny. The book draws on all that this one has gathered over the years from theology, experience, life and revelation. It also fully utilises our God given faculty of reason and logic, which sometimes gets a bad press, but is an integral part of who and what we are as a man or woman, made in God's image.

The book comes in three distinct parts. The first part is a reasoned and logical examination of ourselves, and the God that made us in his own image. It explores the very nature of God and his purpose in making man at all. It then addresses the very difficult question, often asked by all men, of why God should create a world with such a potential for evil, as we observe, and it offers an explanation of how such a thing can be reconciled with the nature of a loving God. God's ultimate objectives of it all are explored. These answers may not resolve the detail of every circumstance, but they are higher level answers that the author personally declares to have completely satisfied him, and have become a solid foundation of faith that in everything we see in this world, God knows exactly what he is doing, and he has done it in a way that only infinite wisdom could have devised.

Central to this theme are the events of the cross of Christ. Again the apostle Paul gives the game away as he points to the cross as the central event of this age, and all the ages to come. He explicitly tells us that understanding the cross is mature spiritual wisdom, and he reveals his all-consuming desire to go deeper into the truth of it as the very central quest of his life. The book therefore seeks to get to the root of this obsession, based on the premise that if we are not equally as obsessed with it, then we are missing something important.

The second part of the book explores God in another way; from revelation, rather than from logic and reason. God in himself is a manifold, manifold being, as can be seen in both the trinity of Father, Son and Holy Spirit, and in the seven-fold spirit of God revealed in the book of Revelation. This multi-manifold revelation of God is explored creatively to reveal something of how all that man is in his complexities of life and relationships can also be seen in God, in whose image he is made.

The final part of the book is more pragmatic as it relates all of this revelation and understanding to our experience on the ground as we grow in faith towards spiritual maturity. In all of this the heavenly perspective of our experience is offered, whilst it explores the realities of life on the ground. Using many illustrations and stories of real events, the author is often open and candid about himself and the challenges life can bring on both a natural and spiritual level. The result is that the book is not milk, but strong meat, as the author intended, designed with a view to pushing on those who have already reached a certain level of maturity to yet higher levels of understanding that should profoundly enrich their spiritual life in this epic pre-age to the ages of ages to come, that God has planned for us beyond this world.

TABLE OF CONTENTS

Synopsis 4

TABLE OF CONTENTS 7

Preface 15

PART I: *THE THEODICY OF THE CROSS* 21

CHAPTER 1: Introduction 23

CHAPTER 2: God – Goodness, Love & Morality 29

    What is God? 29
    What is Love? 30
    Key: Love and Morality – the Highest Good 31
    The meaning and purpose of life 32
    Definition of the word 'Age' 32
    The value of oneself and others 33
    Moral decision making according to our resources ... 35
    Using God's moral imperative for good 38

CHAPTER 3: The Problem of Evil 41

    Theodicy 42
    Controlling behaviour 44
    The Garden of Eden 46

Eliminating eternal risk 47
The losses incurred by the fall...48
The fall of angels..48

CHAPTER 4: God's Plan for Man 51

Man's environment..51
The importance of faith in creation 51
Was the fall inevitable?..52
Free-will and predestination 53
The value of free-willed beings...55

CHAPTER 5: The Cost of Faith Development............................57

Minimum suffering..57
Present example of God developing faith 60
Universalism and the loving God..61
The ultimate goal...63
Errors of Universalism 64
Eternity – the ages of ages...66
Free will and the doctrine of election..69
Angels and reactions to creation..80
Angels and heavenly bodies 82
A revelation of Christian maturity...83
Angels reaction to the plan..84
Doxology and faith development 87
The anthropological argument for creation.....................................91

CHAPTER 6: Faith, the Foundation of Heaven 93

The symbols of faith in the Bible 93
Faith – the foundational fruit of the Spirit.......................................95
Jesus is the author of faith 97
Faith is the key 99

The place of faith in the kingdom of God 100
The empowerment of man through prayer 101
Recap the progressive argument..102
Faith is the reason for the season (age) 104
Faith in the nature of God...105

CHAPTER 7: The Mystery of the Cross 107

Recap of the plan of creation so far..107
Understanding the mystery of the cross 107
The place of the cross in God's plan of creation 109
The suffering of the cross..112
The importance of the cross 115
The security of faith for all the ages of creation............................118
The eternal testimony of suffering 120

CHAPTER 8: The Incarnation of God in Creation....................123

The Son of God 123
Splendour and sacrifice 126
Did the Son of God change?...131
History from God's perspective 132
The physical dimension..133
The work of creation...134
The manifestation of God...135
What form did the expression take? 137
How can God be spirit? 138
The progression of incarnation 140
What is spirit?..141
Levels of incarnation 142
The manifestation of God in the spiritual domain.........................143
The blood of the Lamb 144
Another eternal testimony – hell 145
The anatomy of man and the death of the soul..............................149

PART II: *THE BEING OF GOD* **153**

CHAPTER 9: Coming Face to Face With God **155**

CHAPTER 10: Clearing the Way for Encounter **163**

    Talk of holy fire 163
    So what is the truth about myself as a born again believer? 164

CHAPTER 11: A Vision of a God Encounter **167**

    A vision of an eagle 167
    Interpretation of the vision 167
    The darkness 168

CHAPTER 12: The Seven Spirits of God **171**

    The seven-fold spirit of God 171
    God the spirit of the Lord 173
    God the spirits of Wisdom, Understanding & Knowledge 174
    God the spirit of Counsel 179
    God the spirit of Power 180
    God the spirit of the Fear of the Lord 181
    The masculine and feminine nature of God 185
    The God of relationship 185
    The eternal family of God 187
    The colour spectrum of the Spirit 188
    The royal procession 193
    The significance of marriage 194
    The vision of the throne 196
    The treasures of heaven 197
    Judgement 199
    Our role in heaven 200
    Our attitude to this present age 205

CHAPTER 13: The Wisdom of the Cross 207

The doctrine of substitution – the problem............................207
The demand for mercy...208
Government and the demands of law 210
What did it take to redeem man with mercy?........................212
Why God is worshipped? 214
The cost of mercy 217

PART III: *THE REFORMATION OF MAN* 221

CHAPTER 14: The Reformation of Man by Spiritual Rebirth .223

Reformation and the Cross 223
God's big plan of creation – review 223
Man's need for reformation..225
Man's reformation to Love...226
Man's reformation of Faith 228
Man's reformation of love by faith 229
Two kinds of faith 230
Transitions of faith 231
The function of law 232
Breaking the union of man with his fallen spirit 235
The place of the cross of Christ in rebirth 237
Summary 238

CHAPTER 15: The History of Spiritual Rebirth and Religion .241

The history of spiritual re-birth 241
Other times, places, peoples, eras and religions....................243
What did Christ bring? 246
Increasing revelation of salvation..248
Sacrifice..250

CHAPTER 16: The Fallen Condition of Man 253

A foundation for studying progressive reform 253
The definition of sinfulness 253
Selfishness 257
Deception 258
Cooperatives 259
Religion 260
The values of heaven 262
Faith and the World 262

CHAPTER 17: The Progressive Reform of Man 265

Why does sin persist? 265
What is a nature? 265
The complexity of redeemed man – two natures 266
How can the old spirit persist? 267
How does Sin control the mind? 269
The process of repentance 271
Practicing the presence 273
Dependence – the hallmark of God's way 275
Dividing true & false doctrines 276
Self-denial 278
Self-deprivation 280
The power of the flesh 282
Mortify the old nature 282
Living naturally by the Spirit 283
Living by Conscience 285
Personal struggles with sin 286
Overcoming – the lie of spiritual compromise 289
Overcoming – through reckoning 290
Overcome – resist the devil 291
Is this just positive thinking? 291
The fruit of the Spirit 292

CHAPTER 18: Living by Grace 299

The attitude to grace 299
Mercy 299
Grace beyond mercy 300
Why do many miss the truth of grace? 302
Grace and the two natures 302
The way out of religion 304
The gospel of the early church 304
Grace is radical 305
Legalism and churches 306
Legalism and Leaders 308
Maturity and identity 310

CHAPTER 19: Overcoming the World 315

By faith 315
Overcoming – the lust of the flesh 315
Overcoming – the lust of the eyes 323
Overcoming – the pride of life 324
Overcoming – The World, the Flesh and the Devil 325

CHAPTER 20: Fire 327

Overcoming 327
The symbol of fire 327
The lake of fire 328
The baptism of fire 329
Shadrach, Meshach and Abednego 330
The fire of revival 330

CHAPTER 21: The Final Chapter 333

The wisdom of the cross 333
Faith, hope and love remain 333
The final victory 333

Heaven is coming 334
The final word 334

EPILOGUE 337

Preface

For many years this book has been developing in my heart and mind, but until now I have always felt the restraint of the Spirit of God when considering the prospect of writing it. In hindsight it is not difficult to see why. Had I written earlier, some of the key thoughts, lessons, and experiences I needed would not have been in place. The book is therefore a product of a long journey of faith that has at times been exciting and exhilarating, and at other times difficult and arduous in the extreme.

The learning behind it was, to some degree, compelled by a deep need to resolve my own inner problems as I was experiencing them as a Christian; something I had not expected when I found Christ at the age of eighteen. I suspected that there was some subtle problem in this 'religion' as it had been passed on to me, and it proved to be so. However my path has not been that of theological seminary. Rather I pursued a career in engineering, science, mathematics, and computer software development, with my beginnings and first 11 years in the roughest environment available; the British coal mines. This career path served to prepare me in many ways. It gave me full exposure to the truth about mankind, and of myself, while at the same time it taught me the intellectual discipline of study and analysis, teaching me to break problems down and clarify ideas until truth emerged from the fog.

Though my studies and career have often taxed my mind to the limit, yet such was the compulsion of my inner need, and the problems I was experiencing as a Christian, that I can say on reflection that my study of the Bible, biblical books, and faith, have taxed me further still. Through books I can look back and say that I have been blessed immensely by the ministry of others, and I always therefore hoped that the time would come to give something back in the same way.

The book begins with a logical and theological examination of God, his character and his purposes in creating what we see before us in this world, though it does so, on the whole, without theological language and jargon. It seeks to answer some of the hard questions that naturally arise and continue to be asked by almost everyone that passes through this world. This may seem like an impossible scope for any book, but I can only reflect on my own feelings about it; that the thoughts I have put forward here have come to profoundly satisfy me, and I hold them with conviction.

My intention in writing the book was not to offer 'milk' but 'strong meat', with a view to enriching those that have already experienced some development in their faith, having already become familiar with the Bible. I have therefore written with a view to pushing the reader on to greater maturity. I have personally benefited greatly from some of the theological treatise' that are available, but many of these documents can be a hard trawl, so my desire was to present some of the ideas that have impacted me most in more contemporary non-theological language.

Having completed the book and let it stand and mature for a while, like ageing wine, I can say I am more than happy with the result. My main reason for saying this is that when I review what I have written I become aware that it has gone beyond myself. I regard that as a main indicator that God was involved in both the decision to write and the process of writing it. I find on reflection that there are parts of it that are both old and new; another indicator, and I can confirm that researching and writing it has been a profound learning experience for me.

The book has naturally been split into three distinct and very different sections, though I must say this is a structure that emerged, and was not originally planned. Each of these sections is very different to the others, so I would encourage any who finds one section difficult to try the others before giving up. Though there is a building argument that advances sequentially through the sections, much benefit can still be gained from reading these sections separately. I find the three sections together make up a kind of trilogy that very broadly corresponds to the trinity; Father, Son and Holy Spirit.

The first section has a theological base, using reason and scripture to examine both man and God with a view to gaining some understanding of God and his character and purpose in creation. This section may appeal to those that have an analytical mind and wish to satisfy their desire for reason on matters of faith. There are many authors that contributed to the development of these thoughts, but one I must mention is the *Systematic Theology* of *Charles G. Finney*, who is acclaimed by some to be America's greatest evangelist. As a lawyer, this work has a highly technical and reasoned approach by application of his legal mind. His thoughts led to the first big personal breakthrough I needed to find my way out of the religious confusion I at one time suffered, though his book is one of the most difficult to read due to the legal format, outdated language, and constant repetition. This book had its limits for me, and raised questions as well as answered them, but it laid a base for what was to follow.

The second section will appeal much more to the creative mind. It draws heavily on the symbols and revelation of scripture to unveil the splendour and magnificence of the being of God; the thing that angels seem to make such a fuss about. This section, with its creative emphasis and expression, corresponds to the Son, through whom all has been created. In this section is much that is, as far as I am aware, new and original material in an examination of the being of God from scripture. It was certainly new for me, and as such it was probably the greatest source of blessing to me in the writing of it.

The last section corresponds to the Spirit in that it brings everything to earth, and shows how everything that precedes it finds its practical application on ground level as we seek to live a life of faith. These truths have now been personally worked out in my life over many years, and as far as I am concerned are proven to be the basis of victorious living. I continue to expectantly chart my way into the outworking of these principles in greater ways, as God leads me on in my faith.

Throughout all these sections the meaning, purpose and mystery of the cross is a constant theme, as it should be, given that the cross is revealed to be the pivotal event of all history. This truth is explored and aligned with the study of God, the world, and mankind, to take our understanding of it to a deeper level.

Together these sections form what I think should be a challenging, but balanced diet. I would strongly recommend that those sections that seem to go against the natural inclinations of the reader should not be quickly set aside, because it is often when we break out of our mould that we learn the most.

One other book I must mention, that has been of profound value to me, is *The Healing Presence* by *Leanne Payne*, and many of her other books have been a profound blessing too, for many reasons. Probably the greatest message this book had for me early in my studies was that although the intellectual mind can present a significant barrier to spiritual progress when used to displace the role of the Spirit, it can nevertheless become a profound asset to faith when it is humbly submitted to God, and if given its right place can greatly enrich our lives in many ways.

Beyond this there are many others; *C.S. Lewis* and *Watchman Nee* were both profoundly influential in their season, but there have been many more that are more obscure that have contributed greatly to my development of faith and maturity as a Christian. I am profoundly grateful for them and their contribution to my life and journey.

I have chosen a level of repetition that may not suit everybody, but is judged to help most to follow the building arguments. I preferred there to be too much than too little so that important points, that become the basis of what follows, are not missed. My hope is that if you find this too much for your taste, that you bear with it as a necessity for some.

It is inevitable that the content of this book will provoke some controversy. As with everything it must all be tested to spiritually discern and divide it. However I would urge the reader not to judge it by contemporary thinking, but to use scripture and the direct appeal to the Spirit of God for discernment. For this reason I have selectively included fairly extensive scripture references in the footer of each page to show the source of all key thoughts.

As the book has been written I have become more acutely aware of certain doctrines that are currently invading what is being called 'the emerging church'. This particularly includes the doctrine of universalism that embraces the idea that all men will be saved. As will become clear through the book, I see this as a significant error, and deviation from the authoritative word; the truth. This doctrine is largely based on humanist thinking that prefers to view man as fundamentally good, rather than as a fallen being that needs reform. To those that embrace these ideas they have the paralysing tendency to take all urgency out of the mission to spread the gospel; an urgency that clearly exists in the scriptures, and that existed for the early Christians, many of whom were martyred for preaching and upholding it. These views often seem to emerge where the church gets into a comfort zone, as it has in many places in the west today. However it is a sobering thought to realise that even in our day, the official figure for martyrdom for the Christian faith still stands at hundreds of thousands per year. That amounts to hundreds of people each day martyred for their faith, even on this day!

In the book I have challenged the ideas of universalism, and I try to address both the good news, and the harsh realities of life. But though I believe this is all soundly based on scripture, I don't expect my thoughts to be universally popular, even among Christians.

However, the challenge to erroneous doctrines is not the primary purpose of the book, but rather to know God better, and to understand him as a God of love despite the significant challenges we have of interpreting the world in which we live in terms of his good nature. My hope is that these challenges are answered to the same level of satisfaction I have found for myself, and therefore that through this book you will be significantly enlarged and encouraged in your faith.

Finally, before you begin, please let me add a request to the Lord Jesus; the author of faith, that this book is used to enrich and bless you as you read.

Trevor Maddison – at your service.

PART I:
THE THEODICY OF THE CROSS

CHAPTER 1: Introduction

It seems to be an almost universal experience among Christians, that have grown beyond the initial euphoria of finding faith, that they come to a point of perplexity where they begin to wonder whether they and God are in fact 'singing from the same hymn sheet'. They expected victory from here on out, but soon find themselves in unexpected battles, some of which are new, and some all too familiar with their former life. At this point the WHY? question seems to grow large, and a search for answers begins. They find their faith challenged by doubts, and often fears arise as to whether their experience is real. Or they are led to question if something is wrong or missing. This is normal. It is the beginning of the learning curve of faith as it begins to turn steeply upwards.

It is the job of teachers and leaders to seek to smooth the path of those that follow behind. As such the best way to do that is for the Christian to come into an understanding of God's real agenda, and to lay aside any preconceptions they may be clinging to that are at odds with it. This is sometimes not so easy, but in fact the sooner we find the truth of this the better, because what we come to realise is that God's idea of where he is taking his creation, and us with it, is far greater and more profound than anything we may have conceived. Our hope is therefore to seek to align our minds with his, rather than striving to fit God's ways into our ideas. We therefore intend in this volume to go directly to what the Bible tells us is the very heart of the matter; the cross, and seek through that to understand God's big plan for the ages.

To understand the cross we must understand God. This statement immediately alerts us to the possible futility of the task. God is infinite, and we are finite. He is omniscient; all knowing, and omnipotent; all powerful. Do we have a chance? After all we only have a peanut for a brain, and not the most intelligent peanut at that, relatively speaking of course. For us to fathom God is surely out of our range. Maybe you should shut the book now and go and do something more 'doable'. Or maybe this realisation will help. It was God's purpose in creating us that we should know him. If God is all powerful, then despite the fact that he is infinite and we are finite, would it not be within his infinite power to create us with a capacity such that though we are finite, we could actually know him, at least to some significant measure?

The centrality of the cross – We (Christians) generally recognise that the cross is the central, greatest, and most revealing expression of God in all creation. It has been identified as the pivotal event of all the history of the physical and spiritual universe.

If this is the highest act of God, then the same argument follows for a study of the cross as for God. He surely didn't intend it to be kept as a total mystery. Sure, we are told it is a mystery, but the apostle Paul confirms to us in his letter to the Corinthian church, that we have been given a capacity for understanding it. He says the cross is so wise, it is foolishness to the thoughts and ideas of this world. But for the mature Christian mind, we have been introduced to a whole new sphere of wisdom, and in this sphere the cross is the highest wisdom of all. God has given us access to his own mind as a resource to us for revelation and understanding, so that we can understand it. If this is true, then if we want to understand the cross this is a resource we are going to need. We must access it.

So yes, in studying God and his purpose on the cross as his greatest act, we are studying a mystery. But this does not mean we are locked out of all understanding of it, quite the contrary! What it means is that once we begin to delve into it, using the resources God has given us, we can expect it to become deeper and deeper, revealing ever increasing magnificence and glory as it opens up to us more and more of the truth of our infinite and unfathomably glorious creator.

Understanding the mystery – It is regrettable that some see the word 'mystery' associated with the cross as a barrier. In making no or little initial sense of it, they walk away believing it to be a closed book. It is nearly as regrettable that some obtain a shallow or pseudo understanding of the cross and settle for that. How important is this? Can we really afford to miss it?

If God used this event for his highest revelation to us, and we choose to ignore it, then what else can we expect but to live an impoverished life in terms of our wisdom and understanding. We miss the major revelation of God. We miss the understanding of his eternal purpose. We miss understanding our part in that purpose. And we miss the full understanding of what our life is really all about.

In the book of Proverbs Solomon tells us to sell ourselves out to get wisdom and understanding. The parables of Jesus of *the treasure in the field*, and *the pearl of great price*, tell us the same. Granted the treasure and the pearl is more than just an understanding, it is life itself, but these things come to us through faith. Faith is about believing and therefore in some measure it requires understanding.

We must realise that our mind is part of our being and God wants it to be completely submitted to him. We are not to lean on it, we must lean on him, but we must not neglect it either. God intends that we think his thoughts, and find full satisfaction and fulfilment in the area of our understanding as much as in anything else.

It occurs to me that one day, when we see the Lord Jesus face to face, he may ask us how we managed to miss these vital truths. The apostle Paul makes it clear to the Colossians that the mystery has been made known, and that in Christ there are *treasures* of wisdom and knowledge.

It has therefore been made abundantly clear that for those who would be rich in real terms, the riches are to be found in Christ. We are on a treasure hunt, and we are told in explicit terms that the treasure is there to be found. Too many have been distracted to seek other kinds of treasure in this world. Many have found it only to discover they have been 'sold short'. True treasure is to be found in Christ alone. God did not place a cross at the central event of all history to bar our way to the treasure, he put it there to mark the spot! He made sure we know exactly where to dig! How much clearer can God make it?

So let's begin this quest of exploration relying on God himself to guide us, knowing that it is his purpose that we should be successful. At the same time we must be patient and realise that as much as it is God's purpose to lead us into it, it is the plan of our enemy to keep us away from it. Since the event of the cross the only basis of any power our enemy has over us lies in deception. The cross is the ground of his defeat, and therefore from his point of view it is the most closely guarded secret of all. For us to be aware of that opposition is helpful and should hopefully make us humble, prayerful, and watchful in our quest for discovery.

The strategy for exploration – We started by saying that to understand the cross we must first understand God. This defines our strategy in this study. We must explore the nature of God and his purpose in creation before we can get to the cross. These subjects are interwoven and they progress together. Just as God existed before creation and before the cross happened, so our study should follow the same pattern by seeking to understand God in some measure first.

We must be open to take the scriptures and explore new ground, something that many seem reluctant to do because they are fearful of deviating from the revealed word. However there are a number of places where the scripture itself urges us to press on from the foundational truths to greater understanding. One we have mentioned; that the cross is mature wisdom. In the book of Hebrews we are urged to leave the elementary teachings about Christ and go on to maturity[1]; such teachings about repentance, faith, baptisms, resurrection, eternal judgement and the laying on of hands. It is not that we are intended to leave these doctrines behind, but that we should treat them as a foundation for deeper understanding. In the same way the teachings of the apostle Paul and the other writings of the apostles can be traced back to have their foundation in the words of Jesus in the gospels. The problem is we often go no further than viewing these things from an earthly level.

When the Pharisee Nicodemus approached Jesus with questions about accessing heaven, Jesus spoke to him of spiritual rebirth. When Nicodemus revealed his ignorance of these things, Jesus chided him for professing to be Israel's teacher and yet knowing nothing of these truths[2]. Jesus then said '*I have spoken to you of earthly things and you do not believe, how then will you believe if I speak to you of heavenly things*'[3]. He thereby, in one sentence, declared spiritual rebirth to be an earthly thing, and that there are heavenly things beyond it waiting to be discovered, if only we are ready to receive them.

A preoccupation with church and ministry can be a similar thing; a preoccupation with earthly things. If ever these things expand in the mind and thinking of those who focus on them, to an extent that they become the object of their desire, and displace true heavenly vision, then it is

---

[1] Heb 6:1-2
[2] John 3:10
[3] John 3:12

inevitable that their work becomes a career, and the whole thing shifts into a worldly form, often in the process losing its power and vitality. The condition of those that become caught in this trap can be pitiful. The apostle Paul says *'If only for this life we have hope in Christ, we are to be pitied more than all men'*[4].

The writer to the Hebrews likens these doctrines of repentance, faith, resurrection etc. to milk, and we are encouraged to get onto the solid food that is for the mature, where we learn by constant use to distinguish between good and evil[5]. As immature believers we are blown about by every wind and teaching that crosses our path[6]. But as mature believers we become able to discern and divide truth from error. Knowing God is a huge part of that maturity[7]. Knowing and understanding his plans and purposes are another[8]. God's nature, his purposes, and his ways become the gold standard against which, with the help of the Spirit, we identify and divide doctrines of God from the doctrines of the world, the flesh, and the devil.

The writer to the Hebrews explores some of the rich meaning in the symbolism of the artefacts in the Ark of the Covenant, drawing from it some solid food teaching[9]. At one point he mentions some of the features of its design, but says that he cannot discuss the details of it in the present letter[10]. Here again is a clear invitation for others to pick up the gauntlet and go further. We must not be afraid to explore the depths of the word. Clearly some caution is merited, because we can be led astray, but if we want to reach maturity in our faith we cannot shirk the opportunity to explore the word to a deeper level[11].

Our security is in our ability to trace our learning back to the foundational truths. In this way we avoid the mistakes of the Gnostics, and present day equivalents such as the New Age movement, that tend to absorb every doctrine they encounter into their contradictory belief systems. In the scriptures we have a firm historical and philosophical base

---

[4] 1 Cor 15:19
[5] Heb 5:13-14
[6] Eph 4:14
[7] Eph 4:13, 1:17, John 15:15
[8] Eph 1:9, 1:18-19
[9] Heb 9:9
[10] Heb 9:5b
[11] Heb 5:14-6:1

of truth which underpins all our growth and learning. But to stay with only the surface level of these truths is to be satisfied with a mere foundation[12], and to try to grow up to be an adult on milk alone[13]; something which cannot be a recipe for health. No, our strategy must be to dig deeper and move forward, and God permitting we will do so. That is my intention with this text.

As we move forward our capacity for discerning good and evil will be tested. We will be able to savour the goodness of God and the great things he has done[14]. We will get a glimpse of the powers of the coming age[15]. All of this together will lead us to become spiritually aware of heaven and eternity, and in the process we hope will break us free from living in these temporal earthly realities that will soon fade, but that for the present threaten to blind us to far greater realities beyond[16]. As we begin we must pray that God will open our eyes and teach us[17]. No book can substitute for that. In the end this is about revelation and relationship, not learning for learning's sake. What we hope for is that through learning, by revelation, we will come to personally know the God of truth better, and be more able to align our lives with him and his purposes for us.

---

[12] Heb 6:1
[13] Heb 5:11-14
[14] Heb 6:5
[15] Heb 6:4-6

[16] 2 Cor 4:18
[17] Eph 1:18

CHAPTER 2: God – Goodness, Love & Morality

What is God?

The word GOD comes from the word good. It means 'The Good Being'. One commentary expands its meaning to – 'a fountain of infinite benevolence and beneficence towards his creatures'. This is true but technically it is not a full enough definition because God was goodness and love before he created anything. Love is his eternal nature of goodness. The act of creation was purely and simply an expression of that nature of love.

Jesus gave us a number of statements as to what God is: *'God is love'*[18], *'God is good'*[19], and *'God is spirit'*[20]. It is important that we understand these statements, but we will explore them as we go.

The rich young ruler, who wanted to know how to inherit eternal life, called Jesus 'Good teacher'[21]. It was in answer to this title that Jesus interjected the quick response: *'Why do you call me good. Only God is good'*. This young man may have been taken aback with that response, but it is unlikely that the full import of what Jesus said there hit him, until much later, after he had chosen to walk away with his riches and earthly securities intact. The response of Jesus implied the following:

- That God is good.
- That Jesus is either not good, or if he is good then he is God.
- That this young man could not claim of himself to be good.

After being invited by Jesus to lay down his earthly wealth and follow him, this young man left the scene clinging to his earthly securities, and

---

[18] 1 John 4:8, 4;16
[19] Mark 10:18, 1 Tim 4:4 3 John 1:11
[20] John 4:24
[21] Mark 17:17, Luke 18:18

with his heavenly security still in question. We are told that Jesus '*loved him*'[22]. The gospel writer was struck enough by the emotions he saw in Jesus to mention it.

My suspicion is that when this young man returned to his comfortable life, the Holy Spirit did not allow him to just forget his encounter and the words of Jesus. He had already stepped out of his comfort zone and expressed a measure of faith by visiting Jesus at all. But now, I suspect, as he meditated on the response he had received, he would have been impacted as the gravity of what was said to him sunk in. He may have realised that he needed God more than anything else. That God's goodness would ensure he would get the help he needed. That he had that day encountered the very living God come in the flesh. That he had been made an offer to exchange his earthly securities for a security in heaven that would never perish. It was a call to a leap of faith that this young man was not ready to take.

We don't know who the young man was, only that he was rich. Some speculate that this was in fact Barnabas who later became a prominent believer in the early church[23]. We can't be sure of his identity but it is entirely possible it was him. It is not in the nature of God to let us go at first refusal, or often after many refusals. Not when there is a chance that we will make the response we need to make to receive salvation. The words spoken to this young man were perfect for the moment. They were designed by an omniscient mind of infinite love and goodness to reach this lost one. This is God at work expressing his love and goodness with all the patience needed to give every chance for one of his own to really come to him and live. We can't be sure, but it is quite possible that this young man eventually made the decision he needed to make, and began a life of faith that would lead him to an eternal destiny in heaven.

---

[22] Mark 10:21
[23] Acts 4:36-37

What is Love?

Definition of Love – God's nature is Love. What does this mean? The best definition I know of the concept of Love is – '*To be entirely committed with the whole of ones being (heart, soul, mind and strength) to the highest good of all things*'. This is what it means to love. It involves the wholesale commitment of the will to the purpose of the highest good, which consequentially impacts both the thinking and emotional faculties.

The emotional counterfeit – This foundation of love on the will, rather than the emotions, is important because the reduction of love to just a feeling is to misunderstand a symptom for a cause, and if accepted as the whole deal is to accept a counterfeit that turns it all to mush. True love is ready to put all of its available resources into action to secure what it perceives to be 'the highest good', regardless of how it feels.

The emphasis on love as a commitment to the 'highest' good is a vitally important one, and is a central key to this study. We will shortly explore the importance of that.

Love is the basis of prayer – This wholesale commitment of God to the highest good (i.e. love) is something in God we can completely rely on. It becomes the basis of our faith when we pray. The scripture says that God will not withhold any *good* thing from those whose walk is blameless[24]. Provided it serves the purpose of love/goodness it is available[25]. This is the nature of love.

Morality is Goodness which is Love – Morality is an internal demand we all experience that is based on the principle of Love. Its demands are built into man's constitution in what we call the conscience. This faculty of conscience means that a man finds the value of his actions weighed and judged by his own inner thoughts according to their value for goodness[26]. The demand it makes of us is that in every instance we always do the good thing. Though not just *a* good thing, but *the* thing that is the highest good. To push this further, Charles Finney points out that *for any moral being (God, man or angel) to withhold the good when it is in their power to do*

---

[24] Ps 84:11
[25] Matt 7:11
[26] Rom 2:15

it, is an immoral act[27]. As we will see, understanding this principle is a key to faith. It is also a key to this study, so let's take a moment to stress it.

Key: Love and Morality – the Highest Good

Morality demands a wholesale and absolute commitment to love from all moral beings, which means an absolute commitment with the whole of one's being to the demands and purposes of the highest good of all things. Of course, for any individual this demand is according to their own honest judgement and within their available resources. The moral demand cannot extend beyond a person's limits. But within these limits the highest good is an imperative. It is an intrinsic demand on his/her mind. It includes the interests of God and all of creation, including oneself, but without prejudice to oneself.

To desire or act against the highest good of all things in any instance is an immoral act. This means that *even to choose the second highest good over the highest good is an immoral act*. To choose the second highest good is in effect to withhold the highest good, which I repeat is by definition immoral.

Note: The principle of love as the commitment of the whole of one's being to the highest good of all things is a vital key to understanding God and the age we live in. This principle is morality. It is the very foundation of this study and we will frequently come back to it, so it is worth re-reading and spending a little time absorbing the detail of it.

The meaning and purpose of life

We now find ourselves in the enviable position of being able to define the meaning and purpose of life that some seem to find so elusive. The meaning and purpose of life is: *the promotion and extension of the purpose of love*, the highest good. That purpose, who is God, has now come to include us to our immeasurable blessing, by giving us life through creation in this present age, and by his plan for the ages to come. God has created us to be as freely committed to the same purpose of love, with the whole of our being, as he is.

---

[27] Systematic Theology, Charles Finney

Definition of the word 'Age'

Before we go further we must define the word 'age' as we are using it here. The word age is used in scripture to denote both the ages of this world, and the ages beyond that we refer to as heaven. Here we differentiate these terms. We use the word 'era' to mean the ages, or eras of this world order (e.g. pre-flood era, era of law, era of grace). We use the word 'ages' to mean the whole of this temporal worldly age, with all of its eras, to define the present age, and the following ages yet to come where the very order and principles of life change, as they do in heaven when we move into an age that is truly and wholly spiritual.

An age would therefore be defined as the complete events of a period of eternal history which has a single order, and is governed by a consistent set of natural principles. The present physical age of this world is therefore a single age by this definition. What is clear from scripture is that there are ages yet to come that will have a completely new order and are based on new and higher natural principles.

The value of oneself and others

From our definition of love we come to see that all things in God's universe can be valued in terms of their contribution to the purpose of love. One question that arises from this is therefore: How should we value ourselves?

Jesus was once asked the question: Which is the greatest commandment? He surprised the teacher of the law that asked it when he bypassed the acclaimed 'top ten' and drew the answer from the more obscure parts of the law. His answer was: *'Love the Lord your God with all your heart and with all your soul and with all your mind.' This is the first and greatest commandment. And the second is like it: 'Love your neighbour as yourself'*.

There are several profound lessons here. One is that we are to love ourselves in recognition of the true value that God has placed on each of us in the purpose of love. We are not to devalue ourselves before others, but to regard ourselves as of equal value with them; no more, no less. Of course this must be true. We must be honest about ourselves and others. Any other valuation would mean we all have different evaluations, which would generally mean we all disagree, and truth therefore becomes relative and not absolute.

Secondly we learn that the only one we are led to value above another is God himself. The reason for this is clearly because God is the very principal and sustainer of the purpose of love, and therefore more valuable to it than anything else. God IS Love. To love God is to love Love. Without us in the universe love will continue, but without God love cannot persist.

This leads us to ask: If God can be valued above others then why can't we value one another to varying degrees? Or indeed, why can't we value ourselves as greater or lesser than others? As we are all different we must ask: Don't we all have different values in the purpose of love?

The first answer to this is that we have no way of determining the eternal value of any individual in God's universe according to the purposes of love. To do that we would have to be able to see into the infinite reaches of the ages of ages to know what impact a person will have on the purposes of love, in order to make such an evaluation. Clearly we would have to be omniscient for that to be possible. We may be able to appreciate something of a snapshot of a person's life as we see and experience it at the present moment, but even here we are ignorant of numerous important details. Even if we were able to make an accurate snapshot evaluation, we have to be aware that God specialises in producing good out of evil, so when we look at a person whose life seems to be devalued, they may in fact become one of God's greater triumphs. The only way we could make such an evaluation of any individual is if God revealed it to us, and he is clearly not doing that. Our ignorance therefore leads us to treat everyone as of equal value, and for every person we wait with anticipation to see what will emerge as God's plan for them is gradually revealed[28].

Secondly, a wise parent does not reveal any favouritism. But then an even wiser parent does not have favourites, because they realise that often the more troublesome character can turn out to have the greater potential. It seems that for parents this is almost part of the job description; to see the potential in their children even when no-one else can. God's insight on each of us in this way is complete. He knows the end from the beginning and is able to correctly evaluate us from an eternal perspective, according to his design. This may lead us to think God therefore loves us all in different measure, but in fact we have an explicit revelation in

---

[28] Rom 8:19

scripture that with God there is no favouritism[29]. In fact his love is boundless for each one of his children[30].

It seems that God's plan is to continue to develop each one of us further in love through the infinity of ages to come. We know that the principles of heaven especially value the weak and vulnerable, protecting and honouring them[31]. In this way each continues to develop and care for others, lifting them up to levels they themselves have already attained. God has so designed it that in eternity none are left behind for long, but that they develop as one as each serves the other.

Because this is God's perspective, we can appreciate that his love for each one of us is as infinite as he is, and that he therefore loves us all equally; infinitely.

Moral decision making according to our resources

So we see that love is the key principle and value that we must uphold as moral beings in God's universe. Let's look further at what morality does and does not demand of us.

The limits of the moral claim – Of course for man, as created finite beings, our resources of strength and understanding are limited, and our moral (i.e. loving) decision making has to take account of these limits. Moral demands can only have any claim on us within the bounds of our strength, abilities, opportunities, and understanding.

Morality of mistakes – When I was a boy the younger brother of a friend was helping his parents to wash the car. Being very young, and at that time a little uninformed about the details of car maintenance, he kindly obliged by filling the gas tank using the water hose. In his own mind he was just helping in the task by copying the actions of his parents when they pulled in at the gas station. His parents were suitably annoyed and scolded the poor little guy. He definitely got the point, and as far as I know never did it again. But despite the discipline there was no hint of moral failure on his part on this occasion. He simply lacked any knowledge of the distinction between gas and water. Had he known then the act would have had a

---

[29] Rom 2:11
[30] Eph 3:17-19
[31] 1 Cor 12:23

completely different complexion. Morality does not demand of us to operate beyond our resources, whether of strength, ability, or understanding.

Morality and understanding – Our determination of what is the highest good in any instance must take account of our limited understanding, so it is often the case that due to poor understanding a bad decision is made, but to the person that made the decision it is still regarded as morally right because their intentions were for the highest good.

Politicians are constantly arguing the rights and wrongs of some issue, but they always argue on the basis that their proposed idea or action is for the highest good. They also often seek to prove that they have a superior understanding of what is the highest good over the ideas of the opposition, and through it they intrinsically suggest that they are therefore better qualified to govern.

Politicians will often cast doubt on the very commitment of the opposition to the purposes of the highest good by suggesting an ulterior selfish motive. They may thereby be genuinely seeking to root out corruption, or alternatively they may be seeking to undermine the public belief in the morality of the government. In doing so, as the opposition to the government, they may thereby project themselves forward as more fit to rule by virtue of their higher morality. In all cases the morality of the argument carries the clout. The moral imperative is a strong intrinsic force in all free-willed beings.

Morality and sacrifice – According to the demands of morality, we are not generally called to give or sacrifice to the point of self-destruction because this would not normally be judged to serve the purposes of the highest good. We have to factor into our decision making our own intrinsic value, and therefore the value of our own self-preservation when making assessments on the measure of sacrifice demanded of us.

On occasions our moral conscience may demand of us considerable personal risk, thereby showing this intrinsic demand to exceed our self-interest for the purpose of securing the highest good. For example, we often hear of situations where someone has a stricken conscience over thoughts that they could have done more to save another, even though it would have meant considerable personal risk.

Take for example a case of someone drowning, and those in a place of safety considering risking a similar fate if they chose to try to help. This conflict of conscience shows that the conscience extends well beyond the limits of just self-interest and personal security. It demands the highest good within our resources and abilities, without reference to any personal prejudice.

The circumstances of war often present such occasions where the ultimate self-sacrifice is demanded and made. In other extreme circumstances we may find our moral decision making pushed into positions where the true right moral choice; the choice for the highest good, is the choice for the 'least of two evils'.

In the struggles of World War II, Winston Churchill was faced with many such agonising judgements. For example on one occasion the acquisition of code breaking technology and information had enabled the Allies to break the enemy communication system security codes. This revealed they were heading into an enemy ambush in the campaign in Italy. The problem was that to withdraw was judged to certainly reveal the fact that the Allies had acquired the code breaking capacity. Ultimately the decision was made to proceed into the ambush on the (moral) basis that to give this fact away would in the longer run result in far more loss of life, and jeopardy to the war effort, than to withdraw.

Regardless of whether this judgement was right or wrong, for those responsible the decision ultimately had a moral imperative because their conscience would demand of them to do that which they judged to be for the highest good, or in this case the least evil. We could even turn this around and say that given their best judgement, if to withdraw would have caused more loss of life and suffering in the long run, then it would have been an immoral act to do so. Lesser men may have baulked at the decision under the pressure of self-interest, knowing that there would be a moral indictment from some who did not share their convictions. To act for the good in such circumstances, knowing there will be an inevitable backlash that may even question their character, is what we call moral courage. There are stories of many brave souls, even in the same conflict within the Nazi regime that stood out against the evil of their day in full knowledge that they would bear the brunt of the wrath of those they opposed. For them the moral imperative was stronger than the threat they faced.

In such circumstances the highest good (love) does demand a sacrifice of which the supreme example is that of Christ who *'for the joy set before him endured the cross'*[32], as we will see later.

The authority of morality – On the subject of World War II, as with any war, it is not always realised what weight the moral imperative carries. If the overall cause in fighting a war is seen by the participants to be for the highest good, then the whole weight of the moral demand on all moral beings pulls in favour of the cause. This is why in these kinds of struggles opponents often engage in propaganda wars where they try to 'demoralise' the enemy by challenging their thinking. They know that if they succeed, they relax the moral imperative of their opponents, and therefore reduce the strength and determination that they derive from it.

Using God's moral imperative for good

As we have discussed, as finite beings our resources are limited and this is a factor we must consider in our moral decision making.

For God who is omnipotent, omniscient and infinite he has no such limitations. If therefore, as we have said, there is a moral imperative for any moral being to commit the resources at their disposal to the purposes of the highest good, then it follows that in a very real way we have this awesome and almighty God well and truly cornered. His own moral nature of love empowers us to demand of him that he should conform to these demands[33]. Fortunately he is himself so committed to the purpose of love that he is more than happy about us making such demands. We could even go further and say that he is delighted when he sees his children take up his cause. It is therefore within our scope to lean on this moral imperative, and ask him to do something we know is good, within the bounds of his infinite power, and he will not, yea even **cannot** withhold it.

We are given an explicit invitation to engage God in this way in the parable Jesus told of the persistent widow[34]. She kept coming to the judge demanding justice, knowing that he was under the pressure of his own moral imperative to grant it. The judge could not hold out against her

---

[32] Heb 12:2
[33] Prov 3:27, Matt 7:7, Luke 11:9, John 15:7
[34] Luke 18:1-8

for long, such was the gravity of her demand. God clearly desires to engage us in the purpose of love in our measure to the same extent that he is in his, but not independently of him. He clearly desires that we see him as both the one who has set the standard of love, and as the means for its fulfilment. God is committed to love, the highest good. It is natural that he should want his children to share the same commitment and passion.

By making such a demand we can actually *force* God into a place where he either puts forth his power and might and does the good thing, or he denies his own nature. By this reasoning, for him to deny us would be an immoral act!

However there is a catch to our arm twisting advantage over God here. How do we know what is truly the highest good? We have little peanut brains, and he is omniscient and made the universe. How can we possibly consider all the implications of even the simplest act of goodness? So maybe we don't quite have God as cornered as we thought. Or do we?

To this there is a profound and wonderful answer: Yes we can know! We have been given access to the mind of Christ and we have a resource to *'know all things'*[35]. God has even given us the promise that *'if any man asks for wisdom he will give it without finding fault'*[36]. Through renewed spiritual sight we therefore have been given access to the infinite wisdom of God[37]. It may mean learning to listen and discern good from evil, but the capacity for determining God's mind is there for those who are ready and willing to seek it.

We may not have the capacity to fathom why a thing is good, but God has given us his own mind as a true resource to fuel our prayers. We are able to access intuitive knowledge that comes directly from God, in the form of deep conviction[38], so we can discern good from evil and therefore know with certainty what the right prayer is; the prayer for the highest good.

God has clearly gone out of his way to make sure we are empowered to know and do good works in his universe. If in no other way, then we can always seek to do the good thing through prayer and

---

[35] 1 Cor 2:10,15,16
[36] James 1:5
[37] Eph 1:8
[38] 1 Thes 1:5

intercession[39], which in actual fact is invariably the major part of the work, if only we realised it. Of course these revelations are not entirely under our control. They come out of us seeking his mind, casting ourselves on God in complete dependence, and hearing accurately from him. By ourselves we would even have difficulty forming the questions, let alone discovering the answers. But God engages us with his good purposes by promptings and guidance that lead to the revelations of his own perfect knowledge[40]. We are then able to raise these convictions with God, and lay our requests before him with the whole power of the moral imperative backing us up in our request for him to apply his power to secure it.

This is what intercessory prayer is, and when it is resourced by faith in this way it is irresistible to God because of the moral imperative of his own nature of Love. We can depend on the nature of God to this degree.

If we understand what is being said here: that God is not random in his actions or choices, and that he always chooses the highest good according to his infinite knowledge as a shear expression of his nature; then we can begin to see and appreciate that if we discover his mind on any issue, we have the basis for absolute faith.

---

[39] Eph 6:18, Col 4:12, 1 Tim 2:1
[40] Rom 8:26

CHAPTER 3: The Problem of Evil

The obvious presence of evil in the world has led many to conclude that there is no God, or if there is a God that he is not a God of love as we have defined it; always committed to the highest good. They argue that such a God of love and benevolence would never have created or allowed such things to exist. In answer to this charge against God there are studies of God and creation that have come to be referred to as a 'theodicy'. These studies seek to explain how God can be good despite the obvious existence of evil.

In the book of Job in the Bible we see Job's 'comforters'; Eliphaz, Bildad and Zophar, putting forward a theodicy to explain what were to them circumstances that challenged their understanding of God. They could only conclude that Job had suffered through an act of God upon all that mattered to him in his life. The events seemed just far too coincidental to be any other. The problem was they had a simplistic theodicy that could only explain the situation by condemning Job as wicked and deserving of punishment in order to defend and justify God. Their understanding could not conceive that men may suffer for other reasons than punishment for sin.

Job defended himself, first by refuting their accusations, and then by provoking an indignant reaction in them by suggesting, by his observations, that sometimes the righteous suffer when the wicked escape unscathed[41]. This suggestion struck them like the well-known story of 'The Emperors New Clothes', where up until that time everybody was denying Job's observations because no-one wanted to face this difficult truth and all the difficult implications that came with it. The problem was that it seemed to indict God as unrighteous and unjust, which was a suggestion they were unwilling, or even afraid to entertain.

When the discussion with the three comforters reached deadlock, a young man named Elihu indignantly stepped in and shared his ideas that included the concept that sometimes suffering is used to discipline a man in a way that is intended to ultimately serve a good purpose[42]. This was a

---

[41] Job 21:29-34, 24:12, 35:15
[42] Job 33:14-30

new idea that presented a more advanced theodicy, and which could accommodate Job's observations that it is not always the wicked that suffer. Unbeknown to all of them at this time, the truth of that situation was even more fascinating; that God had in fact seen Job as a righteous man and had challenged Satan to acknowledge it.

This book is partly such a study. It is a theodicy that explains in some measure the existence of evil, while maintaining the assertion that God is good. In the same way that the suggestions of Elihu served to stretch the mind of his hearers, it is essential that we allow our ideas and misgivings about God to be stretched to embrace some potentially new ideas of the way God works in his creation. So here goes. Let's launch out into the theodicy we intend to explore.

Theodicy

To answer the problem of evil we must try for a moment to put ourselves in the position of God as omniscient, omnipotent, and having a nature of Love that must <u>always</u> do the thing that is the highest good in every instance.

Imagine such a God, who is entirely happy in himself, contemplating creating *something*. This God is not at liberty to just make a random choice and create anything good. His nature is Love, which means he must do the highest good. Anything less would be contrary to his very nature. Even the second best idea he has is not an option open to him. As a moral being he must take the highest course. To choose to do any other would be an immoral act. The highest idea he has is the only thing that can serve the purpose of love.

Now if it were actually us in God's position, we can in hindsight speculate that we too may well have considered the idea of creating independent beings that we can relate to in a relationship of love, and that this would most serve the purpose of love. We must then decide how much autonomy these beings should have, and what situation to create for them to live in that will most serve the purposes of love. According to the reasoning of some of the theodicies discussed earlier, we may have come up with an idea that has been called 'utopia'; a society where all are happy and nothing but loving benevolence and care is expressed. We would certainly scrutinise closely any possibility that the society we plan to create would turn bad in some way, and ultimately fail to fulfil the purpose of love.

Considering (as God) that I am already entirely happy in myself, in a place and state of love before even considering creating anything, it is unlikely that a course with any risk of failure to serve the ultimate purpose of love would be acceptable as the highest course of love. To consider such a thing would be to risk moving from a place where love is the reigning principle, to one where something else displaces it. It is not a viable option. The only possible course is one that eliminates all such risk. God cannot, and does not play the odds with love. All his ways are sure.

For God to come from a place of perfect love and gamble, such that the purposes of love may be compromised in his universe, is like a man betting his home and possessions, and risking his family to be sold into slavery should it fail. Even where the odds are stacked in favour of a good outcome, such a risk would be an evil act, unless it was a last resort for salvation in a dire circumstance where there were no better options. However since God was in a perfect state of love before he created anything, he clearly had the option to simply remain in that state and not create anything at all. The purpose of love would then be served. Unless an outcome that ultimately serves the purposes of love is absolutely certain, he will not act. The fact that a loving God went ahead and created free-willed beings, regardless of what seems to us like a huge risk, simply means that he, in his infinite wisdom, had covered all angles such that a good outcome was, and is, absolutely guaranteed. This does not mean that the outcome would necessarily be good for every creature that God made, or that there would not be costs as well as gains, but simply that the final outcome would be guaranteed to serve the eternal purpose of love.

One way for me (as God) to eliminate the risk is for me to give myself sufficient *internal* control over the beings I create so that they are unable to upset my plan. However the obvious problem with this is that love is fundamentally based on choosing the highest good, but true choosing means one must have freedom of will. If I impose some internal control on the will of the beings I create, then I reduce them to automatons, which will in turn prevent them from truly expressing love. This is self-defeating, so I am therefore led to the decision that if I create them then the only option is to give my created beings absolute freedom and sovereignty of will like I have myself, in order that they may truly express love. Only this will truly serve the purpose of love.

I am then left with the problem of removing the risk that the whole thing will break down and ultimately fail to serve the purpose of love by the misuse of that free will. If the risk cannot be completely eliminated, then the whole idea is off, and the path of not creating such beings at all turns out to be the highest path. On the other hand, if in my infinite wisdom (as God) I can see a way whereby the risk can be completely eliminated, then the whole creation idea is back on, and as an omniscient, omnipotent moral being with the power and ability at my finger tips to accomplish it, I have no other choice than to go for it.

The risk is clearly that truly free-willed beings may choose an evil path; a path that is against the purpose of love, the highest good. How can this be prevented? Clearly the only way forward is to somehow ensure that these created beings are as fully committed to the purpose of love in their capacity, as God is in his. They must therefore be *persuaded* never to deviate from that path of love in any circumstance.

When we say never, we mean never in all of eternity, because this is how long God intends to have a fellowship of love with them.

How can God be certain that there will not come a time in all of the vastness of eternity, that a fall from the purpose of love will occur in his created beings, and his creation will turn bad? To proceed he must find a way to establish this certainty without compromising the essential free-will of his created beings, otherwise the whole idea of creating such beings is out of the question.

Controlling behaviour

There are three conceivable ways that God could control the potential for deviation from the purpose of love in free-willed beings, without compromising the sovereignty of their free will. These are to either:

1. Impose external controls that limit their opportunity for sin.
2. Limit their moral understanding.
3. Teach them to voluntarily control themselves to guarantee that they *always* serve the purposes of love.

External Controls – Imposing external controls means creating an environment where the possibility for sin is eliminated, or reduced to a minimum. The problem here is that if all opportunities for sin were removed then it would make the faculty of free will redundant and meaningless, and it would drastically reduce the creative possibilities for the design of their environment because, as we know in our world, almost all choices contain potential for abuse in some way or other.

Also to only *reduce* the possibilities for sin, would leave a measure of risk, so this alone would not be adequate to absolutely ensure the creation is secure in love eternally.

The third option is therefore far more desirable; to create an environment where real opportunities exist for sin, but somehow develop the beings that inhabit it to always choose, with absolute certainty, never to exploit them. *Never*.

Limiting understanding – We have previously explored the effect that limited understanding has on moral decision making. The moral demand can only extend as far as our understanding of right and wrong.

We discussed the fact that moral decisions concern the choice for the highest good according to our understanding.

It follows therefore that to limit the understanding of moral beings is to limit their capacity to discern what path or choice is for the highest good, and is therefore to limit their opportunity for sin. However to limit man's understanding would be to severely limit the greatness of his being. To reduce the constitution of the mind of man is to make him less able to relate to God who has the supreme understanding of omniscience. The greater the capacity for understanding that can be bestowed on his beings, the more they are able to relate to God on the level of understanding.

Once again, rather than limit understanding, the third option is far better if it can be achieved; to bestow a higher understanding but establish grounds for absolute trust that the beings that have it will never violate that trust. *Never*.

The choice of lesser or greater beings – We now see the choice that God had in considering creating beings with free will. He could either create lesser beings by controlling their opportunity for sin by limiting their minds and restricting their environment, or he could go ahead and create greater beings with no such limitations, but only if he found a way to completely eliminate the risk that they will ever use their higher capacities as opportunities to sin sometime in eternity. Reason alone shows us that under the restrictions of Love, if God were to create free-willed beings at all, then this is the choice he had to make.

This leads us to an understanding of the Garden of Eden at the beginning of the history of man.

The Garden of Eden

In the Garden of Eden we initially see both of the first two restrictions we mentioned in place. Man had a restricted environment, and limited understanding[43].

Adam and Eve were in the restricted environment of the garden where their only opportunity for sin was to eat of the fruit of the tree of the knowledge of good and evil. They also had limited understanding of good and evil having not yet been enlightened by eating the fruit from the tree. The only understanding they had of right and wrong was that they should not eat from the tree, as they had been told by God, or they would 'die'.

We therefore see that God initially made man to be the lesser beings we described. He did not remove all risk that they would sin because their free will would then have been redundant, but he minimised their opportunity and vulnerability to sin.

Having done this, we can be sure that because God does not gamble with the purposes of love, and since a measure of risk remained, he had to have a plan in place to respond to the eventuality of man disobeying his instructions and falling into sin.

Here we see the wisdom of God. He arranged things such that in the event that Adam and Eve, as lesser beings, fell into sin by disobeying the only instruction he had given them, the very act of sinning would expand them into the higher beings as we discussed earlier. What we see therefore is that God delegated to man the responsibility to choose which type of being he would become, and proceed into eternity as either the lesser or the greater.

Had they resisted temptation as the lesser beings, they would have chosen a path where they would have continued into eternity as the lesser beings, not knowing good and evil, but avoiding the great suffering and losses we know in hindsight are caused by sin. As such they would have remained in the blissful, but restricted abode of Eden, and the purposes of love would have been served. God would still have had to bring them to a point where they were guaranteed to always resist the temptation, so they would have had to be tested under duress beyond anything they would

---

[43] Gen 3:5

ever encounter in eternity, but when one resists temptation the power to resist gets stronger. No doubt in this scenario God would have somehow led them to such a position.

As history has it, they succumbed to the temptation and disobeyed God, which had several effects. First it brought about a change in their constitution; their minds were enlightened so they could discern good and evil, and in this sense they became higher beings. This enlightenment then blew open a whole range of possibilities for sin, and having opened the door to this knowledge they found themselves swamped with temptations and opportunities for sin. Secondly they were thrust into the whole new environment of this world where the opportunities for sin abounded. Thirdly, they experienced an inner change; their spirit died and was cut off from God, which in contrast to the expansion of their minds, made them far lesser beings than they had formerly been; morally awake but spiritually dead.

What we see here, in the effects of the fall, is God's planned response to sin kicking into action. God and man are now plunged into the scenario where to have an ongoing relationship with man, God must redeem him and teach him to live in his enlightened state, but bring him to a place where he can be trusted absolutely and voluntarily never to violate the purposes of love again from this higher state. The training must be robust enough to stand for all eternity, leaving no element of risk that man would ever use his freedom and powers again as the opportunity for sin, yet without compromising his free will. This would be a difficult thing to achieve, but highly suited to a very big God.

Man chose his own path – In these two paths God had given man a free choice, and it was made in full freedom by man alone. Neither path was a pre-set conclusion, but God had a response prepared for either choice. The former scenario would have avoided some inevitable and immense costs, but man chose the latter which launched him onto a path to become a higher being, as God had planned it, but only by passing through an age of evil that would reform him by involving considerable costs that would serve to eliminate the risk that man, in this higher form, would present to the eternal security of creation.

Eliminating eternal risk

God's plan and answer to the problem of eliminating the eternal risk, posed by man in his now morally enlightened state of mind, was to create an age of pre-history where he would find restoration, and all the risk of further corruption is eliminated once and for all eternity. God's method for doing this is to temporarily create and use the controlled environment of this world in which the whole thing can go wrong once, right at the beginning, in a way that causes a minimum of suffering, and that in the end will eliminate all of the risk that any of his free-willed beings will ever make such a choice again. ***The main factor in this process of eliminating risk is the development of faith in God, in all free-willed beings, through the experience of this age. Faith therefore is to become the guarantee of eternal security beyond this age***. We will discuss this further later.

The losses incurred by the fall

Now that the choice is made, it is abundantly clear that in this evil age of pre-history there will be some considerable losses that would not have arisen on the other path, had man not disobeyed God, and there had been no fall. In other words, there is now a price to pay in order to bring forth the necessary result of the security of faith in all the beings that go through to eternity with God. The cost is a main subject of this book. *What we will see is that it means the unavoidable eternal loss of some of these beings in this age of pre-history, and an incredible personal loss to God*, but all of this was measured to perfect precision by God before the act of creation, in order to fulfil the highest purpose of love and goodness, according to his infinite wisdom.

The fall of angels

Having explored the fall of man, we can look at the position of angels in God's created universe, and their part in the fall. We know and understand less about angels than man, but they too were created as free-willed beings, and as such are subject to the moral demand of love, just as man is. To conform to this demand they too must always choose the highest good.

In creating angels God had the same problem as he had with man; they had the same liability to misuse their free will and fall. However a key difference between angels and men was that they were created all at once at the creation of the spiritual universe. They are not designed to procreate as man does, but were bought into existence together at once. There are therefore a fixed number of angels in God's universe; at least 100 million of them, and possibly many more[44].

We don't know the details of what opportunities angels had for sin in the spiritual domain, or their level of understanding of good and evil, but given that they are the same now as then, it seems they were created with a much higher capacity for intelligence and moral understanding than man originally had in the garden.

It seems that for the angels, they too had an equivalent to the tree of the knowledge of good and evil in their spiritual domain. It appears that their essential area of temptation was man himself. In man they saw the opportunity to become like God; to be worshipped by man and to rule him[45]. It appears that in the process of tempting man to become like God by knowing good and evil, that Satan himself was in the process of attempting to make himself to be as God, and therefore he was yielding to the temptation that was open and available to him by subduing man for his own purpose.

We don't know what specific instructions God gave to angels concerning mankind, but we know they have been given a role to serve man. We can therefore assume that their mandate was to serve[46]. At the fall all angels were sold the opportunity for the same prize by Satan if they chose to follow him and his cause. They were offered the opportunity to be served and worshipped by man, rather than to serve him. It seems from scripture that a third of the angels bought into his offer and fell with him[47].

The result of the fall of angels appears to have been a war in heaven where the offending angels were rounded up and banished to earth, trapped for the time being as the principalities and powers of the air[48].

It may be ironic that in tempting man to sin, that Satan provoked man to take a step that enlarged his being to a higher state that is as great in its moral capacity as that of the angels. He may therefore have inadvertently shifted man into a higher plan of God. However Satan almost certainly knew that in leading man to enlighten himself against

---

[44] Rev 5:11
[45] Isaiah 14:13-14, Matt 4:8
[46] Heb 1:14
[47] Rev 12:4
[48] Eph 6:12

God's command, that man would be spiritually cut off from God, and therefore at the mercy of Satan's manipulation and control. Man would become morally enlightened, but at the same time spiritually corrupted by being cut off from God, the source of love, which reduced his heart and will to a selfish and immoral state[49]. From Satan's point of view, he had taken man captive and found a way to hold him ransom for his own purposes. From God's point of view, man had now been led to a place where he was capable of a higher relationship with God through his moral enlightenment. What remained was for God to take all the necessary steps to redeem man and spiritually restore him. Satan would present a considerable adversary to that plan, but even this could be used by God to develop the necessary faith in those that would survive the era of the fall, which would in turn become the guarantee of eternal security.

It is clear that for fallen angels there is no way of redemption; they are eternally condemned[50]. God's plan for the angels that remained faithful to him, is in one way the same as for redeemed man; that through the events of the fall they too should develop faith that will make sure there is never a repetition of the fall, and that the creation is hereafter eternally secure in the purposes of love.

---

[49] Eph 4:18
[50] 2 Peter 2:4

CHAPTER 4: God's Plan for Man

Man's environment
We have been led to the conclusion that in the event of a fall, the present evil age is an essential age of the pre-history of creation, that God had designed to eliminate the risk of there ever being another fall or invasion of evil in all of eternity to come, by the development of faith in God. This leads us to explore why faith is so important, and how the present environment serves the purpose of developing faith.

The importance of faith in creation
Faith is a highly prized and most valuable asset for all created free-willed beings in the future of God's universe[51]. Faith was the main intrinsic deficiency in free-willed beings that led to the fall of angels and man in the first place. Had they had such faith, none would ever have fallen. However God has used the fall to develop faith both in those that remained (angels), and those that are redeemed (men). Having seen the effects of the fall and God's handling of it, we can see that through the resulting development of faith gained in God's nature, character, and power, even in the most adverse and contrary circumstances, that this faith will result in the eternal security of the universe and all creation hereafter. Because of such faith the fall will not be a recurring theme somewhere in eternity, but this faith will hereafter protect the whole of creation for all of eternity.

To develop faith as eternally robust as this, God had to have a plan that would carry that faith forward into eternity, keeping it an ever present reality, and not as some fading memory. We will come to explore how God has done this.

If it were inevitable that the fall would eventually recur somewhere in the eternal future, then God would probably not in the first place have chosen to create this universe as it is, and the free-willed creatures that inhabit it. His decision to create was contingent on the assurance that the danger afforded by free will could, and would, be eradicated once and for all, right at the beginning, but without in any way

---

[51] 1 Peter 1:7

compromising the most valuable attribute of the free will of his created beings, and turning them into automatons.

If this understanding is correct, then it would mean that the infinite wisdom of God saw that it was worth the incredible cost and trouble to go ahead and create independent free-willed beings like himself, despite the 'inevitability' of a fall in the early stage. Only through the fall could it be made a once only event in the history of creation, and through it God could bring forth something that is so immensely valuable to the cause of love and goodness that it was worth every bit of the cost and trouble for what would be a relatively infinitesimal season (or age), compared to the ages of ages (eternity) to follow.

When we get this perspective on pain, suffering, and distress in this life, as the apostle Paul had, then we begin to react like he did and call them light and momentary troubles that are achieving for us an eternal weight of glory that far (far, far) outweighs them all[52].

Was the fall inevitable?

Before we go further, we should reiterate an issue regarding whether the fall was inevitable, as some have suggested it was.

The question arises: Does this suggest that God engineered the fall as part of his design, and if so how can man be held responsible for it?

By this very valid question we are forced to see that the fall could not in fact have been an inevitable event at all. If God created beings that had genuine sovereign free will like his own, they must have had the choice to either obey, or disobey.

Some have argued that God knows all things, and therefore his omniscience demands that he knew which path would be taken by man. What we have to realise here is that this argument is self-defeating because it denies God's other equally impressive quality of omnipotence by denying his ability to create beings that were able to operate in true sovereignty of will, like God himself does.

Any argument that suggests man did not fall as a sovereign act of his own free will, suggests man has some kind of pseudo freedom of will, and not true free will at all.

---

[52] 2 Cor 4:17

Free-will and predestination

This leads us head first into the old Calvinist/Armenian argument that has raged for centuries over the issues of free will and predestination.

The truth of predestination was first raised by the apostle Paul[53]. Later it was significantly expounded by St Augustine. Then later still by Calvin, and many others. From it comes the doctrines of election[54] and eternal security, that emphasise God is in overall control.

The opposition to these doctrines have argued against the ramifications they perceive from it; that it tends to undermine the truth of free will. The resolution of this argument has only come with the understanding that *predestination and free will can in fact co-exist,* and they are not necessarily mutually exclusive as some have thought. The fact that I can predict the moves of somebody I love because I am familiar with their ways, does not in any way mean I have control of them, or that their will is not free. My knowledge comes from my familiarity with them as a person, but it is not control. In the same way, just because God can perfectly predict the direction and outcome of future events out into the reaches of eternity because he is omniscient, does not in any way compromise the fact and truth of free-will.

To fall into the trap of thinking that because 'it is written', that our actions have no impact or effect on our lives, is to embrace a major error. This type of thinking has become a major part of the belief systems of many in eastern religions, and of many, both now and in church history, that have misunderstood Calvinism. The reality is that every decision we make, and every action we take, has an impact on our lives. God's response and discipline may be designed to bring us back on track with his purposes, but our actions and the effects of our choices profoundly affect our lives, and serve to make our road and life either harder or easier, sometimes to the extreme. The truth is: every action has its reaction. Our will is free and there are consequences to every choice we make.

We must then come to see that although man's will is absolutely free and sovereign, God has controlled man's environment, and is able to respond to his every free choice so that in the end he can still bring him to his predestined conclusion. This means God has a planned response for every possible decision a man can make within the bounds of his freedom.

---

[53] Rom 8:29-30, Eph 1:5,11
[54] Rom 9:11, 11:7, 2 Tim 2:10, 2 Pet 1:10, John 6:44, 10:28-29

God controls man's options by controlling his level of understanding, his opportunities, and his resources. Man is therefore steered towards his destiny by God's great omniscience and omnipotence. Man chooses freely, but God steers by external influences. The end result is that each man reaches his predestined destiny, as God defined it, despite him making his choices freely, and despite having an enemy that is determined to lead him astray. It is witnessing this supreme control, without compromising freedom that serves to develop faith in God's power in all those that see it.

King Solomon expressed it in a way that any child that has ever played on a beach would understand: '*God directs the heart of the king like a water course*'[55]. A water course always takes the path of least resistance. The same is generally true of the hearts of men. In all cases God deals with our freedom and choices by damming us in and blocking our passage. He uses circumstances to redirect us, always guiding us back to the path when we stray, even when we resist. Though the water runs freely, God ensures man invariably ends up reaching his intended destination.

It is beyond us to see how so many permutations of man's free choices and actions can be held and handled within the mind of God, but he is always numerous steps ahead of us. He knows us so well, he knows our next thought to perfection. He therefore knows the one after that to the same precision[56]. This knowledge, and his dealings with us, demonstrate again how great he is. The decisions men make freely decide the path they take to their destination, but their environment is at all times controlled by God in such a way that the final outcome is secure, and turns out exactly how God planned it.

Now that man has fallen, a sobering but essential truth, that comprises a significant part of the plan of God in eternity, is that his plan had to include a phase of suffering. A second truth is that not all men are destined for, or can be led to salvation. The lives of many in this age will, in the eternal scheme of things, be seen to be only a kind of catalyst required to bring others through to their destiny[57]. Here we are beginning to explore the unavoidable costs, but we will explore these truths more fully later.

---

[55] Prov 21:1
[56] Ps 139:2
[57] Rom 9:22

CHAPTER 4: God's Plan for Man 55

The value of free-willed beings

For God, in considering creation, his highest and greatest idea was to make beings like himself with true sovereign free-will of their own, just like his[58]. Only this would serve the ultimate purposes of love; to create beings that were themselves able to love. As love is about choosing the highest good, the attribute of free-will is essential to it, and so is an environment in which choices can be made. The weakness of the plan to create such beings was the possibility of a fall, but God's answer to that was to plan a pre-age in which the essential faith is developed to prevent any further recurrence of the fall, making it an eternally 'once only' event.

To accomplish this God planned the controlled environment of the present age of this world, where evil can be expressed freely, but is handled by God to develop the essential faith in all those that would progress to the future ages, where God would then be able to bestow full freedom on them with complete safety[59]. God therefore went ahead with his highest idea because his plan for the pre-age removed the obstacles to it.

As God's greatest idea, we begin to see that the creation of men and angels, with true free-will, is a truly awesome idea, and they are of supreme value to God and to the purpose of Love[60]. If God had made anything less than this then free-will would be an illusion and we would unconsciously be automatons; robots or puppets that God controls. No, God's idea is supremely higher than this. Our free will is no illusion. It is truly free, and it will continue to be so for all eternity.

The only ways that God has restricted us is by giving us limited understanding, and by limiting the domain he has created for us to live in. But it should be realised that even this pre-age domain that he created is part of the creation idea, and it conforms to the same moral imperative; that it is the highest idea that infinite wisdom and power could devise in the purpose of love.

At the present moment we see a highly restricted temporal domain of this world that lasts only while God develops the assets of faith in the redeemed of fallen men[61]. When he has finished his work with us here he

---

[58] Gen 1:26
[59] Rom 8:21, 2 Cor 3:17, Gal 5:13, Jam 1:25, 1Pet 2:16
[60] Gen 1:27,31
[61] 2 Cor 4:18

will then release us into an eternal domain where we have incredible freedom, which he will then be able to safely entrust to us. This is why the scripture describes us as *'leaping like calves released from the stall'*[62] when we come into the fullness of the eternal domain of heaven that God has all along intended for us. While we are here, we are like the little calves that are full of energy and long to get out into the field to enjoy the freedom to play and frisk around. Instead they are tied up and locked in; bored and frustrated, wondering what life is all about. Here we are groaning for release, and are impatient with yearning because we are so limited and restricted. We have great anticipation of so much better to come, but we must wait for it patiently.

We find the apostle Paul expressing all these sentiments as he contemplates and relishes the prospects of his revelation of our eternal destiny and home.[63]

---

[62] Mal 4:2
[63] Phil 1:23

CHAPTER 5: The Cost of Faith Development

We have previously argued that faith is the asset that God is seeking to develop in his created free-willed beings because it will eternally secure the whole of creation from corruption throughout all eternity, and is therefore of enormous value to God and his creation. But what does it cost?

Minimum suffering

We can be sure from the moral imperative that if there were an easier way for God to develop this incredibly valuable and precious asset of faith, involving less grief and suffering, then he would be under the same moral imperative of his own nature to take that course rather than the present one. *To opt for unnecessary suffering in any instance would be an immoral act that failed to fulfil the highest good.* We can therefore be sure that God has carefully measured every trial and difficulty that stimulates faith to grow[64]. In the final analysis it will bring forth maximum fruit, with minimum suffering, and in no way lead to the long term damage or loss of that most precious asset of faith which makes it all worthwhile[65].

When we are in the middle of the inward and outward '*trials of faith*' that come to all believers[66], it is a comfort to realise that God places great value on our faith, and he is its author and perfecter[67]. As we struggle with the issues at hand we should take heart in the fact that we are not the only one who is seeking to sustain our faith[68]. God will stretch us with precision, using his masterful skill and expertise, but he will ultimately protect and preserve our faith so that each trial turns out to increase faith, and not destroy it. As we struggle we should put our faith in that!

---

[64] 1 Cor 10:13, 1 Pet 1:6-7, Jam 1:2
[65] John 15:1
[66] 1 Pet 4:12-13
[67] Heb 12:2
[68] Rom 10:14, Matt 4:4, Matt 6:11, John 6:48,51

Modern media – On this point I think I see the wisdom of God in the invention of modern media, such as television. I recently heard a statistic that in this modern world we experience more stimulus in 2-3 months than people experienced in a lifetime just a century ago. It is unquestionable that modern media and technology has had a profound impact on the world. Many are unsure whether this is a blessing or a curse. I have on a number of occasions over the years judged myself or my family to have allowed television to become too prominent in our lives, and have taken the step of ejecting it from the home for a season; something we found profoundly beneficial for a while. However I do see how media has been used to raise a huge number of moral issues with us that would never have been possible without it, other than by allowing us to pass through many more difficult and painful experiences of our own. We see both real and fictitious presentations of both good and evil events and situations that make us consider, judge, and decide for ourselves. Through this stimulus our values and faith are developed on many things.

Undoubtedly modern media is utilised by both the realms of good and evil[69], but I do see in it a way that God has developed man's faith in so many areas, without him actually and personally experiencing all the difficult and painful circumstance of the situations portrayed before him. Through the use of shared experience over the media (news), and the use of fiction, I see that God has maximised the development of faith and values with the minimum of suffering. We see the full effects of the extremes of both good and evil in the world, portrayed from the comfort of our living rooms. All of these things lead us to consider and develop what we believe. Through these and other means, God has taught us many things using the pain and grief of others in this age of evil, without unnecessarily putting us through the same experience for ourselves. Clearly we have to have some experience of our own or everything would be abstract to us, but we must trust that our personal suffering has been kept to a minimum, without compromising the work and plans God has in developing us in eternal faith and character[70].

The fact that this invention of modern media has come towards the end of this age, when a significant proportion of the people of history are living (presently approximately one third), may be another act of God in

---

[69] Phil 4:8
[70] 1 Pet 5:10

minimising suffering, and yet developing faith in the multitudes of believers that will populate heaven with us. History has also become a vast resource to us for learning. It is a resource that the media continually draws on.

God made a world where these things are possible, and all of this is ultimately used by him to fulfil his purpose, despite the fact that it is often hijacked by our enemy as he attempts to use it for his own purposes.

We are the branches and the clay. He is the gardener and the potter[71]. What God made us to be we are becoming through his perfect and infinitely wise control of our circumstances and environment[72].

The development of faith is the key issue in this world and age. When we begin to take the leaps of faith that the saints gone by are now famous for, because they discovered (by faith) that this is the kind of God he is, then it makes God roar with laughter and delight[73], because it is good, very good! And it fulfils the very purpose of him tolerating evil for this unique season and age of the pre-history of creation.

Faith is what God delights in because it makes so much possible. This is what God saw in Abraham that made him promise to make him the father of many[74]. On a spiritual level the promise pointed to all those that would emerge through God's dealings with them with the same kind of faith that Abraham had, and who in the end would inherit the ages of ages God has planned for them[75].

The history of Israel – Still on the subject of God fulfilling his plans of love with minimum suffering, as part of the demands of love; we can come to understand the reason for the history of Israel. God used the tiny nation of Israel, early on in human history, to bring a statement of the moral law – the Law of Moses, to the world. This is their message and mission. However as the New Testament makes clear; though the law holds out a good standard, yet it is doomed to failure as a means to bring righteousness because of the broken, and in fact dead state of man's

---

[71] John 15:1,5 Rom 9:20-21
[72] Rom 8:28
[73] Heb 11:6
[74] Gal 3:9
[75] Jam 2:5 Eph 1:14,18 Col 1:12 1 Pet 1:4 Rev 21:7

spiritual being. Unwittingly, through the suffering of failure, Israel therefore taught the world that man could not gain God's favour by his own desire or effort[76], but that God must reform him. However, Israel was setup by God, as a stubborn people, to try to accomplish this first by their own effort as a lesson to prove to all the followed that it was not possible, and therefore to spare the majority the agonies of failure. Of course many have not heeded the warning and had to prove it for themselves, but we at least see that God did everything he could to spare us the agonies of failure through an example by which we all have the opportunity to learn this vital lesson second hand.

We see this lesson in miniature in the life of Jacob, who became known as 'Israel', and through whom the nation of Israel derived its name. Jacob meant 'trickster', which he proved to be in his life. However God brought him to the point of failure and broke him, even crippling him in the process, to where he had to lay down his self-belief and step into dependence on God.

Israel means 'struggles (or wrestles) with God'. We therefore see that the true message of Israel (the Jews) is best represented by those that are aware of the standard of their law and tradition, but are fully conscious of their failure to keep it. Not by those that claim to have become righteous by it. These 'failures' are the ones Jesus came to because their humble condition rendered them open to the message of grace that he brought to them, and by which they may find true righteousness.

Present example of God developing faith

Even at the present moment of writing this manuscript, I find myself in adverse circumstances; something to which I have become accustomed over the years. Though I find myself in this situation by carefully following God's lead in various decisions, and taking the risks I was led to take, God has presently got me cornered such that my only option is to wait for him to come through. Having got me where he wants me, I am guided to 'feed my sheep' and 'hand over the keys of the kingdom', which has translated in this case into the writing of this manuscript. I am therefore forced to act in faith, to maintain the place of rest and trust that no panic measures are necessary, because when God has finished stretching my faith he will once again come through in his own unique

---

[76] Rom 9:16

way. As I quietly depend on him he will send me all the resources of encouragement that I need to endure the trial[77].

Consider the advantage I have from understanding and believing this; that God's agenda in all of it is to extend my faith. Because I understand this the truth has once again set me free[78], and I am so much more able to patiently and peacefully wait for him, while getting on with and enjoying the task in hand. If I were in any doubt about this I may have found myself in the stress cycle of Psalm 73 where the writer looks at his own trying circumstances, then at the easy life of the wicked, and questions whether he had gained anything from his godly lifestyle[79]. Having passionately ranted and raved about the injustice of it all, the psalmist enters the temple and encounters the presence of God. Here he is once again impacted by the realisation of what it is all about; destiny, and declares himself to have been thinking like a '*brute beast*'[80]. He realises again that he is the one who is truly blessed because through his unique trials God is developing in him something that will last and be valued throughout eternity[81].

Once again we must consent to be the clay, and submit to the skilful hand of the potter who we can trust to see to it that our '*faith will come forth as gold*'[82].

Universalism and the loving God

Universalists, who believe that all men will be saved, struggle with the concept that some will not make it into spiritual renewal, and thereby to a spiritual life lasting beyond this world. Once again their argument is that a loving God could not do such a horrendous thing as to create creatures that would ultimately meet with loss and destruction[83].

But suppose for a moment that the enormity of the good of the eternal result of this short age were so great that it was totally dwarfed and eclipsed by the loss and cost. Would God then go ahead with such a plan?

---

[77] Rom 15:5
[78] John 8:32
[79] Ps 73:13
[80] Ps 73:22, 17
[81] Ps 73: 24
[82] Rom 9:20-21, 1 Pet 1:17
[83] Ps 73:18-20

Does this not put God in exactly the same kind of position that Winston Churchill was in when he made that excruciatingly difficult decision to allow men to walk into the ambush? His conscience demanded that he must choose it for the higher good.

We may find it hard to understand or accept, but it was God's call on this and not ours. It was his infinite wisdom that determined what cost was, or was not, worth paying in the event of the fallen race scenario, and what was and is the value of the outcome. We are living in the highest idea of God, not of ourselves. In the ages to come, when we come to understand better, we will undoubtedly agree with him.

The apostle Paul speculates on this very theme as he postulates: What if God put up with the objects of his wrath for a time in order to accomplish what was necessary for the objects of his mercy[84]; to secure this eternal future? In other words: What if the highest good demanded that some men and angels become catalysts in a short age of pre-history, and in the end are unavoidably lost in order to precipitate the thing that his highest idea could produce in creation?

Could God back away from this opportunity and ignore this decision that his own infinite wisdom demanded of him, albeit the source of excruciating pain to his heart of infinite love? We have far more reasons to believe that God would go ahead and do it – that he must do it – when we look at the evidence of what must also have been another inescapable demand of this supremely high idea; that of the cross.

Any lesser being would have chosen a lesser course than the cross, and accepted a lesser result. But because God is the God that he is, for him there was no other option. To fully weigh the costs against the outcome of God's chosen path is beyond our capacity for understanding. Our answers to these dilemmas in life lie primarily in faith and trust, but we are not entirely bereft of the ability to appreciate some of the immensity of the issues involved, as this text proves. It is likely that the events of the cross, and the cost and outcomes of this age, will stand throughout eternity to perpetually deliver ever increasing wonder to us. It will be there for all created beings to examine and explore it, and the nature of the God that chose it[85].

---

[84] Rom 9:22-23
[85] Phil 3:10

It is no wonder that angels long to look into these things![86] In eternity the opportunity of all created beings, like us, to investigate these things will be a never ending pursuit. What it reveals will be among our highest pleasures[87].

The ultimate goal

As this study progresses it is like a vortex that is gathering pace as we begin to come within sight of its centre. The more revelation we get, the closer we come to that centre, and the clearer it looms into view with its vast and terrible aspect that dwarfs us like the very universe itself. We become inescapably drawn to it like an eternal magnet.

Paul had come within sight of it and lived longer in this world to tell the tale, but he desired with all his heart to leave and move on as it became for him his passion and overwhelming desire. Nothing of this world any longer held any significance for Paul, other than to tell others about it[88]. His life was sold out with urgent and overwhelming longing to return to go deeper into what he had glimpsed. He saw himself as *'pressing on heavenwards'* to *'gain Christ'* and to *'know him and to share the power of his resurrection and the fellowship of his sufferings'*[85]. He glimpsed the centre of the vortex in the cross, and knew beyond doubt that this event, though it seems the greatest folly to men, was in fact the greatest wisdom of God[89]. He was captured by it to the extent that he was committed and determined to preach nothing else, because nothing else came within sight of it[90].

The passions and ideas of men Paul discarded as rubbish compared to this all surpassing desire. He saw religion as worthless[91]. All of his efforts became devoted to leading his brothers towards this all-consuming centre of Christ and him crucified. If he preached or taught anything else, it was perpetually geared to leading people to the place where they were mature enough to see this central, most awesome, and glorious truth of the cross of Christ.

---

[86] 1 Pet 1:12
[87] Ps 16:11
[88] Phil 3:21-26
[89] 1 Cor 1:18
[90] 1 Cor 2:2 Gal 6:14
[91] Phil 3:7-9

Many in our day miss the real point of the cross and God's eternal plan, and instead get enthralled in church, church service and their own ministry as if this were the end and not the means. To make this mistake is to mistake and miss the very point and purpose of it all, and to exist in an unenlightened and backslidden state. It is to play with the wrapping paper at Christmas.

These are hard hitting statements, but we should appreciate that on this issue the stakes are extremely high, and if we miss the point of it all we have much to lose.

At this point we may well ask ourselves – As a Christian is there something I am missing? Yes we know about the cross and have registered the Apostle Paul's fixation on it, but what are we to make of it? Do we put it down to Paul's eccentricity, or are we ready to take the hint that this, above all else, is where it is at? If we have any respect for any of the profound things Paul wrote, we must be deeply cautious of dismissing his expositions on this point as mere enthusiasm. Here he is pointing us to all that matters in our lives. Nothing we own, and nothing else we desire in this world should come near it, other than in love that we should desire it for our fellows as much as we desire it for ourselves.

The cross is the vortex centre of creation and all history, and although we may not yet have grasped what the fuss is all about, we must trust that we are being led to something of vast importance to us on the eternal scale of things.

Our study must press on to lay the ground work for us to explore this all important revelation of the cross. It will help us to know that this is where we are headed, and that we can expect it to have radical implications on the whole of our lives if we reach and grasp it.

Errors of Universalism

The doctrine of universalism is an idea that has crept into the belief systems of a significant number of Christians, both today and throughout the centuries.

In many instances it has found access by implication rather than through explicit teaching. At times it has been subconsciously granted access to the Christian belief system as a possible answer to some of the difficult questions of God being a loving God, yet creating or allowing a situation to arise in which some, or even many, will be lost. It is partly a humanistic reaction for those that at root believe that humanistic thinking is in fact greater than the doctrines of scripture, including the words of Jesus. Humanism is based on a belief that man is fundamentally good, whereas Christianity categorically teaches that man, having fallen, is fundamentally corrupt[92].

Of course many Christians would be horrified at the suggestion that they are deviating from the Bible by embracing the ideas of universalism, or even that they are embracing the doctrines of humanism. Many would attribute the belief that some will be eternally lost, to a failure to correctly interpret the Bible. However there are some extremely explicit parts of scripture that show that not all men will be saved[93].

If we can casually set these scriptures aside on the basis of either abhorrence of the idea, or a hunch that God would not do such a thing, then we are likely to eventually put the whole of scripture in the dock on the same basis, as many have.

The importance of the idea of universalism and its impact, if it is in fact in error as we have said, is huge, because it has the effect of taking the urgency completely out of the gospel message. One scriptural indicator that universalism is in error is the fact that scripture emphatically contains that urgency, whereas this doctrine of universalism invokes the casual response that absolves us of any need to transmit our faith to others because we believe they will definitely make it anyway. In fact the truth is much simpler, and it is that *men will actually be lost unless we act.*

Of course this could evoke in us the equally problematic responses of either condemnation for our failure to act, or panic that forces us to confront people. Both of these responses would be wrong. First because there is no condemnation and we are free from any such load[94]. And second because winning men is like fishing; we can't just rush into the water and grab the fish no matter how hungry we are. To win men requires strategy and wisdom. We need God to show us the way and resource us with direction, courage, faith, and compassion to act. Blundering actions in our own strength will only spook the fish and make them harder to catch in the long run. This will only lead to the discouragement of failure on our part. However we must not let this persuade us to give up, but

---

[92] Matt 7:11 2 Pet 1:4 Mark 10:18
[93] 2 Thes 2:10 John 3:16 John 5:40 Rom 9:22 Matt 7:13 Matt 23:23 2 Pet 2:4-10
[94] Rom 8:1

rather to look up. We must learn to fish, and it is God that must teach us to do it[95].

We stated it earlier and reiterate it again now: universalism is a failure to see how high the bar is set, and the enormity of the stakes in this fleeting age of pre-history that we are in. Those that are too horrified to contemplate the thought of souls being eternally lost should take a close look at the horror of the cross, and ask themselves what could ever warrant such an extreme action on the part of God.

Eternity – the ages of ages

The truth that some are headed for destruction is not easy to accept because we can feel our security challenged or even threatened by it. For many the response is to draw on the wisdom of the Ostrich, but as ever the better way is to face up to the truth, and by faith seek to understand the loving but awesome God behind it.

We have said that the only way we can understand a truly loving God creating such a situation, is for the product of his actions to vastly, or even infinitely, outweigh the cost. To begin to understand this we need to grasp something of the vastness of eternity. Or as it is more accurately translated, the '*ages of ages*'.

The word 'eternity' does some real damage to our concept of the plans God has for all beings that have a part in it because it suggests some kind of static unchanging state. The better translation of 'ages', or even the 'ages of ages' suggests the exact opposite; that beyond each age there is still greater to come, and that in every age to come this will ever be true[96].

We see God reflected in the fact that our present physical universe stretches out towards the infinite before us. Equally the ages ahead of us stretch out with the same incomprehensible vastness of infinity. We cannot possibly comprehend the scale of it.

In this study we explore something of just the next age of man which we know as heaven, but our appreciation of it and our ability to understand it is very limited, and much of it is abstract when we try to imagine it in terms of the present age because what follows is so much greater. The Bible therefore uses earthly symbols to describe it, but these

---

[95] Matt 4:9
[96] Eph 3:21

are at best a faint reflection of the reality that at present is beyond us to fully appreciate[97].

To think of yet another age beyond the next that is equally greater, is clearly way beyond our capability to imagine at the present time and with our present constitution, except to simply know that it exists.

The fact of an eternity of ever greater ages is a revealed concept that we can only grasp in the same way that we can contemplate the infinite. It is really an abstract thought to us because we are unable to come anywhere near a true appreciation of what it means.

Julian of Norwich – We have the writings of a nun from nearly a millennium ago known as Julian of Norwich. In them she shares some visions she was given by God.

In one of them she sees Jesus standing before her and he stretches forth his hand towards her, opening it to reveal a hazelnut in his palm. He then says to her 'this is all that is created'.

The revelation here is that God is vastly greater than all that is created in the physical and spiritual universe.

We cannot rule out the idea that God has not finished creating for all eternity and all ages to come. It is quite possible that in the ages to come we will see his creative hand move again and again to bring the greater and greater ages into being.

Even within the present age, we see man creating things that are vastly greater than himself in terms of their physical dimensions. We see immense buildings and structures, some of which strike us with awe, even though they are a product of our own hands.

Equally if God has gone no further than the hazelnut, relatively speaking, in creating the physical and spiritual universe so far, then shouldn't we anticipate that his creative expression may be far from complete at this present time? There is some degree of speculation here, but we have tantalising hints in scripture that God intends to go on creating in the ages beyond. We are already aware that having created the spiritual domain with all the angelic beings, he then went ahead and created the physical sub-domain as the angels watched, at which they sang and rejoiced with shouts of joy.

---

[97] 1 Cor 13:12

We can appreciate the wisdom of God in including the angels in this creative act right from the beginning; that they would have seen it in all of its original goodness, and would have formed a personal bond of love with it as the place where so much of their work would be focused. We can also understand the passion they have to see its restoration, for which they work so hard, knowing that God's plans are not just to restore it, but to produce something vastly greater than the original through the events of the fall. Their love and passion for us and the creation is seen in the way they rejoice whenever a sinner comes to Christ.

What we can be sure of from the whole testimony of scripture, including the words of Jesus, is that if we make it beyond this age we will have an unending part in all the ages of ages to come. In a similar way we may therefore come to see God's creativity in action like the angels did for our present physical world. We are repeatedly assured that if we make it through, we have eternal/everlasting life, and our dwelling place is with God forever. Jesus explicitly said on this matter '*if it were not so I would have told you*'[98]. This is the God of truth speaking directly to us. Our hope of eternity is true and it is real, therefore he has told us so.

It follows, as we have already discussed, that this age with its sufferings is merely an age of pre-history where the vital essentials of eternal beings to live securely in eternity are brought into existence.

If God were to have backed away from this age because of its sufferings he would have lost the opportunity to create the ages of ages to come. The future for us, for him, and for all eternal beings to enjoy this vast eternity of the ages together, would have been lost. The sufferings of this age were a cost he was unable to refuse because of the immensity of the goodness of what is to come through it.

As we begin to grasp the immensity of God's plan we are forced to reflect on the folly of living for this age alone. Jesus spoke of the deceitfulness of wealth[99]. Many in our day, even in the church, have a fixation on wealth and rarely emphasise these words of Jesus, unless they give a token acknowledgement or a dismissive reference to them. This treatment is a hint that they themselves are under its deceit, and are focused on this age alone. Many claim to seek wealth for the kingdom, and if they truly have this eternal perspective, and God's call to it, they may

---

[98] John 14:2
[99] Matt 13:22 Mark 4:19

have a valid claim. However we should see that the trials and experiences of seasons of poverty[100], and other challenges that cause us to cast ourselves on God and rely on him to supply our need, develops something of great great value. The result stretches out into the eternity of ages, as we have discussed; faith[101].

When we lead a soul to Christ, or do something that results in the development of faith or character in believers, the effects of what we do are like single strands of golden thread that stretch infinitely and eternally before us into the vastness of the tapestry of the future ages. Its implications are huge. No wonder angels rejoice at these things[102].

To seek the comforts of this world, and thereby forego the development of faith and all that is built upon it, is to pay a high price indeed[103]. It amounts to shear folly. If we have the truly eternal perspective we will despise anything that displaces the development of faith and character in this age of man, and seek to follow God into whatever challenges his wisdom has laid out for us in this world.

May God give us the wisdom to regard this world in these terms, and live our lives accordingly!

Free will and the doctrine of election

Referring back to the Calvinist/Armenian argument that has raged for centuries, with Calvinism emphasising predestination, and the Armenian emphasising free will; We explored the fact that the conflict in these ideas is resolved by the realisation that these doctrines are not mutually exclusive as they at first seem to be, but that they can actually coexist.

We saw that God can predestine without removing free will because he is able to control the external circumstances of every free-willed being to ensure that, although they make free choices, they are always led back to the path and destination that God predestined for them.

We therefore concluded that free will is no illusion, and all actions have their corresponding consequences, but that God works with these choices and he never subverts free will. The will of man is truly sovereign and free, but God controls the environment in order to work out his

---

[100] Phil 4:12
[101] 1 Cor 13:13
[102] Luke 15:10
[103] Luke 12:20

purposes. Of course men and angels may cooperate with God, so his control may be partially via their voluntary submission to his will, but for all other areas where they are either ignorant of God's will, or in rebellion against it, he is able to control their actions externally to ensure that his purposes of love are accomplished.

We then went on to explore the truth that due to the immensity of the plan of God, as the Bible makes clear, not all men will be saved. Some will be lost. Together with the ideas of free will, what follows is that men choose their own path. Some choose to accept God's offer of redemption from sin and are saved. Others refuse it and are lost; both as an act of their own free will. This raises the question of where the doctrine of *election* fits into this scheme of things. The doctrine of election teaches that it is God and God alone that decides who is saved and who is lost; that he elects/chooses those who receive salvation[104]. Once again this is a Calvinist doctrine, but also a biblical one that seems to contradict the freedom of man to choose his own destiny by either accepting or refusing God's offer of redemption. How do we resolve this?

Once again the doctrine of election can coexist with free-will when we consider that God is able to use circumstances to lead any man to a point where he is ready and willing to accept salvation. BUT, under the current scheme of things, in the way God has configured his creation, it is not possible that all men will be saved. I repeat: God can lead any chosen individual to salvation, but not all can be saved; some must be lost.

Why must some be lost? – As discussed previously, the short answer to why some must be lost is that, according to God's infinite wisdom, only through this path and plan can the highest good be served because the result is eternal, compared to an infinitesimally short period of pre-history where evil happens and the losses are incurred.

The longer answer is more difficult because we struggle to understand the detail of God's paths, but we can speculate that God's purpose in this age is to eliminate any possibility that a fall will ever happen again, once and for all eternity. He desires to release his creation into an environment where they are incredibly happy, and have full freedom together with incredible power and responsibility, without risk of corruption. It is therefore essential that the security of faith in all beings that survive the

---

[104] Rom 9:11 2 Thes 2:13 2 Tim 2:10 1 Pet 1:1-2, 2:9 Phil 1:29

CHAPTER 5: The Cost of Faith Development

present age, be bought at great cost by them developing faith in the following:

- A full appreciation of the horrors of evil.
- A full appreciation of the genuine losses of evil.
- That redemption is only possible at an immense cost.
- That only God can possibly pay the cost of redemption.
- That God's redemption is a once only event in all eternity.
- That for some there was no possibility of redemption.
- That redemption was only possible at all for any man because they fell from a position of relative naivety to evil.
- That redemption by God's grace is entirely unmerited and undeserved favour.
- That God is both merciful and unswervingly just.

We can appreciate, in some measure at least, that this essential faith cannot be achieved unless genuine losses are incurred in this fallen age while the essential eternal lessons are learnt, and faith is developed. It is not too difficult to appreciate that if God had acted to redeem all, then the very reverse of some of these items of faith would be the result, and that would inevitably destabilise all future security, virtually guaranteeing another fall somewhere in eternity, based on the belief that all losses would ultimately be recovered.

We can even consider that this present age of evil is part of the essential creative process of God to create the beings that he has planned to occupy eternity with him. That is why we are calling the present age an age of pre-history, because it is merely in preparation for the ages to come where the goodness of what God has created is seen in its fullness[105].

Who will be saved? – We are now led to consider that if God can lead any to salvation, but not all, and that he must choose some, who will he choose (i.e. elect)? Once again this is not a random decision by God. As for everything God ever did, right from the decision to create at all, God must choose those that will fulfil the highest purpose of love and goodness throughout eternity. From his perspective of an intimate understanding of

---

[105] Eph 2:7

each and every individual that he has made, he is able to make this choice. He is able to see the effects of choosing one individual over another right out into the reaches of eternity.

This is well beyond our wisdom, knowledge and understanding to appreciate for any individual person. It is an amazing thing to reflect on the fact that to choose one person over another will always have an impact on the eternal outcome. God considers everything. To choose one that will evangelise in obedience, over another that will not, may have a radical impact on the actual number that come in. On the other hand to choose the one that will evangelise, over another that will disciple others, may have a huge impact on the eternal fruit that is developed through this age. Of course God is the one that gives the gifting for such service, but he knows what can be done with one individual over another.

Only God knows the optimal choice to achieve the highest possible good into all eternity, and this is the choice he has made. We therefore find Jesus speaking of those that are *'worthy'* to take part in the coming age[106]. Here we see the criteria of worth as the deciding factor. But worth to what? The answer is: worth to love, and therefore worth to God who is love.

We must be careful here and realise that this is not an assessment based on self-achievement. Rather it is related to the ability of God to individually lead us to fulfil the purposes of love. Only that which is done in his power and enabling can have an eternal impact for good.

So there is no hint of some legalistic or competitive idea in this idea of worth, as if man were able to achieve his own worthiness. This is purely a matter of sovereign choice based on God's knowledge of every individual, and their potential impact on eternity based on his infinite wisdom and foreknowledge[107]. God has the capacity to bring any man through to surrender himself and receive salvation if he reveals enough to him of the future consequences of refusing it. However, now that man has fallen there is a cost, and it is unavoidable that some must be lost. He therefore carefully measures the revelation men receive so that though many are called, only the elect come through to true repentance and salvation[108], and through this means of election and selection the eternal purpose of love is served, all without compromising man's free will.

---

[106] Luke 20:35
[107] Rom 9:10-18

As a general rule we can reason that those that accept the truth of their fallen condition and receive salvation more readily, are those that are more fitted for eternity because it is they that show themselves to be more ready to face the truth, and to have a more honest and humble heart that will therefore better serve the purpose of love in eternity. However such reasoning is futile[109], and we will always see God calling the unexpected, often in preference to those we would expect, based on his own infinite reason, not ours[110].

The implications of God's choice are so far reaching that the only way we can recognise a chosen one is by seeing them come to faith, and then by them producing good fruit as evidence of their rebirth[111].

As we consider that God must make this choice of who is saved, and who is lost, we realise that this is part of the unavoidable cost of creating free-willed beings in the act of creation. The other part of the cost is nothing less than the cross of Christ, as we will see later.

We may feel it is unfair on those that did not receive salvation, but what we must realise is that it is an entirely free choice on their part, and really every man deserves condemnation. It is only the action of God's grace that sets the natural consequences of sin aside for some.

The parable Jesus told of the workers in the vineyard demonstrates the point that it is entirely at the discretion of the master to give beyond what is deserved[112]. This act of God is an act of grace; the undeserved favour of God on some that could be reached[113]. If he were able to give it to all, and still fulfil the purposes of love, he would have done it gladly[114]. However the plan is so immense that this is not possible, and God must make this choice in the purposes of love, regardless of the pain these losses cause him. As a result we see God calling many, but only the few that are chosen/elect accept the call[115] because they are the ones God has conditioned and prepared through their circumstances to be ready to receive it. They are brought to a place, through their circumstances, where

---

[108] Matt 13:15
[109] 1 Cor 3:20 Ps 94:11
[110] Is 55:9
[111] Matt 7:20
[112] Matt 20:1-16
[113] Eph 2:8-9
[114] 2 Pet 3:9
[115] Matt 22:14

they are ready to accept his salvation as an act of their free will. God reaches out to them by offering them the enlightenment of faith that if accepted, brings with it spiritual rebirth[116].

A personal testimony of salvation – My personal journey towards God stretches back to my childhood and youth. I was raised in a Christian home as the son of a Pastor, and as such I heard the gospel many times. Many times in my childhood I was profoundly impacted when I heard the gospel preached, but like all 'Christian kids' I had to come to the point of making my own decision.

Though my home was a place of safety, I nevertheless experienced many influences from outside of the home that were less protective. As a result, to some degree, I accepted the values I was offered by my peers and the world, and as I reached my mid-teens I became involved in an intimate relationship.

The experience led to the inevitable conflicts, crashes and mistakes one would in hindsight expect. As I faced up to the pain and consequences of my sinful juvenile choices in my mid-teens, I turned to God in a prayer of desperation.

At this time I had developed many questions of faith that I felt must have answers for me to progress any further in a life that included God. At this point I therefore appealed to God for answers, hoping that he was there and would hear me. In my ignorance I made a request that if God be real, he should make himself known to me before I reached eighteen years old, because I had no desire to live my life in ignorance of him if he really did exist. Strangely I left this prayer with a profound sense of peace, as if God had agreed to my request, and from this point the turmoil in my life seemed to recede. The relationship continued. I finished my schooling and began work in the coal mining industry as an engineer in training.

The next thing that happened to me was completely unexpected; my partner found Christ. I was unprepared for the reaction that this provoked in me, probably rooted in the guilt I experienced from my own spiritual condition. It was then that my relationship problems and issues began to surface again, and my world began to fall apart. Not only was I distressed at home, but the job was tough both physically and

---

[116] 1 Thes 1:5

psychologically, especially as I observed many men that seemed to have little hope of anything but what I saw before me in the mines, for the rest of their lives. I had come from the naivety of youth, with hopes and dreams, to an experience of many men that had none, or at least nothing that impressed me. I found the impact of it oppressive.

As the trouble intensified I continued to attend my local church under the duress of my parents. At this time I had become used to the experience of hearing the gospel, followed by an appeal to respond. Almost without exception I would feel the pull and impact of God in these appeals. However, over the years I had learnt to resist them, and walk away without any response. I had learnt that the impact soon subsided as I did so.

On this occasion, as my whole life seemed to be under siege, I yet again heard the gospel, and the appeal to respond, and was again profoundly impacted by the draw of the Holy Spirit. Again I weathered the experience until the meeting ended, and I walked out of the church and headed home. However instead of the usual subsiding of the experience of deep conviction, the experience continued.

I reached my home, took off my leather jacket, and lay on my bed. But the Spirit of God was still upon me strongly. As I lay there a deep conviction came to me that tonight I must make a choice. I must choose the path of my life. The gravity of it was unmistakable, the choice was clearly now or never. I knew that if I would not voluntarily respond to God under the level of conviction I was now experiencing, then I surely never would.

I soon reached the point where I was ready to surrender. My circumstances of life at the time were painful, and had already impacted me severely. I really felt I had little reason to resist. As I got up from my bed, I put on my jacket and headed back to the church. Several times on the way I changed my mind and turned back home, hoping to resist the deep conviction within me. Each time the conviction intensified, and each time I responded again and turned back towards the church. Only this gave me relief, and a sense of peace, but the urgency persisted.

When I finally made it to the church where the after meeting was still in progress, I asked a respected member to help me to pray the sinners prayer. There and then I surrendered my life to God. Nothing in my life has ever been so dramatic. In the intensity of my emotions I was suddenly and unmistakably born again. My spiritual eyes were opened. I suddenly saw beyond any doubt that the message of Christ was true and real.

One of the remarkable things about this event was that though I had long forgotten my prayer of two and a half years earlier, I had surrendered my life to Christ on the eve of my eighteenth birthday. It was a mere three hours before the very deadline that I had laid down in my request to God.

In all of this two things are unmistakable; the hand of God, and my freedom of will to choose. Not all people experience such dramatic conversion as I did, but this path was right for me. I have seen many others come through a much slower and more gradual experience, but what is clear is there always comes a point where they surrender and become inwardly spiritually aware. God is sovereign in his dealings with us. However the will of man is also sovereign, and though God devises the circumstances that lead his elect to him, they nevertheless surrender their lives as an act of voluntary and perfect free will.

Why must some be lost, the detail? – We can appreciate in some measure the detail of why some must be lost in this great plan of God. It is essential that the effects of sin be seen and understood in their entirety by all that pass through this age and on into the eternity of ages to come. It is partly this experience that will ensure eternal security hereafter. It is therefore essential that many who are ultimately lost push the godless life to its full conclusion, so that those that find eternal life may learn the true cost of the fall. If God always intervened to prevent evil developing to its full potential, this would never be appreciated. The more completely the horrors of evil are appreciated, the more this aspect of eternally protective faith is established in the fact that God's way is the only way. For this faith to be properly formed the full horrors of departure from God's ways has to be revealed. This includes testimony to such things as: the gruesome violence we constantly hear about in our world; the lustful abuse of the body; the vanity of man; and the power mongering and brutality of tyrants and despots.

For this reason we see God withholding judgement on the earth in some cases while the sins and wickedness of certain people and nations reach their full measure (e.g. Sodom and Gomorrah, the Amorites[117]).

---

[117] Gen 15:6, 18:20

But this is to speak only of the plight of man. If we also consider the spiritual corruption of fallen angels with their diabolical malice and power systems, the picture is a dark one indeed.

For man these are the more dramatic things that often get the focus in this world, but the truth also includes the reality of the emptiness of life without God, and the dissatisfaction and lack of fulfilment that many experience on a daily basis, which is itself a true evil.

In the end we only have a simplistic understanding of God's reasoning for allowing all this, but we must hold to the belief that despite the horrors of this evil age, the only reason some are lost is because the plan is so great that it had to be so. We must believe that God is bringing forth the essential faith in those that survive that has made the ages to come possible, and that he has done it with the least possible suffering in this age of evil.

So the conclusion is that God calls and elects, but at the same time men receive or refuse as an act of their free will. The doctrines of election and free-will do therefore coexist.

The sufferings of believers – This understanding of election leads us to an understanding of the sufferings of believers.

We mentioned earlier the case of Job whose faith was tested severely as he suffered great loss. The suffering was then exacerbated by his 'comforters' and their theological view that only the wicked suffer. Later another young man spoke up who could see God's use of suffering in favour of man as a means to discipline and reform him.

We now raise the bar again to say that God uses our sufferings to bring forth a crop of faith that has an eternal value and purpose that is so great, it is beyond our ability to fully appreciate[118]. The outcome of Job's suffering was that he became a greater man of faith that would never again readily question or doubt God's character, even in the most extreme suffering and circumstances. Though Job probably never appreciated this during his lifetime, because it was not yet revealed, he was being profoundly enriched for heaven and eternity.

This is now a revealed truth of the New Testament. As a result the tables are now completely turned, and we are led to rejoice in our sufferings because we know that in the end, if we endure it, we develop

---

[118] 2 Cor 4:6-8

invaluable eternal faith[119]. As we will come to see; the result is genuine treasure in heaven[120].

Ironically for believers, the pursuit of comfort and security in this life, as an alternative to relying on God, often translates to a pursuit of spiritual poverty in heaven[121]. Fortunately God is on the case of each individual, as the potter and gardener are to the pot and the branch, to stimulate the maximum result[122]. Therefore when our thinking gets out of step with God's we don't always achieve what we hope for, thank God[123].

Evangelism – The doctrine of election means that we meet some in this world that are not destined to be among the elect, and who are therefore ultimately and eternally lost. Only God knows for certain who these are. We could only know for certain if he revealed it to us, but generally this does not happen and we are instructed instead not to judge, but to wait for the appointed time of judgement when all is revealed[124]. This applies to all individuals we meet, and to every action we see an individual take.

Motives are something that God has allowed men to hide in this world. By hiding this from us we are compelled to treat all men equally, showing love to them all. In evangelism we are forced to try to reach all in order that some may be saved[125]. Even then we can never be absolutely sure about those that profess to believe. If they produce fruit in keeping with salvation, this is a good sign[126], but ultimately we are told not to pre-judge, but that we should leave it to God who knows those who are his[127].

When I meet people on the streets in my evangelistic efforts I am led to be hopeful and open hearted towards everyone I meet, treating them all as future believers[128].

---

[119] 1 Pet 1:6-7 Jam 1:2-4
[120] Matt 6:19-20
[121] Luke 6:24 Jam 5:5
[122] John 15:2,5,8
[123] Jam 4:3
[124] 1 Cor 4:5
[125] 1 Cor 9:22
[126] Luke 6:44
[127] 2 Tim 2:19
[128] 1 Cor 9:22

The sufferings of unbelievers – Earlier we put forward a moral principle; that it is immoral to choose a path that causes *unnecessary* suffering. This is the same principle as the demand to always choose the highest good, or in certain circumstances to choose the least of two or more evils.

We see this principle at work in the way God handles unbelievers. If it were possible, God would spare all men their sufferings. However in the case of believers we have discussed the fact that God can use their experience for the higher purpose of developing faith, but how do we account for the suffering of unbelievers?

Again, if it served the purposes of love, God would spare unbelievers their sufferings too. However it is essential that the effects and sufferings caused by sin are clearly seen and appreciated by those that have a destiny beyond this age. Unbelievers are therefore not exempt from suffering by any means. Though as both Job and the psalmists observed; the wicked do not always suffer for their wickedness[129]. Sometimes they experience all the earthly blessings and comforts of this world[130]. We can be sure that either God is using this circumstance in some way, or it may be a case of God not causing unnecessary suffering, even to those that will ultimately be lost. As Psalm 73 and other psalms declare: it is only the perspective of eternal destiny that can make sense of these things[131].

Sinners and Pharisees – Once we understand these principles of election we begin to appreciate why Jesus came to the sinners, and not to the self-righteous.

The redemption and reformation of sinners would carry vastly greater value through to eternity than the beliefs of such self-righteous people as the Pharisees ever could. For sinners their testimony of the horrors of evil, their faith in the mercy and grace of God, and the power of God to overcome evil and to reform them, are of immense value in eternity. It is these assets of faith that will underpin the security of the ages[132].

---

[129] Job 21:29-34, 24:12, 35:15
[130] Ps 73:2-12
[131] Ps 73:17
[132] Luke 7:47

By contrast the Pharisees were in denial on all these points, abounding in self-belief rather than faith in God, having little need for forgiveness or mercy they became of no value in eternity[133]. They thereby lacked any value to God and creation to become one of the elect.

Of course many men that have never plunged themselves into the depths of evil are chosen, but never those that cannot, or will not appreciate that they too are part of a web of evil in this fallen world.

For those that are brought up with good discipline, and thereby manage by training to avoid many of the traps of sin, God often applies special grace to reveal the hidden depths of their need. On the whole the most important qualities that give value to an individual in eternal terms are honesty and humility, because only this will lead to faith. It was precisely the dishonesty of the Pharisees, with their control and manipulation of the truth that drew such scathing and revealing words from the mouth of Jesus[134]. Even this was not issued to condemn them. By revealing the depths of their depravity Jesus was seeking to give them the best possible chance they could have of seeing the truth, because only this could give them any chance of being found among the elect.

Many are preoccupied with seeking to live a good life in this world in order to give themselves a measure of eternal security on earth, because they think that through their works they may obtain eternal life.[135] Often, for these, the greater need they have is to seek to discover the truth about the need of their inner self, rather than seek to mask it with good works and the approval of men. Job was one of the most righteous men that ever lived, but he sacrificed daily in case there was any transgression in his family[136]. This is how aware and careful he was when it came to being honest about his inner state, or that of his family.

The demand to be truthful is fundamentally important because truth and life are closely bound together in the way of the one who said *'I am the Way the Truth and the Life. No-one comes to the Father but through me'*[137].

---

[133] Luke 18:9-14
[134] Matt 23:13-33
[135] Rom 10:3
[136] Job 1:5
[137] John 14:6

The diversity and testimony of the elect – What we do know is that the elect people who come through this age and make it to eternity, will be a great multitude from every people, language, tribe, and nation[138]. We can assume that they also come from every era of this present age. In this way there will be a full witness of this age, with all its diversity of good and evil, carried forward as a testimony in the ages to come.

It seems we may possibly spend another age sharing our experiences of this present age when we come into the fullness of the intimacy of the union of the Spirit in heaven, together with all our fellow believers. The combined testimony of it all will then be carried forward by all, and will become part of the guarantee of faith that there will never be another fall in all of the ages to come.

Angels and reactions to creation

It is not only man that is being developed through this evil age. Angels are profoundly engaged in these events as *'ministering spirits sent to serve those who will inherit salvation'*[139]. They are aware of it all and are direct observers of the heavenly events, and of God's handling of it all[140].

In the book of Job, God himself recounts how the angels sang, rejoiced, and shouted with joy as they observed God in the process of creating the physical universe[141]. This display of the raw power of God must have been a profoundly breath-taking experience for them as God did something that was so infinitely beyond their own power to do; he created. They could discern, to the level of their own capacity to appreciate it, the profound and awesome goodness of what God was doing.

We recall in Genesis that God himself stood back after creating the universe and declared, according to his own infinite wisdom, that *'it is good'*[142]. The angels would have appreciated in some measure this goodness of what was done.

It is a remarkable thing that God chose to create part of his creation first, including the spiritual realm with the angels, then in another

---

[138] Rev 7:9
[139] Heb 14:1
[140] Luke 15:10
[141] Job 38:7
[142] Gen 1:31

phase of his plan allowed them to witness the creation of the whole realm of the physical universe, including man.

We humans as a race can sometimes get so self-absorbed in our own race to forget that God has created angels too, and he has a relationship with each one of them, just as he does with us. He is profoundly interested and careful in their development, as he is with us, correcting them and engaging them with us as servants, even though at present they are superior beings to us[143]. This is part of God's great plan to develop both them and us together into the beings he wants us to be, with all the values and faith we and they need in place so we can together populate an eternal future with a happiness that is entirely and eternally secure.

Through all these events and experiences the angels were, and still are witnessing the true nature of God, exposed in ways that would never have been seen or appreciated without it.

Angels and heavenly bodies

Cherubim are one kind of angel that appear to have a major role in the service of the human race and God's kingdom here on earth[144]. Other kinds of angel exist, like the Seraphim whose focus seems to be more primarily on direct ministry to God in worship. They cannot bear to be away from the inner courts of his presence for long[145].

Incidentally, as an aside, I should say that I have come to believe that in the race of men, among the people of God, there are similar divisions. Some focus primarily on service, others are made more for direct ministry to God and they often have a more secret, but incredibly intimate walk with him[146].

Like Obed Edom in the time of King David who had the Ark of God stored at his house for three months[147]. He was thereafter incurably hooked on God's presence. He pops up several times in the record of subsequent events, always involved in service in pursuit of the Ark and God's presence, and seeking to serve in the inner court[148]. His heart's

---

[143] Job 14:18 Heb 2:7
[144] Ezek 28:14,16
[145] Is 6:2,6
[146] 1 Cor 7:7
[147] 1 Chron 13:13-14

longing echo would be *'to be even a doorkeeper in the house of God'*[149]. No doubt King David and others watched his progress closely, and it was perhaps what inspired the psalm.

Some major on service as their form of worship, others on the worship of praise, and others on prayer. Each kind of person is convinced they have the best of it, but as C. S. Lewis provocatively puts it: 'God made all men unequal'; we are all made differently.

I suspect that when we reach heaven and embrace our new immortal bodies, where we see one another clearly as we really are, then just as Seraphim, Cherubim and other angelic beings are easily distinguishable by their kinds, we will see the same spectrum of variety in the kinds of men that God has made[150]. To some degree this is visible now. We see in each other a reflection of the real spiritual being beneath these temporal bodies that are like husks concealing the real fruit.

It is like comparing the chrysalises of different species of butterfly, which some experts are able to identify and distinguish. How much easier is it to see the difference in the species when they emerge in their full glory?

A revelation of Christian maturity

Once as a young Christian, in the middle of many inward and outward struggles, I visited Chatsworth House; a famous stately home in Derbyshire, England.

From a place of inner turmoil I was taking some time out, and I remember standing admiring two impressive marble statues of huge lions that were so finely carved they looked like they might stand up and roar at any moment.

As I stood there another visitor on my left spoke to me and said, 'magnificent aren't they'. In an instant, through that simple contact, I got a glimpse into the spiritual state of the person that was speaking to me. I discerned that this was a mature Christian, and sensed the tremendous peace of his inner being that seemed to be revealed and shared just for a fleeting moment. What was revealed to me in that moment seemed for me to be such a completely opposite state to the state I was then passing

---

[148] 1 Chron 15:18,21,24,25, 16:5,16:38,
[149] Ps 84:10
[150] 1 Cor 13:12

through, with its 'strange trials' and inward suffering[151]. God was able to use this fellow Christian to re-envision me, and show me that despite my present experience of seemingly interminable darkness, and my battles with the mind and the sinful nature, that there is in fact a time when the *'day dawns and the morning star rises in our hearts'*[152]. A time when we rise above the sinful nature as if moving from night to day, and we come to know God in a way that makes us yearn for heaven as the apostle Paul did[153].

In this moment I saw what was not only possible, but in fact was already eternally secure through God's determination to deliver me into it.[154] Little more was said by this fellow Christian stranger, but nothing more was needed.

I have to say now, many years on, that between then and now there have been many trials and many easier times and seasons, but I have undoubtedly closed in on what God revealed to me there.

I believe this kind of vision or revelation, where we see one another clearly, is precisely the kind of thing that will be the ongoing experience and norm in heaven, where we share ourselves with each other and become one with God and one another in what is presently almost inconceivable fellowship[155].

Angels reaction to the plan

There is a hearsay story in the kind of C. S. Lewis's Screwtape letters where two angels are discussing in heaven the events they are witnessing on earth.

The two angels are talking with some dismay at the rampant spread of evil in the earth. If we understand something of the horror of sin and evil to God as a holy God, and as revealed in the cross, then we should be able to appreciate something of the 'feelings' of the angels towards the events on earth and the prevalence of evil there, given that they are in spiritual union with God.

---

[151] 1 Pet 4:12
[152] 2 Pet 1:9
[153] Phil 1:23 2 Cor 5:2
[154] Phil 2:12-13
[155] 1 Cor 13:12

They had seen God deal radically and justly with those of their own kind that rebelled and were expelled from heaven and God's presence, but here they saw God apparently tolerating the ongoing existence of evil. This would have been a trial to them like the sins of Sodom were to the soul of righteous Lot[156], and they would have longed for it be resolved in one way or another.

It is itself a situation that would demand faith on the part of angels to wait for God to act. As the story goes, one of the angels says:

First: 'Have you heard the news?'
Second: 'What News?'
First: 'You mean you haven't heard? God is going down there!'
Second: 'Going where?'
First: 'To Earth!'
Second: 'Finally he's going to sort this lot out. I was beginning to think it would go on forever. Thank God! He's going to put an end to it. Thank God!'
First: 'No you don't understand; he's going to become one of them. He's going to become a Man!'
Second: 'He's going to WHAT?'
First: 'It's true. He's going to become a Man!'

This is a simple story to convey the total incredulity that angels would have felt at hearing this news for the first time.

Again in the words of C. S. Lewis – for God to become a man is like an arc-angel condescending to become a garden slug, only the descent is far, far greater. For the angels to know the awesome breath-taking glory of God, and then see him consent to descend from such glory to such incomprehensible grime, would have given them the greatest shock of horror and wonder that they are ever likely to experience in all eternity. Any one of them would desperately prefer to take this plunge than let the God of glory in the highest do such a thing.

The incarnation is such an incredible thing to them that we find the New Testament writers telling us that *'angels long to look into these things'*[157]. They know that through it God is revealed to both us and them in ways that would never have been possible without the fall.

---

[156] 2 Pet 2:7

Again as the book of Job points out, angels are fallible. They make mistakes, and God corrects them so they learn[158]. These are not sins or moral failures, but merely errors, born out of the fact that they are finite beings like us. For them God's handling of both fallen angels with justice, and fallen man with mercy and justice, is a profound learning experience, and they are first hand witnesses of these events from the beginning in ways that we are not.

On the other hand, we are first hand witnesses of what it is like to be a sinful fallen being, and to find the forgiveness and mercy of God in a way that they have not. In the coming ages of ages, God has destined that we will intimately share these things, including our lives, our faith, and our experiences, as we come into awesome levels of friendship, intimacy, and union with him, and with each other, together with all his created beings, in a way that will eclipse even the most intimate relationship we have here in this age.

The Bible says there *'we will fully know and be fully known'*[159]. The question that is often asked about heaven – 'Will we recognise one another?' – shows our deep poverty when it comes to our knowledge of the things of heaven. There we will realise that we have only so far seen each other as a dark shadow, and as a poor reflection. We will realise we have seen no more than a silhouette of even our most intimate partners and friends. The recognition we have in heaven will finally be complete, and we will suddenly realise fully who we have been living with and relating to for such a long time.

Though we may have known a wife, or friends, for many years, and though they may be our most intimate companions, there we will know them, and they will know us, with greater intimacy than anything we have on earth. When we are there, what we had here will be considered totally obsolete. Here we are a work in progress, and as such we are partially hidden and not yet on exhibition. There we are complete and ready for God to show us off as his handiwork, and all his glory in us[160]. There the faith developed in this age will ensure the security of the happiness of all beings for all eternity.

---

[157] 1Pet 1:12
[158] Job 4:18
[159] 1 Cor 13:12
[160] Eph 2:6-7

Let's be sure about this: God's nature is infinite goodness; he is Love. At any and every level his purposes are beyond our comprehension, and he has prepared for us in heaven a place for which a Persian garden of paradise is only a faint shadow of the reality[161]. There he will totally satisfy us with himself, each other, and his creation. It is essential for now that both we and this future be revealed only as *'through a dark glass'*[162], in order that God may finish the work he must do first in order to secure it for us for all eternity.

Let's take the advice we are given to rejoice in our light and momentary troubles[163], doing all we can to cooperate with him in his work with us, making this temporary life deliver every atom of faith it has to give us, and every other aspect of God's nature that can be built upon it.

Doxology and faith development

In the letter to the Romans, having explored some of the mysteries of God's dealing with man, the apostle Paul spontaneously breaks out into a torrent of praise and wonder that someone has incredulously labelled a 'doxology'.

I have to also marvel at that, and wonder if the person who ascribed that word to Paul's expression really got it! This is no 'ology', this is the apostle Paul leaping and dancing around the room and shouting WOW! WOW!! WOW!!! What an awesome God! I feel at this point, as I ponder the subject, I must do the same: *'Oh, the depth of the riches of the wisdom and knowledge of God! How unsearchable his judgments, and his paths beyond tracing out!'*[164]

I am profoundly convinced that God knows his business, and it is wise beyond my comprehension. And where does that lead us? Well it leads us to the challenge to deny the apparent desperation of our circumstances, and throw ourselves wholly on this God who hides his face and waits for us to decide how to react.

I look back over more than 30 years of my Christian walk and remember passing through dire straits, when only a miraculous intervention would avert disaster. Having passed through considerable

---

[161] Luke 23:43 Rev 2:7
[162] 1 Cor 13:12
[163] 2 Cor 4:17
[164] Rom 11:33

anxiety in the early experiences, and then seen God pull me through, I had to come to the point of saying: 'You can't fool me God. I know you're there so you might as well come out'.

He really is ok with that kind of prayer, and I think has some real delight in it. It's like a huge game of 'hide and seek' with a real dangerous and thrilling edge to it. Waiting for God to come through can be an emotional roller coaster ride, but boy does faith grow!

If we are only able to accept it, we have all the safety nets we need. God has promised never to test us beyond that which we are able to bear, and to provide escape routes whenever they are needed[165]. That should be good enough, but we should also remember that God is not wasteful, and these experiences are used efficiently by him to bring forth the fruit. He takes us right to the edge, and will stretch us beyond what we think are our own limits[166].

There are many brave souls in the victorious history of the true Church that have realised that God is infinitely more dependable than we have even contemplated, and have gone pro-active in their risk taking ventures expecting God to see them through.

Finding mercy and help in times of need is a great thing, but this bold leaping of faith to advance the kingdom that these souls have launched themselves into, is when the adventures really begin. At this point the growth of faith in these adventurous souls turns rampant and the rest of us are left to marvel in its wake.

George Mueller – One amazing example of this kind of faith is George Mueller who moved from Prussia to Bristol, England in the 1830's.

Having been a youth who indulged his youthful passions to the extreme, and developed irresistible patterns of dishonest and corrupt behaviour that even disgusted himself, he was faced with deep dissatisfaction of soul, and at this point found Christ.

From there he began to radically change and manifest the very opposite in the form of honesty to himself, God, and everybody he met. In so doing he discovered and believed the promise of God to meet his every need if he would '*seek first the kingdom of God*'. As an act of obedience and faith, he gave up all sources of worldly financial support, and found

---

[165] 1 Cor 10:13 Heb 2:18
[166] 2 Cor 1:9

that though he often lived on the edge, God always came through and met his need. Then, having discovered that the believers in general had such small faith in these things, he chose to take a radical step, partly to do some good for orphaned children, but specifically and primarily to demonstrate to his fellow believers at large that God's word has rock solid dependability.

He audaciously opened orphanages and schools, and rather than simply depending on God for himself and his family, he demonstrated to the world that without asking men for a dime, God was able to meet every need of these whole institutions, simply by prayer and faith. Though he ran these benevolent institutions for no less than 45 years, and though God constantly tested him by bringing him to the point of having no provisions for himself or the children in his care for the day, his faith grew and God never failed to come through to meet his need.

These are the kind of people that prove to the rest of us that in this world we are living under what Jesus called the *'deceitfulness of wealth'*[167]. God is our only real resource and security. When men discover it and trust it, God absolutely delights in it, because faith is such an eternally profound, good, and valuable thing.

Personal Stories of Faith Development – Over more than 30 years there have been numerous occasions when God has developed my faith through testing and trials, and then led us to his providence. God deals with us individually in these things, but for me and my family there have been some considerable financial trials. Of these I will briefly share three occasions where God came through in ways that grew our faith incredibly, marvellously enriching our spiritual lives and liberating us from the belief that we are in any way dependent on this world for provision.

In the first instance, after some clear direction from God, I had set up in business and begun developing software, having left the receding UK mining industry with a redundancy payment. The development took the best part of two years. No sooner had I finished developing the software than the country was plunged into recession following what has become known as the 'Black Wednesday' stock market crash. At this point I was at the end of my resources and was left wondering where I had gone wrong. The result was mortgage arrears that after a while extended to

---

[167] Matt 13:22 Mark 4:19

£1800, which was a considerable sum for me in those days. We were called in to the court where both the judge and the bank representative were extremely sympathetic to our predicament, given the present recession, but were forced to issue a time limit of six weeks for us to clear the arrears, or face repossession.

At the time I had three young daughters, so this was a devastating prospect. Up until this point I had been experiencing considerable anxiety over our situation. We constantly prayed and scraped through, finding some clear and timely provisions from God for what we needed, but the repossession was a looming shadow. Up until this point I had held on to hopes of finding a solution, but as I left the court that day I remember a real peace descending on me as I realised I had come to the end of myself and that there was nothing I could do. We were completely in God's hands. Five weeks and five days went by with nothing. Then I had a phone call. A company had heard of the software I had developed and invited me to visit them on that very afternoon. Until this point I had sold nothing, and this was unprecedented. I went out, sold them a license, and used the software for them to fulfil an urgent job. That day I came back with a cheque for £1836. The cheque cleared exactly on time to pay the arrears, and I also had a critical bill for £36, required by the telephone company, that would otherwise have forced me to cease the business. The boost this experience gave to our faith was indescribable.

Secondly, during the same period, before the mortgage miracle happened, we came to a day where there was absolutely no food left for the day. I was still growing in faith but this was my worst nightmare. My faith teetered on the edge at times, with me even saying to those close to me 'now we find out if there's a God or not'. It was a Sunday and church was seven miles away. We had a car but no fuel in it, so we were unable to make it to church. I had not really learnt at the time to rest in God in these times, so the circumstances were really impacting me. The situation was just too hard to face so I decided to go out for a walk and try and hear what God had to say about it. I was really too anxious to hear anything. Eventually it got to 3pm and I decided I had to go home and face this dire situation. As I walked in the door I was met with a lively, cheerful family that were a bit irate with me for staying away so long because they were 'waiting for me to drive them out to get a burger'. They had already had breakfast, and lunch, and clearly now really fancied pigging out again. It turned out that a nearby neighbour had gone to church and a person in the church, who I knew was in the same dire straits I was, had given them some money for us that had been owed to us for more than a year for the sale of an item I had made through them. The person they had sold the item to had not paid up, but 'coincidentally' had finally only come through with the money just the day before. My local friend had been given the money at church and dropped it off on the way back. In all of this we never told a soul of our predicament. Not because of pride, but on principle, knowing that if we were to lean on others to get us through, then we would quickly come into the same predicament again. We understood that the only solution was for God to be as good as his word and come through for us. This is the only time I came so close to the edge with provisions for the family, but you can imagine how our faith grew through it.

Finally, again during the same period, I went to church on a Sunday morning and was invited to visit another church in the evening with a view to giving some much needed ministry. I felt the deep conviction of God that I must go, but I had no fuel for the car journey. I agreed to go and when I got home I began to pray about the fuel problem. As I prayed God dropped into my mind to look through the drawer in which I put all my till receipts. Had I ever thought before that there might be some money there I would have had it, and spent it, long before now. As I rifled through the receipts in the draw I suddenly came across a £5 note; exactly what I needed for fuel that evening. Needless to say the meeting turned out to be significant and I was called on to play a major part.

Through all these occasions, and many more besides, God has shown me over the years that he is as good as his word, and he will come through in his time. These are now great memories that have provided for me a firm foundation of faith that means now, when things get dire, I just rest in God. Such faith is true freedom. We can depend on it to the ends of the earth. Even the richest of the men of this world have no such guarantee of security as we have through the faith God has developed in us.

The anthropological argument for creation

To return to the main discussion, we have justified the creation of the world around us in its present form, including all the aspects of it that temporarily tend to call us to question the character of God, by accepting it as an essential phase for developing faith, which in turn will ensure the security of all free-willed beings in God's kingdom throughout all eternity.

We have accepted that this creation is the highest idea of infinite love and wisdom combined. We accept that this level of wisdom has even extended to the point of demanding and accepting considerable cost to God in order to yield that which is of supremely higher value; faith, and all that is built upon it. High enough to make the cost worth it to God.

We accept that these costs have taken the form of the fall, the loss and judgment of a portion of free-willed beings, including men and angels, and the extreme action taken on the part of God in the sufferings of the cross. However the outcome of all this in the beings that remain is worth the cost. It is necessary so God can fulfil his highest creative idea of the infinite wisdom and love of God; the creation of free-willed beings. The result is that these beings can live with him and each other in love for the eternity of ages to come.

We have also said that by virtue of God's own nature of love, which demands the highest good, he was not at liberty to create anything less than his greatest idea, but that there was and is a moral imperative for him to do the greatest loving thing of which his wisdom could conceive.

We further accept that this highest idea required the creation of free-willed beings. We accept that they should be centred on God in voluntary and complete dependency for their life and being. That God should be their highest delight. That they should also commit to one another in love and intimate fellowship as part of God's highest creative and loving idea.

In essence, in much of this we are using what is known as an anthropological argument; that things are the way they are because this is the way they had to be. This is a statement of faith. The detail of what God has done, and how this served the purposes of love, will forever be a quest of exploration for us. But in all of it we should remember that this is the way it had to be because this, and this alone, is God's greatest and highest idea. It is the only thing that satisfied the demands of love. We are only glimpsing an understanding of these things, but they have unfathomable depth that will take us 'ages' to appreciate. What we do come to appreciate here in some measure we marvel at, and it becomes for us the basis of greater faith. Therefore, given the importance of faith development in this age, the more revelation we can aspire to on the goodness of all that God has done, the more the purpose and goal of this age is served in us.

CHAPTER 6: Faith, the Foundation of Heaven

The symbols of faith in the Bible

We have been driving at the importance in God's design of the development of faith in man, and all created beings in his kingdom, as the foundation of eternal security.

Having accepted this point, we can go on to discuss what other attributes God is seeking to establish in man, and what relative importance they have to faith and to God's eternal purposes. This is best discovered by first being clear on the place of faith in created beings.

We have some biblical images to draw on for this purpose. The Bible is full of symbols. For example: silver represents purity, being a white metal with perfect reflection[168]. Bronze represents strength and power, in the good and holy sense, as the material of weapons and structures etc.[169]. Iron represents cruelty and oppression, and power in the bad sense, given its hardness and tendency to corruption through corrosion[170].

In a similar way, faith has the symbol of another metal; gold. Gold is the most precious of metals and is extremely weighty. The symbol of gold is used directly in scripture in the context of faith. Speaking of times of testing it says: *'your faith will come forth as gold'*[171]. A wider study of gold as a symbol reveals this parallel to be consistent throughout the scriptures, as is revealed to be surprisingly true of many such symbols. In this parallel the scripture is alluding to the value of gold, as we have discussed the value of faith to God's creation. The weightiness of gold may also indicate the weightiness of faith as an asset and solid foundation of character. We are led to two interesting places in scripture where gold is clearly used in the same symbolic way.

---

[168] Ps 12:6 Ps 66:10 Prov 10:20 Mal 3:3
[169] Ps 18:34 Ps 107:16 Jer 1:18
[170] Ps 105:18 Dan 2:33-34, 2:40, 7:7
[171] 1 Pet 1:7

The New Jerusalem – The first is the heavenly city, the New Jerusalem, that is referred to as our 'mother'[172]. The study of the use of the symbol of mother for the New Jerusalem is a fascinating study in itself, which we can only cover briefly for our purposes here.

The New Jerusalem is heaven, and when Jesus spoke to the thief on the cross of paradise[173] as a place they would go to together, he was referring to her. The descriptions of her show she is breath-taking in her beauty. It also describes her in three dimensions[174]. Our cities are laid out on the earth's surface, and in this sense are two dimensional. Of course our buildings reach up into the 3rd dimension to some extent, but the New Jerusalem is symbolised to have a full occupation of three dimensions, showing it to be an entity that has a higher existence that we cannot fully appreciate by comparison with what we know at this time.

To understand this a little further, it is useful to remember that the scriptures describe believers as living stones that are being built together into a spiritual house[175]. Jesus is also similarly described as the foundation, or cornerstone, and capstone[176]. Although we may associate ourselves with earthly cities as our birth and dwelling places, we don't consider ourselves to actually be part of its fabric, even though our bodies are fundamentally of the same stuff; clay[177]. However with the heavenly city of the New Jerusalem, we ourselves are part of its very fabric, and rightly consider her our mother because we are '*born from above*'[178]. We are spiritual beings as she is, made of the same body and substance.

God is in the midst of her and fills her[179]; he fills us and unites us[180]. This shows that this city is our home in the ever present and eternal sense, and is the place where the very intimate union of the ages to come, that we have alluded to earlier, will be experienced and enjoyed forever[181].

---

[172] Gal 4:26
[173] Luke 23:43
[174] Rev 21:16
[175] 1 Pet 2:5
[176] Matt 21:42 1 Pet 2:6
[177] Gen 2:7,3:19 2 Cor 4:1,7
[178] John 3:3 – See footnotes. Gal 4;26
[179] Ps 46:4-5
[180] Eph 1:22-23
[181] Rev 22:2-4

The purpose of delving into these truths is to point out that the very streets of this city are described to be paved with gold[182]. Gold is the main fabric of the city. This symbol is used in one way to show, by comparison, the glory of that place, compared to our present environment on earth that stands on clay, earth and dirt. But it goes further in the way that it shows faith to be the very foundational material of the heavenly kingdom. This is borne out by the scriptures that declare faith to be real *'substance'*[183], like we might consider rock to be to the substance of the earth. Faith is the rock material of heaven.

In the New Jerusalem we see how, in this symbolism, faith is depicted as the very foundation of our eternal dwelling.

The temple – Another place that gold is very definitely used as a symbol of faith is in the material for the building of the temple[184]. Here we see that virtually everything is overlaid with it. In the same way this speaks of it being the very basic fabric of heavenly things. It is often used to overlay acacia wood, which speaks of life.

Together life and faith become the very fundamental fabric of heaven on which everything else is built, including the heavenly city who is our mother, and we; the true church, as the bride of Christ, are of her[185].

Faith – the foundational fruit of the Spirit

In scripture the lists of the fruits of the Spirit include faith. Some versions translate this as faithfulness, but it should be literally translated as faith[186]. Faith is the foundational fruit on which all other fruits grow[187]. It comes directly from hearing the voice of God[188].

In other places it is called a gift, but this refers to special faith, given for a specific occasion and purpose; perhaps for some healing or miracle. As with the gift of prophesy; once this gift of faith is applied it is fulfilled and therefore ceases because its purpose is complete. Gifts of

---

[182] Rev 21:18,21 Rev 18:16
[183] Heb 11:1
[184] 2 Chr 3:7
[185] Gal 4:26
[186] Gal 5:22 – See KJV for correct translation as 'faith' not faithfulness.
[187] 2 Pet 1:5-7
[188] Rom 10:17

faith are therefore transient. However saving faith, which is faith in God, is as eternal as God is. This faith grows incrementally as we hear and discover more and more of God, and as it is applied to more and more areas of our life and understanding.

The parable of the mustard seed shows faith to be something you either have or do not have. I am aware that some still talk in terms of faith growing to be as big as a mustard seed, or only having half a mustard seed, but that misses the point of the parable entirely. Faith is a black or white affair; you either have it or you don't. Faith only grows in the sense that it is extended to apply to new things. It is not a case of size and strength, but merely application. We believe we are saved or we don't. We believe we will be healed or we don't. Faith is primarily a thing of the heart, and the absolute nature of faith is defined in the heart. The only complication to this is that the alignment of the mind with the heart may at times vary and differ from the heart to some degree.

The certainty of our faith for any specific thing may be challenged in various ways; perhaps by deception, or rational questioning, but at any given instant, at the level of the heart, we either have it or we don't for any specific application.

Faith is delivered to the heart by the heart hearing the word of God. This word then translates into faith, and the faith becomes the first fruit and foundation on which further fruit can grow.

We are told that: *'the only thing that counts is faith expressing itself through love'*[189]. Love is the ultimate fruit of the Spirit, and therefore the ultimate expression of faith. In fact all the fruits of the Spirit are built on faith and are an expression of faith. Faith expressed as joy. Faith expressed as peace etc. Faith is truly foundational to our whole spiritual being and it underpins all the other fruits of the Spirit.

Often one hears of the salvation of souls referred to as fruit, and the scriptures also sometimes speak in these terms[190]. However it should be understood that strictly speaking, new believers are not fruit in themselves. Rather they are like a new branch, or new ground on which new fruit can grow[191]. The actual fruit is the faith that they receive as they become a new believer.

---

[189] Gal 5:6
[190] Col 1:16
[191] John 15:5 Matt 13:1-23

CHAPTER 6: Faith, the Foundation of Heaven

In the description of heaven (the New Jerusalem) and in other places in the Bible, fruit is often symbolised as precious jewels; thus giving us one of those dual symbols we sometimes find in Biblical text and images. These are the fruit that last that Jesus spoke about. These jewels are all set in the gold of faith. Faith is therefore the first fruit, and it provides the setting and foundations for the progressive development of all other fruit that is built upon it – *knowledge, patience, tolerance, forgiveness, self-control, perseverance, humility, sensitivity, truthfulness, protectiveness, goodness, godliness, brotherly kindness, compassion, hopefulness, peace, joy* and *love*. This defines the approximate order of development as given in the scriptures[192], culminating in the supreme fruit of love.

We can appreciate the effects that our growing faith in God has on us, and how it impacts the focus on self that otherwise dominates us in its absence. Faith allows us to trust another with all of our cares, concerns and interests. It therefore allows us to relax from the strain of self-sustenance and we begin to become outwardly focused, instead of inward looking. It therefore leads us into a place of peace and rest as we trust God for what would otherwise be our burden of care. Out of this comes the joy of freedom from such a burden. Having found a firm guarantee that God cares for us, and is perpetually working in the background to secure for us not just the good, but the best, we are then free to express care, compassion, and ultimately love towards others.

Of course as we reach this place of faith, the source of our stability is God himself, so he naturally becomes our greatest resource when it comes to reaching out to others in the form of things such as patience, kindness, compassion, tolerance, and love. We can therefore understand how the first fruit of faith becomes the very foundation of all other personal fruit bearing, and how our faith as a fruit then seeds out through love, and spreads to others.

Jesus is the author of faith

In the book of Hebrews it says Jesus is the author and finisher of our faith[193]. He also sustains it at every moment[194]. Therefore, though faith is our

---

[192] Gal 5:22, 2 Pet 1:5, 1 Cor 13 Col 3:12
[193] Heb 12;2
[194] Is 46:4

foundational fruit, God is the foundation to faith itself. Our faith is built directly on Christ and his word, so he is our rock; our immoveable substrata[195].

Faith grows in the sense that we begin by believing for salvation, and we end by having it applied to all areas of our lives as we hear the word of God, and are taught the truth by the Holy Spirit[196].

I once had a weird experience that taught me something of my dependence on God as the one who sustains my faith. I woke up after a short nap, and found myself without any assurance even of the existence of God, let alone of saving faith. I was aware of the tricks that feelings play, and the fact that we often do not feel what we believe, but this was something else. I believe it was a genuine temporary loss of faith as this was the key subject in my spiritual study and learning at the time. The experience was unnerving, and lasted only about an hour, but I believe God used it to teach me a real truth; that I am wholly dependent on him as the author, sustainer, and perfecter of my faith.

Our faith is sustained by the inner voice of God at all times. In fact the Spirit of God perpetually bears witness within us to the truth, including the most fundamental truth; that we are children of God[197]. This is how dependent we really are on God as the sustainer of our faith. And in this we can understand something of what Jesus meant when he claimed to be the Way, the Truth, and the Life. Faith in the Truth is our means to Life, and this is God's Way, from first to last[198].

Jesus said: no man comes to him unless the father draws him[199]. We come to Christ by faith. We can therefore put this together and say; no-one comes to faith unless the father draws him. In Paul's letter to the Ephesians it says: you are saved by grace, through faith, and this is a gift of God, leaving no room for boasting as if it were something of ourselves[200]. The gift is given through the voice of God that both creates and sustains the fruit of our faith.

---

[195] Matt 16:18 Matt 7:24 1 Cor 3:11 Eph 2:20 2 Tim 2:19
[196] Eph 4:13
[197] Rom 8:15-16
[198] Rom 1:17
[199] John 6:44, 14:6
[200] Eph 2:8-9

CHAPTER 6: Faith, the Foundation of Heaven

Faith is the key

Many years ago, when I had been a Christian for only about seven years, I began to be given prophetic words through various sources that all brought the same message – that God was going to give me *'the keys to the kingdom'*[201]. I didn't know what it meant, but at the time I was about to take a business trip to Scotland where I visited an engineering manufacturing company. This company had its own foundry where they cast metal components. I spent a whole day learning their processes. Towards the end of the day one of the workers came over to me and said they would like to give me a souvenir to commemorate my visit. He then held up a casting of a large ornamental brass key that had just been poured (see the cover image). The casting was still warm and connected to the core through which it was poured. I was left to saw it off and polish it up. What a great confirmation!

This kind of thing does not happen to me very often, but I believe God went to some lengths to impress on me a lesson that I was learning at that time. The lesson can be summarised as follows – *all things come by grace through faith*. I started to realise that here God was giving me not just a key, but a master key. It was the key to the key cupboard. This realisation was a revelation that revolutionised my life.

The message of grace was the first revelation; that everything we get from God comes to us undeserved and free.

This marked the beginning of the end of years of striving in my Christian walk. I began to lay down all attempts to receive from God on merit, and I began to receive by grace alone. The whole idea of receiving undeservedly runs counter to this world that wants to maintain its pride and independence, and receive only by right. The self-life has an arrogant independence of God that prefers to avoid any obligation to him. In time I began to discover how deep this rabbit hole goes; it is the very root of the corruption of the fallen nature. God delights in us receiving by grace alone because by doing so we move back into the pre-fallen state of recognising our entire dependence on him. We lay down our pride and self-belief, and receive God as our supreme source in all things. This change is effectively a transfer from self-belief to belief in God, which brings us to the second part of the principle – by grace *through faith*[202].

---

[201] Matt 16:11
[202] Eph 2:8

We receive all things through faith[203]. God's way of working is always to give us more faith, which means to apply our faith to something new. The evidence that we have received it is that the appropriate actions naturally and unavoidably follow[204]. We find ourselves able to depend on God by faith in new ways, and able to take risks that confirm it.

The point here is that faith is fundamental to both our regenerate being, and the way we live. Successful Christian living is that which produces fruit that lasts[205], and this is only possible through living on a solid foundation of faith.

Sometime later in my Christian walk I began to get a new and equally revolutionary revelation of another truth; the part that the cross of Christ must play in our lives if we want to see victory in our living.

Later this will become a key part of this study when we come to the subject of the reformation of man.

At the time that I began to receive it for myself, I happened to come across the old brass key. It tends to pop up now and then when I am searching for something. I had now possessed this key for many years, but as I looked at it closely I suddenly realised that in the metal at the end of the key that fits the lock, there was the shape of a cross. I had not noticed it before because the cross was seen in the negative. You had to look at the spaces rather than the metal to see it. Once again I believe God was stressing to me the importance of the cross of Christ as a revelation of truth.

At present, in this study, we are still exploring the truth of God's nature and his eternal plan. We will cover the place of the cross from that perspective, but we will later come to see how the cross of Christ and faith are together highly instrumental in the reformation of man, even after rebirth, and we will explore the impact it has on victorious living.

The place of faith in the kingdom of God

So now we have an understanding of the place of faith in the Kingdom of God; it is the very foundational rock substance on which the Kingdom stands, and it has many precious things built upon it, some of which are

---

[203] Rom 1:17
[204] Rom 4:4-5 – Compare – Jam 2:22
[205] John 15:16

symbolised in the heavenly city by jewels, pearls, crowns, and numerous other things.

What is clear is that these are all spiritual and living things of great splendour beyond anything of this earth, but faith is clearly the substance on which it is all built and which holds it all together. It is not God's plan that our spiritual development stops at the foundation of faith[206], though it is clear that there are some who will stop there and not progress further[207].

If we go on to '*live by the spirit*' by abiding in Christ, we produce the fruit of the Spirit which starts with faith, and is followed by extremely precious things that are built upon it; fruit/jewels[208]. These are the highlights of heaven that reflect God in all his wonder. Some men spend their whole lives after spiritual rebirth living almost entirely in '*the flesh*', and in the end produce no real fruit, escaping with only their foundation of faith in Christ[209]. This is salvation, but also loss in terms of what could have been. They come through as the base foundational substance of heaven, but have nothing of the exquisite beauty of all that could and should be built upon it.

The empowerment of man through prayer

In considering the issues of prayer, and of God doing good things in his universe, the question arises: Why doesn't God do the good anyway without our asking? Isn't there a moral imperative on him as a moral being to act to do the good thing, regardless of whether we request it or not?

To understand this we must realise that in God's infinite wisdom, he has so created and configured the universe in this age of pre-history in a way that man has a domain of responsibility assigned to him[210]. In this domain God has made his own actions to secure the 'highest good' dependent on our participation. We are called to exercise delegated authority by asking and interceding in prayer[211].

---

[206] 2 Pet 1:5-
[207] 1 Cor 3:11-15
[208] Gal 5:16-22 John 15:5
[209] 1 Cor 3:15
[210] Gen 1:28
[211] John 15:7 2 Cor 1:11 Eph 6:18 Phil 4:6 Col 4:12 1 Tim 2:21

In other words, as things are designed; if man does not act to discharge his God given responsibility within his own domain, then it is not normally good that God should go ahead anyway and act because this will not serve his ultimate good purpose; it will not develop faith. Instead he makes himself and his power available to us through the channel of faith and prayer, and gives us delegated responsibility over it. He has therefore configured our allocated domain in such a way that it is only good for him to act if we accept our part and ask for him to intervene. In fact God has even gone beyond this by giving us authority to speak directly to the mountain in faith to produce change. All of this is designed to make us develop our faith.

Of course there are many exceptions when for special reasons God does act independently within man's domain, but these are the exceptions and not the norm. On the whole God's intervention without our participation would circumvent the primary purpose he has of developing faith in mankind. God has therefore set a principle in place that means he must restrain himself from doing many good things in the world if men do not take responsibility for it.

Why did God design it this way? – The short answer is because in his infinite wisdom it was the greatest and highest good thing for him to do! He saw it was good to empower man in this way. Empowering man results in his development in ways that are supremely valuable to God in the eternal future he has planned. It is therefore an act of goodness that God should so empower man and make his interventions dependent on him. We should therefore realise a profound truth: that when we expect God to act independently of our prayerful participation, we are expecting him to set aside his higher purpose in favour of our short term purpose. Something his very nature forbids him to do. Those that diligently pray have either explicitly or intuitively realised this truth.

We only have glimpses into the detail of the reasoning of God behind the decision to make things this way, but we can at least see in it the wisdom that by empowerment, God has put man under the same moral imperative that he himself has (and is), and has thereby forced man to act in faith if he is to secure the good for his domain. It follows that through the pressure of that responsibility, man is thereby forced to grow in faith, which in turn fulfils God's higher purpose.

CHAPTER 6: Faith, the Foundation of Heaven

Recap the progressive argument

In our discussion so far we have found ourselves getting into some serious 'joined up thinking', where one thought becomes the basis of the next, so let's recap on the main progression of the discussion:

- Man's root problem since the fall is independence of God. God's answer to that is for man to return to total voluntary dependence on him through spiritual rebirth, and then to learn to live by faith.
- This faith is an implicit trust in God, and the belief in man's need of God. To have such a faith man must learn the trustworthy nature of God.
- Man has been placed, by God's wisdom, into a domain where he has authority, but relies on God's power to maintain it against a formidable adversary.
- God's nature is Love, which means to commit the whole being to the highest good. To do the highest good is the very definition of Love, and therefore morality. To serve the highest good is therefore an imperative of all moral beings.
- Man is made in God's image, and is also a moral being like God, with an obligation to love and commit himself to the highest good.
- God has given man authority in the domain of this world, and has made himself, his wisdom, and his power, an available resource to man through faith, accessible through prayer.
- Faith is based on the imperative that God has it in his own nature to do good. As man trusts in God he can secure the highest good in his own domain by appealing to God in prayer.
- Man can only be certain of (i.e. have faith in) a response from God by being certain of God's good nature, and that what he is asking for is for the highest good[212].
- Man has limited intelligence and is unable to ascertain what is really ultimately the highest good by his own reason. In response God has made his own mind and wisdom accessible to man through the intuitive faculty of his renewed spirit, so he can know with certainty the mind of God, as God reveals it[213].

---

[212] Heb 11:5-6 Ps 84:11
[213] 1Cor 2:16 Rom 8:26

- Staying informed of God's thoughts and wisdom requires man to cultivate a communicative relationship with God[214].
- By experience in exercising faith, man grows in faith[215].
- Faith is the fundamental product and asset that God is seeking to develop and establish in created beings in the present age to ensure their eternal security, and make them invulnerable to another fall.
- In this age man learns the true horror of departure from God as his resource of truth, goodness, and ultimately Life.
- God has tolerated evil for a season in order to ensure it is a once only event in the story of creation, and he is ensuring it will not recur throughout eternity, despite continuing to include free-willed beings. All these beings will voluntarily remain throughout eternity in a loving relationship with their creator.
- God has gone ahead and created free-willed beings, and allowed for the fall and a season of evil because in his infinite wisdom he knows it will ultimately yield the highest good that the infinite wisdom of God could determine.
- If there were a higher creative idea, according to God's infinite wisdom, then God would, by virtue of his moral imperative, have chosen to create that instead. However this is it.

Faith is the reason for the season (age)

Within these simple reasoning's are the beginning of answers, on one level, to the problem of pain and evil in this world that is so often postulated by man as evidence against the goodness of God when we observe the suffering and corruption around us.

For this present age our answers to this are partially answers of reason, but are mostly answers of faith. The questions of man that are raised surrounding these things are often a challenge to the goodness of the nature of God. The Christian can only put faith in God by believing that despite the many horrors he is witnessing in the world at large, that God will exonerate himself absolutely in the end by the proof that this has

---

[214] John 15:15
[215] 2 Thes 1:3

produced something that is worth it all, and that God has done it all in a way that ultimately demanded the least suffering.

In many ways these questions highlight the very root of evil and the fallen nature of man; that he is more willing to trust his own independent reasoning than trust that God knows best despite all the appearances to the contrary[216].

Those that come to faith in God in this world do so through the most adverse circumstances, thereby developing in them a faith that is incredibly robust, and not dependent on circumstances or appearances[217]. Compare this kind of faith to that of Adam and Eve, who being naive to the very language of lies and deceit, were led to doubt the goodness of God almost at the mere suggestion of it[218]. Through the present events, this inherent weakness in the plan to create truly free-willed beings will be eliminated for all eternity. The happiness of God's creation is then secured, and God is free to enjoy what he has created (us) for all the ages to come; because it is good, very good!

Faith in the nature of God

We have taken some time to answer the question of the nature of God because this is the thing on which all of our faith is based. We have seen that despite everything, God's nature is good! Each individual must find faith in this truth for himself, and that is only possible by us finding another source of truth that we can trust more than the contrary evidence in the world. It requires us to see and hear the truth with new eyes and ears; eyes and ears of the spirit[219], as we will explore later.

Faith development is therefore something that is only accomplished by man entering into a new communicative relationship with God as he is invited into it, and finds the path to do so[220].

If goodness/love is the truth about God, then we begin to appreciate something of the freedom afforded by this truth; that we can live our lives trusting ourselves to the care of a good God. By understanding and believing the truth of God's nature, despite everything

---

[216] Prov 3:5
[217] 2 Cor 5:7
[218] Gen 3:1,4
[219] Eph 1:18
[220] Rom 10:17　2 Cor 4:4　1 Thes 1:5　John 6:44　Phil 1:29

we see in this evil age, we find that *'the truth has set us free'*[221], as promised (by Jesus), in so very many ways; not least the freedom from fear.

As we become confident of the nature of God, we become confident in his intentions and love towards us[222]. It only remains that we should find faith in his omniscience and omnipotence for us to believe that he has the power to carry it through, and therefore that *'God works all things together for good to those that love God and are called according to his purpose'*[223]. This evil age therefore serves a huge purpose by testing and revealing God's power to accomplish his purpose of love to an incredible degree, even in the face of extreme adversity. By observing this our faith in his supreme omniscience and omnipotence will be eternally established.

It follows that anything that reveals the truth of God to us is of incredible value to us because the more we understand, the more we believe, and the more our faith is increased. This leads us to the thing that we have said all along is the central and most stupendous event in all the history and future of creation; the cross of Christ. Next we begin to explore the mystery and truth of the cross in the hope that in it we will discover the greatest revelation of God, his nature and his love.

---

[221] John 8:32
[222] 1 Tim 3:13
[223] Rom 8:28

CHAPTER 7: The Mystery of the Cross

Recap of the plan of creation so far

We have so far explored, through scripture and reason, God's purpose in choosing to create at all; that he did it as an act of Love, to accomplish the very highest good purpose of Love that could be conceived in the mind of God, according to his infinite wisdom.

We have explored the fact that this highest of all ideas required provision for the inclusion of a pre-season of evil, with some considerable costs associated with it, but that was demanded as the path of least suffering to allow the future happiness of all creation to be secured for all eternity.

We have discussed the part that faith is to play in guaranteeing the security of the future ages, and that the primary goal of the present age is to develop such faith within all the created beings that will participate in eternity, including men and angels.

We have explored the fact that this faith is faith in the goodness of the nature of God, and that it is made to withstand the most adverse and contrary circumstances that even appear to challenge and contradict the belief in God's goodness. The development of faith that extends beyond sight[224] is the foundational objective that justifies this temporary toleration of all that is evil in this age because it will ensure that the happiness of all beings, in all of the coming ages, is beyond the bounds of corruption, even though God's creation is populated with beings that have true, sovereign, and independent free will of their own.

We can be sure God's plan for the ages to come is high indeed and beyond our comprehension, though we can glimpse something of the glories of at least the next age by vague and shadowy comparisons with the things of the present.

---

[224] 2 Cor 5:7

Understanding the mystery of the cross

Understanding a mystery – From here we must take our exploration of God's purposes a step further and begin to explore the main and central theme of it all; the purpose and meaning of the cross.

Some have suggested that the cross is a total mystery[225], and that we are not intended to understand it, so therefore attempts to explain it are futile. This is something that I cannot accept. It may be true in the sense that the extents of the wisdom of God's act of going to the cross, in the form of the Son, is the most stupendous and incredible event of all history and the future of creation, but I believe the very central purpose here is that we do explore it, and come to greater and greater understanding of the God we worship through it.

We must be cautious not to lean on our understanding and try to wrap this whole thing up within the bounds of our very limited mental capacity[226]. We recognise that the temptation to do so stems from the arrogant and sinful independence of man, but it is not inevitable if we approach it humbly and allow the Spirit of God to lead us into the truth.

We can approach this in the same way that we should for most honest studies of anything on earth where we have to carry unknowns and variables. These unknowns don't necessarily prevent us from progressing in the study and carrying these things with us, if we keep them always open to God for more light and understanding.

Handling unknowns – My background and early career training was in engineering, which included an extensive use of mathematics. I reached a point in my study course where I had the opportunity to move up to another level, but I had my doubts about my ability to handle the demands of it.

I discussed the matter with a wise tutor who explained to me that the difference between students on my present level, and those on the higher level I was considering, was that students on the lower level would meet an unknown and at this point would be stuck and unable to progress further. On the higher level the students would meet the same unknowns, but would have the skill and knowledge to recognise it, and assign it a variable name. They would then continue to progress whilst carrying the

---

[225] 1 Cor 2:6-7
[226] Prov 3:5

unknown variable forward with them. Often this would eventually lead to the unknown being either resolved, eliminated, or at other times it would simply continue to be carried. In each case the study was not limited by it, nor its progress halted.

I believe that this approach is really appropriate to the mysteries in scripture. They are not there simply to tease us and make us aware of our shortcomings, though that may be part of it; for the purpose of humility. Rather they are primarily designed to spur us on to further exploration, knowing there is more to discover.

We are encouraged in scripture itself to sell ourselves out to get understanding at all costs[227]. We are left in no doubt about the value of wisdom and understanding. The cross is the greatest of mysteries, but rather than respond to it in a way that abandons hope of understanding it, we should regard it as the greatest opportunity to come into a fuller understanding of God and his nature, and ways.

The place of the cross in God's plan of creation

The unavoidable losses – We have discussed the fact that faith is the foundation of all future eternal security, and that God is seeking to establish this faith in all created free-willed beings through the events of this present age of sin and evil.

We have seen that God has determined to accept considerable cost in this age of pre-history in order to achieve this faith, and accomplish his end of eternal happiness for all his creatures that have a part in all the ages to come.

We have explored the fact that these losses include the initial eternal loss of a proportion of all the created beings in the fall, including many men and angels[228]. And though this loss is considerable, and a cause of heart wrenching pain to God[229], just like the cross is, it is nevertheless the path of least suffering to the awesome eternal future he has planned for those that have a part in it. Universalism is therefore a dangerous error. The reason some are lost comes down to the greatness of God's idea in creating genuinely free-willed beings such as men and angels.

---

[227] Prov 4:5,7 Prov 16:16, 23:23
[228] Rom 9:22-23
[229] Ez 18:32, 33:11 2 Pet 3:9

Mitigating the charge of selfishness – We have already alluded to the fact that God's wisdom showed him that in accepting the loss of a proportion of his created beings, in order to secure the eternal future for the rest, that he himself would also have to bear a considerable personal cost.

There could be no room left open for the charge that God accepted the cost to others in order to secure himself and his own interests. This charge would undermine the very faith he was seeking to establish. The truth is that God in himself was already secure in Love; nothing would change that. But for these created free-willed beings the loss was essential so that at least some of them could come through to that same level of security in love. However the possibility of the charge of selfishness on God's part had to be mitigated.

If God had no alternative, in his highest idea and scheme of creation, than to leave this charge of selfishness open, then this idea of accepting the loss of some beings would probably have been out of the question, and he would have abandoned it as an unworkable design. Of course if this were so, then the opportunity for creating the eternal future of happiness we now see before us in the ages of ages to come, would also have been lost for all beings – forever. However God saw the immensity of its value, and not willing to give up on it, in his wisdom he saw another possibility; that he himself should bear a personal loss that is great enough to overshadow the loss of some of his created beings, in order to nullify the charge of selfishness in the sight of the rest, and secure this eternal future, founded on the faith of those that remained.

The scale of the cost of redemption – With this thought we begin to approach the very purpose and meaning of the cross from the eternal perspective. We are led to the question of what measure of cost could possibly be acceptable for such a course of action. The short answer is clearly this: the cost must be huge! The scale of it must reflect the immensity of God himself, showing that he is committed to the cause of love with his whole being. However we must also answer that the cost could not be so huge as to remove God himself from that eternal future he desires. This clearly could not happen because it would clearly defeat the purpose of the highest good; of Love.

CHAPTER 7: The Mystery of the Cross 113

God believes in himself – God has no will or desire to self-destruct. He believes in himself absolutely. He is perfect Love and is committed to the cause of highest goodness, and therefore committed to himself as its very source. All he ever considered creating was always inseparably tied to that purpose. He cannot abandon that purpose because to do so would be for God to become other than he is. God only went ahead with this immense scheme to create beings like himself because his wisdom saw its value to the purposes of Love, and he was unable to refuse it by virtue of his very nature.

To see the possibility of creation, in the interests of the highest good, as an achievable option, and then refuse it, would be God denying his very self. To even accept a second best idea would be the very same; a denial of himself. No, although the costs are immense, the immensity of the result dwarfs the cost so much that God was unable to refuse it. So he faced up to the personal cost, even despising and scorning its shame[230], and he went ahead and created!

The immensity of the plan – From the perspective of a human being in this world, we may have some difficulty in seeing how it could be acceptable for God to choose to sustain such a cost and lose any being. How could such a cost ever be justified no matter how great the result?

In answer to this we should see that this thinking may be the result of our dim view, and total failure to grasp just how immense God's big plan actually is. If we were to see heaven and the extent of its joy, peace and happiness in the coming age of heaven, then we may come to understand and appreciate the balance in the wisdom of God when he accepted these costs.

If we were then able to project the effects of this decision on to the age beyond the next, which is likely to be equally greater in glory, and for which we will only be ready after the next age of heaven is complete, then we would probably find ourselves completely and utterly disarmed of our questionings.

How many ages would we have to project forwards before we agree with God's wisdom to accept an initial fall, rather than lose the ages to come? – I suspect not many, if we could only appreciate what that meant.

---

[230] Heb 12:2

Then consider that God has set before us not just one, two, or even a few ages, but 'ages of ages'[231], and that all of this would have been the loss of baulking at the cost of creating this first age; then we start to get closer to God's perspective on it all[232].

Of course there is no way that we can comprehend the extents of all this, and no matter how far we go it will always stretch out infinitely before us. We are therefore trying to see the extents of God's wisdom in creation by abstract thought, which rapidly becomes more and more vague and mystical. Is it possible for us to overcome this limitation? Clearly the more we can see of the goodness of God's dealings and plans, the more our faith is established. But unless we become infinite like he is, it is always going to be beyond us. Perhaps we should simply accept that to glimpse the coming ages is enough for us, however we see that God had a better plan.

Once again we see that God's wisdom is greater than ours, and that he has in fact made a way whereby something of the immensity of his plan can be set before us in a way that we can see and explore its vast extents without ourselves somehow becoming infinite or omniscient as he is. He has made this possible, not directly, but by comparison. That comparison is found in the cross, and as we will see, this is something that has been set in full view before men and angels, both now and for all eternity in the person of the Son of God.

The suffering of the cross

The cross happened about 2000 years ago. We have several written records of it as a testimony of those who witnessed it, but we were not there to see it for ourselves. We also have the record of the life of Jesus up to the cross, and the prophetic record that predicts his sufferings, and tells us he was *'a man of sorrows and familiar with suffering'*[233]. At the same time we are told that *'God has set you above you companions by anointed you with the oil of joy*[234]*'*, so he was not heavy spirited, but very light in spirit, full of joy and gladness, showing one of the many paradoxes we

---

[231] Eph 2:7 3:21
[232] 2 Cor 4:7
[233] Is 53:3
[234] Ps 45:7

find in him, and that becomes reflected in those who are his; the peculiar people[235].

Prior to Gethsemane and the cross, we have no record of Jesus suffering, but his familiarity with suffering may have stemmed from his experience of passing through this broken and suffering world that he himself had made. If the soul of righteous Lot was tormented by the sin of Sodom and Gomorrah[236], how much more Jesus must have suffered in the same way. He was always full of compassion when it came to suffering, and to see all this as the creation of his own hand must have been an awful burden to his soul. As a man, this whole experience of the suffering of mankind would have steeled him to face the demands of the cross. It was *'the joy set before him'*[237] that made him determined to see it through.

We see from the historical record the psychological and spiritual struggle that took place both in the garden of Gethsemane, and in the cruelty of his crucifixion. Even in just the physical aspects of this suffering we stand in awe of it as an act of love for mankind, and wonder how a man can suffer to that extent and still be focused and determined enough to go through with it for the love of his friends, let alone his enemies.

Many have agreed that the physical aspects of the suffering on the cross were just the tip of the iceberg. Beneath the water line the spiritual struggle was truly epic. We only glimpse this in a few places in the record; Jesus sweating drops of blood and begging for an alternative to the cup God had given him to drink, if any were possible[238]; the agonising cries of *'Father forgive them'*[239]; and most chilling of all the cry of *'my God, my God, why have you forsaken me'*[240] as the full darkness of the sin of age was thrust upon him.

We have other glimpses too from the prophetic record, written beforehand to foretell of the events that were to come on the cross. Most notable are the writings of Psalm 22, and Isaiah 53. In the Psalm the physical agonies are foretold with statements such as: *'my bones are out of joint'*[241], *'my strength is dried up like a potsherd and my tongue sticks to*

---

[235] I Pet 2:9 Titus 2:14
[236] 2 Pet 2:7
[237] Heb 12:2
[238] Luke 22:42-44
[239] Luke 23:34
[240] Matt 27:46

the roof of my mouth[242]. The emotional torment and rejection is revealed in statements such as *'I am a worm and not a man, scorned by men and despised by the people. All who see me mock me, they hurl insults...'*[243] and *'people stare and gloat over me'*[244].

These statements show incredible physical, emotional, and psychological suffering, but the true depth of the struggle is only revealed by the metaphorical statements that show this to have reached the spiritual plane as the clash of the ages took place, and the principalities and powers came for their 'pound of flesh', hoping in their wretched arrogance to defeat God – *'Many bulls surround me; strong bulls of Bashan encircle me*[245]*'*, *'Roaring lions tearing their prey open their mouths wide against me'*[246], *'Dogs have surrounded me'*[247] and *'save me from the horns of the wild oxen'*[248].

Some of these expressions undoubtedly refer to the people on the ground, such as the Romans and the Pharisees, but they clearly also point to the fury of the demonic spiritual realm that was unleashed upon him. Even those on the ground were incited to the full fury of these evil and malicious beings as they sought to maximise the suffering of Jesus as he went to the cross.

In Isaiah 52/53 we get the same kind of expressions with some that reveal much more of the physical horror – *'his appearance was so disfigured beyond that of any form of a man and his form marred beyond human likeness'*[249]. The suffering clearly reached every dimension of his being. Nothing of him was spared. For him there could be no mercy. He was taken to the edge, and then into the darkness beyond where he was *'crushed for our iniquities'*[250].

One of the most revealing scriptures on the depths of the suffering that Jesus went through, during the period of his death, comes from the

---

[241] Ps 22:14
[242] Ps 22:15
[243] Ps 22:6-7
[244] Ps 22:17
[245] Ps 22:12
[246] Ps 22:13
[247] Ps 22:16
[248] Ps 22:21
[249] Is 52:14
[250] Is 53:5

CHAPTER 7: The Mystery of the Cross

prayer of the prophet Jonah. Jesus himself drew the parallel with Jonah saying that as Jonah was in the belly of the whale for three days and three nights, so the Son of Man will be in the heart of the earth. This prayer reveals how near to the edge he came with statements like: *'the earth beneath barred me in forever*[251]*'*, and: *'my life is ebbing away'*[252]. It is a picture of total despair. To limit our understanding of the cross to the physical suffering is to almost miss it entirely. This journey to the underworld was clearly an epic struggle.

The physical suffering was specifically designed to agonise every nerve centre of the body, short of inducing the release of unconsciousness. Nails were driven into the nerve centres of the hands and feet, and the flesh was ripped and shredded to extract the maximum agony that could be induced from it. The fact that no bones were broken, or body parts lost, would, it seems, enforce this view, because pain cannot be induced in a part that is severed from the body, nor are there nerves in the bones that can induce pain.

If, as I suspect, this physical suffering was a mirror of all the suffering that took place in the spiritual realm, in a spiritual form, then we have not yet even begun to perceive the extents of it. Jesus may well have run the gauntlet of demons that caused his spiritual being the maximum possible suffering their evil minds could devise in order to break him.

The fact that no bones were broken, or body parts lost, reflects the fact that in the end Jesus comes through with his frame and his being intact. Only that which will ultimately heal is surrendered. God did not suffer loss to his being through the cross. He is the same yesterday today and forever[253], so such a loss would not have been a true reflection of him. In the book of Genesis it is likened to a bruised heel from crushing the head of the serpent[254]. This bruise may be eternal, as we will see later, but the point is that he comes through it complete, and entirely victorious in the end.

---

[251] Jonah 2:6
[252] Jonah 2:7
[253] Heb 13:8
[254] Gen 3:15

The importance of the cross

From our earlier discussions of what would be demanded to fulfil God's purposes in creation; we can suppose that the full depths of what happened here on all planes was sufficient to fulfil these demands. The significance and extents of this event must therefore have been huge.

The limits of suffering in man – First of all, when we think of the extents of the physical suffering of the cross, we realise that when God created man, and determined the kind of body he should have, he set the degree to which suffering would be possible, and chose the limits to which one man may cause another to suffer.

When God made beings that have free will he clearly knew that they may fall into sin, and that in such a scenario, in their sinfulness, men would push their persecution of each other to these limits. According to the principle of love he must therefore have set these limits according to his infinite wisdom, for the purpose of the highest good, and to achieve the highest eternal outcome in his handling of this fallen race.

According to his perfect wisdom we observe, therefore, that God gave us bodies that are capable of both considerable pleasure, and fairly extreme suffering; perhaps to a greater level than any of us would have chosen for ourselves, had we had the choice. But, he also built into our physical constitution a limit to the measure of suffering that was possible by the mechanisms of both unconsciousness and death, both of which bring an instant release from suffering.

We can therefore speculate that for fallen man to have the best possibility of redemption, and to produce maximum eternal fruit in his character, that this level of sensitivity, and the ability for us to hurt one another to this degree was an essential thing. Through it men are both empowered to fully enact their sinfulness, and to realise through their own suffering how the sinfulness of others affects them. Both of these effects are designed to best enlighten fallen men to the full consequences of sin with a view to leading them to become aware of their desperate need for reform.

In choosing this level of sensitivity in man's physical being, we are also led to understand one reason why God also chose the cross as a necessary step for him to take in the process of redeeming man from sin. Here we see God taking on the form of man and allowing his own body to be pushed to the very limit of the suffering that he himself had made possible in these earthly bodies. We can see how this is an expression of the righteousness and holiness of God. He is not willing to impose on men the possibility of suffering, even for the good of man, without showing himself to be perfectly prepared, and indeed determined, to suffer to the very limits of the pain and agony that he had made possible.

Though the sufferings of some men in this world have been extreme, no other person has been pushed to these limits. But for God, as the Son – Jesus, as a consequence of his own good nature and selflessness, it was not possible for him to escape it. His goodness demanded that he demonstrate his readiness and determination to take upon himself the very extreme of possibility for suffering that he had chosen to lay upon others.

The concept of substitutionary sacrifice – Many expositions of the cross expound only the simple truth of a substitutionary sacrifice. We will come to examine this later. For many this explanation of the cross is enough, but it raises many perplexing questions of justice, faith, and understanding. It is these questions that give us clues to the fact that here, at the cross, we have a tremendous opportunity for profound learning about God and his plans and purposes in creation.

We read that in the beginning, after Adam sinned and fell, an angel was appointed by God to guard the way to the tree of life in case man should eat of it and live on in his sinful state forever[255]. The tree of life is Christ who said: '*I am the way the truth and the life*'[256]. In him is all life, and it is through him we must find the way to access it.

God's plan for fallen angels was, and is, destruction. No way of redemption has been found for them[257]. Let us be sure that if this highest plan of God's infinite wisdom could have been formed such that it could also include the redemption of fallen angels, then the opportunity would have been taken by God to secure it, and the cost paid. So would a plan for the redemption of all men, but this was not possible without God reducing the immensity of the plan, and the outcome, and probably reducing men and angels to far lesser beings than they are under the present plan.

---

[255] Gen 3:24
[256] John 14:6
[257] 2 Pet 2:4 – From the book of Enoch

As we have said: it was God's judgement that prevailed on this, not ours. What is clear is that for some men there would be redemption, and this was made accessible through the cross.

The fact that life is accessed through death is part of the profound mystery of the plan. Having lost the battle of the ages at the cross[258], the realms of evil continue their struggle for their cause by deception and lies[259].

Part of their campaign is to keep man from the cross, so they guard the road to it hoping to prevent man from finding his way back to God through 'the Way' made open for him in Christ. Satan is a master at counterfeit and disguise, and in his efforts to guard the path to the cross we see him raising another counterfeit of the actions of God. Just as God placed an angel to guard the way to the tree of life from sinful man, so it appears Satan seeks to guard the way to the cross to prevent man from finding a new life of righteousness.

The cross is both the greatest truth, the gospel (good news) to the world of fallen men, and at the same time the most closely guarded secret of the evil realm. For both fallen and redeemed men, Satan desperately tries to minimise its importance because he knows that here is the ground of his defeat[260], and if men discover the truth of it the last hopes of him maintaining a kingdom are ended.

For the same reasons we here maximise our resolve to pursue this truth, regardless of the resistance. Let's realise that we have not yet scratched the surface of the full meaning of the cross. We will not be satisfied with the meagre pickings we now have. Yes the cross is foolishness to fallen man, it is a mystery to the new Christian, but it is the most profound wisdom to the mature Christian[261].

Maturity is a matter of faith[262], which implies that we must find a deeper understanding and faith in God's purposes in the cross, if we are to become mature. Let the cross be our passion and our quest because it is here that we will find the truth, and the source of life in all its fullness.

---

[258] Col 2:15
[259] 2 Thes 2:10 John 8:44
[260] Col 2:15
[261] 1 Cor 1:23 1Cor 2:6-7
[262] Eph 4:13

The security of faith for all the ages of creation

We have discussed the truth that God's plan was to bear a personal cost that exceeded the losses incurred in the fall of created beings, and that this personal cost reflected God's estimation of the loss of these beings. He did this in order to demonstrate the measure of his commitment to the purpose of the highest good as the only way to counter the suggestion made by the losses that he only acts in self interest in the same way that fallen and sinful beings do.

It is only through God's acceptance of this personal cost that his highest idea for creation could be made possible. Countering a suggestion of selfishness may on the surface seem to be slim grounds for taking such radical action as the cross, until we reflect on the fact that faith in God is the very foundational requirement of a free willed creation; to secure its eternal happiness. If any of the issues of faith were left with room for any doubt, then this would leave open potential for a further rebellion and fall somewhere in the ages of ages to come; a risk that the love of God was not willing to accept.

God was not happy to create anything less than beings with a sovereign will of their own just like he has, and in his determination to create beings as great as this, all the measures he has taken to make the creation secure through the ages are profoundly important. This includes faith in the following:

- The fact that God is just, and therefore some are eternally condemned.

- The fact that God is merciful, and, as far as possible, those that are fallen are redeemed.

- The fact that God was willing to accept a personal cost beyond any other loss in order to secure the purposes of love.

- The fact that God is proving, through the events of creation, that his power and wisdom is sufficient not only to defeat evil, but also to turn every detail of the events of the fall to serve the purposes of Love. This reveals his omnipotence and omniscience.

The facts are designed firstly to establish unshakeable faith in God as a God of Love, and secondly to establish faith in the omnipotent and irresistible power of God. Both of these areas of faith in God serve to underpin and secure the happiness of creation for all the ages to come, forever.

Because of this faith, all free-willed beings in eternity will have their own inbuilt and unshakeable defences against any suggestion that God is not a God of Love, or that his power cannot secure the purposes of Love in any circumstance. Redeemed men learn these truths whilst in the most adverse and contrary circumstances in this world. It is therefore not surprising that God is raising them to entrust them with huge responsibilities through the ages to come[263]. In future ages they will no longer be assailed by evil from every side as they now are, yet in this present age they learn to remain firm in their obedience and faith, regardless of these trials, once they have become mature in their faith towards him.

The scriptures declare that it is faith that overcomes the world[264]. This includes all temptation and all pride. We can now begin to appreciate that this security of faith opens the way for God to do incredible things with us in the ages of ages to come without danger of another fall or loss.

We should also understand that God is not happy for his creation to proceed in a manner where we watch each other with a suspicious eye as we see governments and institutions behaving in this world. God's plan is true freedom for all free-willed beings[265] and for this there must be complete trust. His plan was never for anything less. The development of faith therefore has to be great enough to enable him both to entrust us with incredible power, and with total freedom.

None of us come close to appreciating the extents of his plan. He is the author and finisher of our faith[266], and in his passion and determination to proceed with this immense plan, he will carry the development of our faith on to completion in us by his sovereign power.

---

[263] 1 Cor 6:3 Matt 25:21,23
[264] 1 John 5:4
[265] Gal 5:1 2 Cor 3:17
[266] Heb 12:2

The eternal testimony of suffering

We may detect a weakness in the plan of God for the ages to come, as we have discussed it so far. The weakness I refer to, by this understanding, is that in the ages to come much will depend on the memory of a bygone age of evil. The further we move into the coming ages, the more distant and foreign this evil age of pre-history is likely to become.

In some ways this idea is already reflected in the way we use scripture and the fact that so much of it relates to a time and country that is now far departed from our modern society. Having said this, we can see that the memory of that time and culture in Israel is the stuff of factual legend and it has been effectively carried forward to our day with all its lessons intact for us, despite the fact that it belongs to such a different time and culture. In many ways we enjoy and benefit from the historical context of this record, and we find there are some things about the character of man that never change. We can expect this to continue to be so in eternity as redeemed men and angels carry the experiences of this age, and all its lessons, with us as a living testimony in the ages to come. If in the ages to come God has destined to create new races of free-willed beings, then our relationship to them, and the experiences of this age will be of supreme importance for them to prevent another fall. We will effectively deliver to them our faith, thus giving them the same security we have from repeating the fall and loss we are now experiencing in the present age.

This idea is reflected in the way God instructed the Israelites to pass on the memory of God's wonders when they came out of Egypt[267]. In the Bible Egypt is a symbol of this present world and age. No doubt in heaven our ability to pass on our experiences of this age will be greatly helped by the intimacy we have there, and the ability to share oneself through our spiritual union with others.

The idea of a living testimony is a marvellous thing, but there is more. The truth is God has not left it to the history of the events of this age, and the faith developed through it, to be carried forward by our testimony alone. His plan is much greater than that. God always uses several witnesses to important truths[268]. The steps he has taken will ensure that this age of evil will never (ever) be forgotten, no matter how many

---

[267] Ex 10:2 Ps 78:4 Joel 1:3
[268] Deut 17:6 Matt 18:16 Heb 10:28 John 8:13-17

ages pass. This other eternal testimony is also living, and it comes directly from the cross, as we will see.

CHAPTER 8: The Incarnation of God in Creation

The Son of God

It was Jesus, the Christ, the Messiah, and the Son of God that died on the cross. His name is also *'Emmanuel'* – God with us, *'Mighty God'*, and *'Prince of Peace'*[269].

The apostle Thomas is remembered most for his doubting, perhaps because it is this that encourages us most when we wrestle with doubt. He was however a great character who in the end surrendered his life to martyrdom for his Lord (in India), as did the others on their own mission field.

Not much of what Thomas said is recorded but when he does speak we gain some valuable insights into him as a man. It appears he was perhaps a pragmatist, a man of courage, and he always 'called a spade a spade'. He was profoundly practical and 'down to earth' in his outlook, but perhaps as a result was slow to discern the spiritual.

When Jesus decided to return to Bethany near Jerusalem, to pay a memorable visit to his friend Lazarus, where the Jews had recently tried to stone them, it was Thomas that piped up with the comment: *'Let us also go, that we may die with him'*[270]. He may have been a practical man but he was gutsy and no-one could question his commitment to his Lord. He was ready to make a mistake with Jesus if that was what was demanded of him. I have no doubt that Jesus loved Thomas; they had a great relationship. He probably chose him as one of the twelve to maintain some real backbone in the group.

Later, on the eve of the last supper, Thomas again chips in when Jesus tells them he is going away and that they know the way to the place he is going. Thomas comes up with the same old earthy logic – *'Lord, we don't know where you are going, so how can we know the way?'*[271] I am guessing that the famous answer of *'I am the way and the truth and the*

---

[269] Is 7:14 Is 9:6
[270] John 11:16
[271] John 14:5

life...'[272] didn't do much for Thomas; he would probably have preferred a map reference. Neither, I guess, did he make much of the answer to Phillip's request in the same conversation, when he asked Jesus to show them the Father. Jesus answered, *"Don't you know me Phillip, even after I have been among you such a long time? Anyone who has seen me has seen the Father. How can you say 'Show us the Father'? Don't you believe that I am in the Father and the Father is in me?"*[273]

A little while later Thomas witnessed the crucifixion first hand. I am certain that he was deeply saddened and horrified by it, but his pragmatism and courage led him to admit that the adventure was over, and he went off quicker than most to get on with his life. Perhaps that is why he was missing when Jesus first appeared to the disciples in the upper room after his resurrection.

When they told Thomas of the visitation he refused to believe it, and demanded the evidence. He had seen the body of his Lord mutilated beyond the form of a man[274]. He saw the major killing wounds inflicted. He needed proof. He demanded not just a body, but he wanted to see the scars and evidence of the damage. Lazarus was one thing; he thought even that had some possible explanations, but not this; no way.

He didn't believe, but he was intrigued. He could sense that something was going on, so it appears he decided to stick around and see what was happening. Then, with the doors locked, Jesus appeared in the room once again, this time with Thomas present. I imagine at first that Thomas would have been completely stunned; it would have been just too much for him to process, with all that it meant. I have seen the same effect on those that have witnessed a miracle for the first time from a place of unbelief. Jesus invited him to examine the scars. All Thomas could do was fall down and worship him and say *'my Lord and my God'*[275].

There would be no going back for Thomas after this. His scepticism had given way to faith. He was now bounding ahead of the others that were still grappling with what they were seeing. Thomas knew beyond doubt for the first time that he was talking directly to the living God.

---

[272] John 14:6
[273] John 14:9
[274] Is 52:14
[275] John 20:27-28

CHAPTER 8: The Incarnation of God in Creation

There are two purposes in raising this here. One is to show the work Jesus did to develop faith in Thomas, along with the revealing lesson that *'blessed are they that have not seen, and yet have believed'*[276]. Here we see the great value that Jesus places on us coming to see with the spiritual eyes of faith over seeing in the flesh, or in any other way[277]. The lesson reflects the universal eternal value of faith. This is the reason Jesus often holds out for so long before we see the answers to our prayers; he wants to see the greater thing appear first; the faith that will form the bedrock of eternal security.

A second lesson we get from Jesus appearing to Thomas is that here is Jesus appearing to the disciples in his resurrected and immortal body, and he bears all the scars and evidence of the crucifixion. We are not told exactly how extensive the damage appeared on his resurrected body, but what is clear is that it was visible as major scarring. The scars from the nails in his hands appeared as holes that Thomas could put his fingers into[278]. The same was true of the wound in his side. We can only speculate on the condition of his back that was *'like a ploughed field'*[279], and his body as a whole that was *'marred beyond human form'*[280].

In this world our bodies bear a faint reflection of what will be seen in heaven when all is revealed. The faith, the fruit of the spirit, and the character of God that has been developed, all have a way of shining through in the life of the mature Christian[281].

In this instance with Jesus we see something of the reverse of that. The scarred body of the resurrected Jesus in the flesh carried a physical reflection of him as he is in his spiritual body in the spiritual realm. This is borne out in the book of Revelation where we are introduced to the awesome scene of the throne of God in heaven. The splendour of it is radical; jewels, crowns, gold, 24 elders sat on thrones around the central throne, thunder, lightning, 7 lamp stands representing the 7-fold spirit of God, 4 awesome living creatures representing the whole of creation and

---

[276] John 20:29
[277] Eph 1:18 John 12:40 2 Cor 5:7
[278] John 20:24,27
[279] Ps 129:3
[280] Is 52:14
[281] I Cor 3:12 2 Cor 4:7

worshipping with exclamations of 'Holy, Holy, Holy'. Most importantly there was *'someone'* of great glory and splendour sitting on the throne, who is later identified as God[282].

We then see, in the hand of the one sitting on the throne, a scroll, but no-one was found who could open it.[283] The scroll contains God's judgements on the fallen, sinful, and unrepentant creation[284]. Justice was about to fall, but who would administer it. No-one in heaven was worthy of this. Only one that had proved his love for that which was to be judged could be worthy to open it, because no being in heaven or earth could be left in doubt that this was anything but an essential and unavoidable act of judgement, demanded by the highest purposes of Love for all of creation.

Then, standing in the very centre of the throne, we suddenly see; not the glorious someone, but *'a Lamb, looking as if it has been slain'*. We are told he is *'the Lion of the tribe of Judah, the Root of David and he has triumphed'*[285]. This is the Lord Jesus; the Son of God himself who has come from the cross[286]. His love for the world is proven beyond any question of doubt by the evidence of his sufferings right there before every creature in the kingdom of God, and he is therefore the one through whom the Father has chosen to judge[287].

Splendour and sacrifice

All of the imagery in the book of Revelation is earthly symbolism, used to give a faint reflection of real events in heaven. What is described to us is the very throne of heaven with God sitting on it, and the myriads of beings in all creation worshipping him.

An amazing thing about this scene is that in one view we see the throne, with God upon it, represented in all the glorious splendour and beauty of rainbows and jewels. In the next instant we see the glorious image of God replaced by the Lamb that is slain. What an awesome contrast this is; one second immense beauty, the next the horror and mess of a sacrifice.

---

[282] Rev 4, 4:2
[283] Rev 5:1-3
[284] Rev 6-
[285] Rev 5:5-6
[286] John 1:29
[287] John 5:22

Here we see God the Son, standing before all creation, showing the evidence of his unimaginable sufferings at the hands of men and demons. The scene reveals all; the pain, the terror, the humiliation and the agonising suffering of the cross, leaving nothing of it hidden.

The Lamb has now returned to glory, but he carries all of the evidence of the cost of creation and redemption upon him, and all the creatures that look on him see it. The effects of my sin are there, and so is yours. It is no longer ours but his. He took it from us and here we see the effects of it on display before all of heaven and creation.

We may ask: Will my sin be on view in heaven? I answer no – it is eternally covered – but like a person that has had a near fatal injury may show the scars of their trauma, or like a soldier that has been in battle may show their scars as full evidence of their struggle, so we see Jesus bearing the marks of what it took to deliver us from sin and the eternal judgement that he must now administer in opening the scroll[288]. It is this parallel to the cost of our sin that will bear the eternal testimony, and Jesus himself is the one that bears it.

Why the scars? – A favourite pastime of soldiers, in the lazy and boring waiting times between terrifying battles, has always been to show off and compare battle scars, and tell the stories of courage, strength, and bravado behind them. These scars are the evidence of real action and they have always been a source of great pride and respect for those that bear them. They are the proof that they have risked their lives for their cause, and the cause of those for whom they fought.

The scars also serve another purpose; to spur their fellows on to great deeds so that they too may do their duty, and have their tales of glory.

Now imagine a soldier that has been so traumatised by their experience in the arena of war that they only reluctantly and unwillingly consent to show the scars of a near fatal encounter where the struggle was so immense that even the memory of it is hard for both the bearer and the observer to face. Those that see the evidence are hushed and silenced with horror, wonder, and awe at the sight of it.

Such revelations as these have a very different effect of humbling both those that see them and those that bear them. With the onlookers

---

[288] Rev 5:7, 6:1

there is the humble realisation that the seriousness and radical nature of such an epic struggle would have swallowed them up, and been far beyond their ability to bear. For those that bear the scars, the very memory of the anguish they have passed through is the source of the very deepest humility of heart. This is the kind of wounding that is evident on the saviour from his battle of all ages to redeem man from his sin. This is the humility he spoke of when he said: *'Take my yoke upon you and learn from me, for I am gentle and humble in heart, and you will find rest for your souls'*.[289]

It is the Father's will that the Son should bear all this in the sight of all creation for all the ages to come. The Son asked to be released from it if another way could be found, but it was the Father that required him to do it because there was no other way[290]. Does this diminish the glory of God? Not in the least! In these wounds and scars are both the awful and the awesome combined; awful suffering, and awesome glory.

Artists know that among the works that have the greatest impact on their admirers are those that show stark and radical contrasts. As God has received this evidence of these real and actual sufferings of the cross into himself, in the form and on the body of his Son, he has not diminished his glory but has greatly enhanced it, though in a way that shows the most profound humility.

Humility is part of the nature of Love, and therefore of the character of God[291]. In God's kingdom the strength of the strong is devoted to the care and protection of the weak. The strongest become the servants of all, and the weak are given special honour and valued to an even greater measure because of their weakness and vulnerability[292].

These things are in awesome contrast to the values of this world and of the evil realm. The truth of the humility of God, as shown on the throne in the wounds of the Lamb that was slain, is something of him that calls forth unending worship from all creatures in heaven that see it, even as much as the splendour of his being. It reveals, more than anything, the vastness of the Love of God.

---

[289] Matt 11:29
[290] Luke 22:42
[291] Phil 2:3-4,5-8
[292] 1 Cor 12:23-24 1 Cor 13:7

CHAPTER 8: The Incarnation of God in Creation

When respected men take the humble step of sharing their failures we respect them even more. If it is humbly borne we appreciate their transparency and honesty. God is a perfect being. If he has any faults they are well out of range of the perception of his creatures[293]. However he has, in a similar way, revealed himself to us by giving us an insight into an event that, even for him, was immense suffering. Yes, it was on our behalf, but his nature forced him to bear its consequence in a measure that reflected the full extents of his hatred and revulsion of all that sin is.

The evidence of sufferings act like the flaws in a diamond; they refract the light that shines through it with a myriad of colours. It is these 'flaws' in precious jewels that make them more unique and valuable than ever. The display and record of suffering in God's Son is the same; his scars have the same kind of effect. This is something of God that is unique in all heaven, and it is carried through all of the ages of ages to come in the being of God himself. All other beings are perfectly formed, but here, in an aspect of the form of God, is the unique expression of something indescribably traumatic.

God has eternally set the view of these sufferings right at the focal point of all of creation, including all beings, by setting it in himself; who is the object and centre of their worship. Because of this none of them will ever forget, or fail to see or appreciate the cost. This time it is not just a testimony of an age gone by; it is direct and first hand evidence, held before all, as part of God's being and constitution, and all that know him know also his sufferings in the same way the apostle Paul longed to know them[294].

Paul was one who was called to share the sufferings of Christ in his experience of this world, and as such came to bear a reflection of this most awesome aspect of God, thereby fulfilling his heart's desire. Of course all that pass through this world come to share in it to some measure, but though the suffering is sometimes intense, we should see that this is a source of immense glory on an eternal scale, and therefore the reason God does not readily withdraw us from it, but chooses instead to pass through it with us, suffering alongside us in our pain.

To explore the depths of God is the passion, desire and pleasure of all heavenly beings. This aspect of God's being will forever fascinate and

---

[293] 1 Cor 1:25　Ps 50:12
[294] Phil 3:10, Col 1:24, 2 Cor 4:17

enthral those that chart a course into it. For us to bear a reflection of it, as an aspect of God, is therefore a great honour and privilege.

No Christian should doubt that in suffering the penalty of their sin, Jesus paid an eternal price for it. This is the answer to those that cannot correlate the ultimate destruction of the unredeemed sinner to the cost Jesus paid to redeem them, even though he himself is not eternally destroyed through it. It is the infinity of eternity for which the cost is carried that makes the cost of the cross equivalent for God, as an infinite and eternal being, to the destruction of a finite fallen being. This was the ultimate possible cost for God.

If Thomas was compelled to worship Jesus on seeing the scars on his physical resurrected body in the flesh, then none of us should doubt that when we see him as he is, with the evidence of his sufferings for our sins there upon him before us in the form of the Lamb that was slain, we will be able to do nothing other than worship and thank him, with inexpressibly grateful hearts, as we marvel and delight in his inestimable love and goodness to us.

The church of Christ is the bride of the Lamb. When the wedding supper of the lamb is complete and we come to the consummation of the ages, then the most revealing and intimate moments between them will bring the closest and most intimate revelations of the sufferings Jesus endured to save her. In these times she will know beyond measure his love for her. Like a bride whose heart longs to be wed to her beloved, the apostle Paul expressed these very deepest yearnings of the body of Christ when he said: '*I want to know Christ and the power of his resurrection and the fellowship of sharing in his sufferings*'[295]. We can be sure that even beyond the revelation of the glory of God in heaven before all creation, there will be the private and intimate revelations of love between Christ and his bride that will be the very fulfilment and consummation of love for all the ages. Our most intimate experiences of worship on the earth only ever foreshadow this, which will be the fulfilment of our deepest desire in heaven.

A testimony of a vision of Jesus – As a testimony to this truth I recently heard the story of a young woman that had been involved in a car accident, and the physical and emotional trauma of it had caused a reaction in her

---

[295] Phil 3:10

body that meant she was infirm and permanently racked with pain. However, she was a Christian and had an intimate walk with God through her years of suffering, with a full assurance that she would come through to healing and live a normal life. She fought a faith battle and won, eventually realising, by faith, that she had authority over her body, and as she realised it she received an instant healing, rather than the progressive healing she had previously hoped for.

During her battle she shared some of the intimate visionary encounters she had with Jesus, and described how he had revealed himself to her like he had for Thomas; his body scarred with all the evidence of the cross, including the deep gashes in his back where he had been scourged.

What I found most interesting in this testimony was what this young woman said of Jesus's face. She said; as she looked at him, and the scars and evidence of crucifixion on his body, she saw that one cheekbone was higher than the other. She realised that in the suffering of Jesus he had been truly brutalised and tortured to death, and that even his face and been smashed out of shape. This would confirm the scripture that speaks of him as *'marred beyond the form of a man'*; the face being the main form and feature of recognition. She also spoke of blood being still apparent on his hands, and when she asked the Lord why it was visible Jesus said to her, with great delight, that it was to remind Satan of his total defeat through the blood.

This is, at least, an interesting testimony that is strongly supported by her physical healing. And it expresses the truth of the eternal cost of the cross that Jesus has carried, and of which this vision is only a shadow of an unimaginable spiritual reality that we have yet to fully encounter in the spiritual realm.

Did the Son of God change?

We are told in scripture that *'Jesus Christ is the same yesterday, today and forever'*[296]. We may therefore ask – In bearing the scars and evidence of sufferings for sin that is laid upon him as the slain Lamb, has he changed in form?

This is a very valid question. The answer is that Jesus has not changed; he was slain from the foundation of the world (cosmos).[297]

---

[296] Heb 13:8
[297] Rev 13:8

Therefore he has not changed. The concept is hard for us to understand because it takes us outside of the dimension of time. We see Jesus slain just 2000 years ago, but the reality is that this extreme expression of his love was incorporated and accomplished in the plan of God right from the very conception of the idea of creation.

The cross displays something of God that is an eternal reality. This is exactly who and what God is; and always has been. As the act of Jesus washing the disciple's feet shows God to be what he is[298], so the cross gives an eternal view of his sacrificial heart of love that readily condescends to the level of a servant, even at immense personal cost, in order to ensure the purpose of love is accomplished[299].

History from God's perspective

To understand this further we have to view time and history from God's perspective. Think of it like a tapestry, such as the Bayeux tapestry that depicts the battle of Hasting in England in the year 1066. In this conquest the Norman king 'William the Conqueror' won his campaign against King Harold to claim the throne of England and open the Norman era of English history. The tapestry shows the events of the battle sequentially from left to right, including King Harold who was defeated and killed as he was struck in the eye with an arrow, later dying from the injury.

To God the whole of the history of the age, and all that is created, is laid out in a similar way like a tapestry before him. Jesus is the Alpha and Omega, the beginning and the end[300]. To God a day is as a thousand years and a thousand years as a day[301]. God is outside of time. He made the time dimension. He is above time and is in no way restricted by it as we are.

As the weavers of the tapestry were not limited to weaving from left to right in the order of the events as they occurred, so God is not limited to work on the history of this age in the order that the events appear. From our perspective Jesus has appeared in time and was slain on the cross towards the end of the present age. From God's perspective this only fixes the location of the cross towards the right edge of the tapestry of

---

[298] John 13:1-14
[299] Phil 3:10
[300] Rev 1:8, 21:6, 22:13
[301] 2 Pet 3:8

the age[302], but in terms of the sequence in which he put the events of history in place; the cross was woven in first, before anything else. Everything else was then woven around it. The scriptures can therefore accurately say that he was slain from the foundation of the cosmos[303].

The physical dimension

In our day we are better informed than any previous generation on the concept of time as a dimension. This is largely due to the numerous fictional works that now exist exploring the ideas of dimensional time in the form of science fiction films and books. However this knowledge is by no means confined to fiction.

Einstein introduced us to the theory of relativity that transformed our whole space-time concept, revealing that neither space nor time are the absolutes they appear to be. The theory of relativity shows that time may pass at different rates for different observers in the universe; as becomes more evident in certain extreme conditions. Time is relative, and so is space. These theories have been scientifically proven beyond doubt and are now accepted as facts that underpin some of the latest technological developments.

We observe that in the physical universe man is limited to a 3½ dimensional environment – 3 spatial dimensions and a ½ time dimension. I call the time dimension a ½ dimension because we observe that physical man is only able to travel forwards in time and not backwards.

We may be forced once again to speak in the abstract here, but it is perfectly feasible to understand that God is not nearly as limited as we are. He has full freedom in the fourth dimension of time, and undoubtedly has made for himself many more dimensions. Perhaps he has 7 dimensions to play and work with that we know little about. He may create or reveal more in the coming ages; who knows?

We know there is a spiritual world that gives further dimensions to move in, but we really are not equipped to appreciate this in more than an abstract way, other than that we are aware of 'moving in the Spirit' as people who are born again[304].

---

[302] Heb 9:26
[303] Rev 13:8
[304] John 3:8 2 Pet 1:21

What is clear is that God moves in some higher dimensions than we do. One of these appears to be the very dimension of persons[305]. We see him manifest as one being in three persons in the Trinity. We also see him filling all beings that unite with him in his universe. This is God moving in the dimension of 'us' (created beings) which is a dimension entirely of his own. Heaven itself, as the New Jerusalem, may be a higher experience of this dimension with God inhabiting her in this way. In this we see a little clearer how we can be regarded in terms of a structure or dwelling, as living stones[306], and as the very fabric of the New Jerusalem[307]. The scripture says God inhabits her, which we see in another way; he inhabits us[308].

The work of creation

On the subject of time and the order of God's creation; Jesus said that both the work of the Father and his own work is ongoing, even though the scriptures say that God completed his work and rested from it[309]. This is Jesus speaking from the perspective of both man within time, and God with his view of the tapestry of time. His words show that from within time we may see the work in progress, but from God's perspective it is already complete. He sees the end from the beginning. Despite the fact that men and angels have sovereign free will and make free choices, yet God sees the completed work. His design has never changed and he sees the end from the beginning. His work within time progresses unstoppably towards the conclusion that God designed[310].

The angels also operate from the eternal spiritual domain. As spiritual beings their view on the physical domain is the same as God's. They see the whole work like a tapestry as he does, each of them participating in the weaving, choosing the next place in history to play their part according to the wisdom and guidance of God that they access to direct them as they play their part in this age. The scripture says: '*are not all angels ministering spirits sent to serve the heirs of salvation*'[311]. They

---

[305] Eph 3:19, 5:18 Acts 2:4, 4:31
[306] 1 Pet 2:5
[307] John 3:3 – See footnotes Gal 4:26
[308] Rev 21:3 Ps 46:5
[309] John 5:17 Gen 2:2-3 Heb 4:3
[310] Eph 1:11

CHAPTER 8: The Incarnation of God in Creation 137

are keenly interested in its work, its progress, and us as the objects of their work. When the physical domain was created they danced and shouted with joy as the blank canvas of all the physical creation and time was placed before them[312].

The angels see the plays of the enemy and his cohorts to corrupt God's design, intervening in the affairs of men and history wherever they believe they will advance their malicious cause. At times this is distressing to the angels of God; until they see how every malicious action of these fallen ones of their own kind is used by God, through their work, as he directs them to turn every evil action to his good purpose. They marvel as they see the complete tapestry emerging, with the work progressing in all areas of history at the same time from their eternal perspective.

As this work of art forges towards completion they begin to see that this is precisely what God designed it to be. They marvel at its wisdom and the sight of it invokes in them irrepressible expressions of praise and worship from the very depths of their being, with excited exclamations of *'The Lord has done this and it is marvellous in our eyes'*[313]. If they danced and shouted at the beginning, imagine their joy at the completion of the age[314]. In all of this we see how God has worked to establish even the angels in unshakeable faith. Through all that has happened in the age of the fall, we see both men and angels emerging with the faith that will ensure the eternal security of all creation for all the ages upon ages to come.

Mission impossible – As a boy my family first possessed a television at the age of eight. In these early days I was enthralled by the Mission Impossible series. The key feature of these programmes was not reflected in the films that were made at a later date, based on the series. This key feature was that a plot unfolded where the team accepted a mission with a particular intended political outcome. The team were then seen to set about the mission, and on a number of occasions it appeared to go completely wrong. Then, as the story progressed, all the problems and errors suddenly came together to prove that all of this was actually part of

---

[311] Heb 1:14
[312] Job 38:7
[313] Ps 118:23
[314] Heb 12:22

the original plan, and it had all been worked together by the team to accomplish their goal.

In taking on the work of creation, God took on an impossible mission. However God specialises in the impossible, and as a result what we see emerging, to our amazement, is God's perfect design and conclusion from all that we see going on around us in and through this world.

The manifestation of God

Jesus said: '*God is spirit and his worshippers must worship him in spirit and in truth*'[315]. God is spirit! God is described elsewhere as invisible; the invisible God[316]. What does this mean? It clearly does not mean that God cannot be seen at all because many scriptures show that God is seen by angels and sometimes, as in the case of Moses, by man. David held to the promise that beyond death he would '*awake and be satisfied with seeing his face*'[317]. So, when God is described as invisible, does it just mean in this physical world? Or does it mean something deeper?

It is important to understand that both the domain of spirit, and the physical domain, are parts of creation. Only God is 'uncreated'. He is '*before all things*'[318] including the spiritual realm, and he is '*for whom and through whom everything exist*', including the spiritual domain. He is not therefore subject to the spiritual domain in any way other than the ways he has made himself subject to it. God defines the spiritual domain; it does not define him. It follows that God is not primarily and fundamentally spirit because he pre-existed the creation of all things spiritual.

To try to understand this we must try to put it in terms we understand by using the concept of time. Imagine God in a time before he decided to create either the spiritual or physical domains. God existed, but he had not yet made any creative expression. It is clear that, to their delight, the angels saw the physical domain created, so the angels and their spiritual domain must have been created first[319].

---

[315] John 4:24
[316] Col 1:15 Heb 11:27
[317] Ps 17:5
[318] Col 1:17
[319] Job 38:7

Of course the idea of there being a 'time' before God created anything may not be strictly correct because time itself is part of the present creation, but it does help us to describe it in terms we can understand.

In this time before the creation of the spiritual domain, God had in himself a full expression of himself waiting to be released. This expression was in God and has always been in God. It is a perfect and complete expression of all that God is. It is not **'a'** creative idea of God, it is **'the'** one and only perfect expression of himself. Nothing else would fully express him, not even something that differed in the minutest detail. This expression is the perfect representation of his being.

As such we can truly say, this expression 'is' God, just as when we see someone that we recognise we would say this is my friend 'John' or 'Susan'. In truth we see only the physical body of John or Susan, and this is what we recognise, but we have to acknowledge that here we see their full being, including all their visible and invisible parts as a human being.

This expression that was in God, and was God, has been called both the *'Word of God'* and the *'Son of God'*. It is clearly incorrect to say the 'Word of God' is part of God because it is the whole expression of him, not part of him. If we encounter the 'Word of God' we therefore encounter God in his fullness[320].

The 'Word of God' is also called the 'Son of God' because he came forth from God; he was 'begotten' and not created because he was always in God. The use of the term 'son' is the closest we can identify this with in earthly terms; however the reality is that he did not come forth as another being; he came forth as a full representation of his Father, the invisible God, and is one and the same as him.

It is only through this expression of God in the Son that God can be seen or known. Consequently, when Phillip asks Jesus to 'Show us the Father' Jesus responds with *'Don't you know me Phillip even after I have been among you such a long time. If you have seen me you have seen the Father'*[321]. Jesus was not now claiming to be the Father because the Father is the term that describes the invisible God that pre-exists the begetting of the Son and the creation that is in him. He is claiming to be the Son, who

---

[320] Heb 1:3 Col 1:15 John 1:1-3,18
[321] John 14:9, 17:3

is the one and only expression of the Father, and in him is all that there is to see of God, including the spiritual and physical creation.

What form did the expression take?

God expressed himself perfectly and completely in the 'Word of God' as the 'Son of God' came forth from him. The Son is the whole expression of God; the exact representation of his being[322]. As such the Son of God came forth, and as he did so the creation was created in him as the form and detail of that expression.

This does not mean that the Son of God was created, or that he was at this point within his creation. He was not created; he simply came forth, or was 'begotten' as a perfect expression of God[323]. At this point we see that the creation was in him, not him in creation[324].

As the next step in this process we see that the Son of God then stepped into his own creation and became 'incarnate' within it[325]. We therefore see that the creation is in the Son of God, and he is now also in the creation.

In reality this would not have been a step by step process, but it all came together in a single act; God begetting the Son, and the Son coming forth from him complete with the creation in him. It all happened in a word from God. There was therefore an act of creation, but that act was not of creating the Son, but of the Son creating all in himself as he emerged from the Father and was begotten.

How can God be spirit?

To take the next step in our exploration of the being of God, we see that the 'Word of God' has been expressed and come forth in the form of the 'Son of God' who is a full representation and expression of God. In the process the creation is created in him as part of that expression.

This creation came forth primarily in the form of the spiritual domain. For this expression to be complete the next thing required was that the Son of God must express himself *within* that spiritual domain. He therefore places himself within his own spiritual creation as a spiritual

---

[322] Heb 1:3
[323] John 1:18
[324] Col 1:16, 17
[325] John 1:14

being, with a spiritual body and form in that domain. Here God is made manifest as a spirit; the Spirit. Here we see the first level of incarnation where God appears visibly in his created spiritual domain in the form of the Spirit of God. Through this Spirit, angels see him and he is now fully represented and expressed in that domain[326]. In fact the very purpose of the creation and design of the whole spiritual domain is precisely to give God perfect and complete expression of his being through it and in it[327].

Other spiritual beings are created to occupy that domain with him, having free-will like God but wholly dependent on him for their being. The Spirit of God relates to all these other spiritual free-willed beings (angels) in a full expression of his love and goodness.

The angels are created spirits[328] but in some inevitable ways the spirit of God is different to them. We will explore this later, but one important way in which he is different is that he is not a created spirit. God as *the* Spirit is the only uncreated part of the spiritual domain. We could in the same way say he was begotten within the spiritual domain. When angels look on him as a spirit, one of their marvels is that they see him as a unique pre-existent uncreated spirit in their spiritual domain. They are aware that they themselves are created, and as such, like us, they are not the source of their own being. But in the Spirit of God they see one that is uncreated, who is his own source, and who is in fact their source too.

These finite free-willed spiritual beings we call angels are part of God's complete creative expression in the spiritual domain, but the highest of all spiritual beings is the Spirit of God himself which exists to fully reflect the complete fullness of God in this domain in the form of a spirit[329]. The Spirit of God is therefore glorious and full of splendour in the extreme. The being of God is also reflected in the Spirit by the fact that all other spirits depend on him as their source and sustenance of their being[330]. We therefore see the suffix 'el' to both the word 'angel' – meaning messenger of God, and the names of all angels such as 'Gabriel' and 'Michael' – 'El' meaning God in the Hebrew language. We see these

---

[326] Matt 18:10
[327] Heb 1:3 Col 1:15-17
[328] Ez 28:13 Rev 10:6
[329] 1 Cor 13:12 Ps 11:7, 17:15 Rev 22:4
[330] Heb 1:3 Col 1:17

beings totally dependent on God for their being, and therefore we even see God reflected in their very names.

As we explore this progression of creation, we begin to see it is like holding up two mirrors facing each other. As we look into one of the mirrors we see the other reflected. In the reflection of the first mirror we then see the reflection of the second. The reflection goes deeper and deeper disappearing into infinity.

In a similar way; in creation what we see is God creating a domain, and then putting himself within that created domain in an incarnate form. We then see him make a full expression of himself through his incarnate being, and then putting himself within that expression in whatever form that expression takes, and on it goes.

The progression of incarnation

To reiterate this and put the actual progression of incarnation in a nutshell in real terms:

- The invisible God was fully expressed in the 'Word of God' coming forth as the 'Son of God' – he was begotten.

- The creation of the spiritual domain came forth within the Son of God as a full expression of himself in a perfect form, complete with free willed spiritual beings – angels.

- The Son of God then became incarnate and gave himself spiritual expression within the spiritual domain he had created, in the form of the uncreated 'Spirit of God'.

- Through the Spirit the Son of God then created the physical domain in full view of the angels as a temporal sub-domain within the spiritual domain.

- The Spirit of God then gave himself full expression in the physical domain by taking physical form as the man Jesus. As a sub-domain of the spiritual domain the angels were able to witness the whole event unfolding in the physical domain.

CHAPTER 8: The Incarnation of God in Creation 143

- The Spirit of God then filled the physical man (Jesus) with himself, who then gave a full expression of the Spirit of God within the physical domain in all his words and deeds in the earth and on the cross.

- The scriptures were written to embody the words of God and provide a full expression of God throughout the present age in the form of the written word; which we also call the Word of God, which is also a form, or sub-form, of the incarnation of God.

- Each created domain includes a creation that is packed with design that reflects God[331], including each having its highest expression, apart from the being of God, in the form of other free-willed beings like God[332]. These beings always relate back to the being and form of God in their own domain in a relationship of worship and complete dependence on him. In the spiritual domain we see angels as spirits relating to the Spirit of God with worship and dependence on him. In the physical domain are men who are made in the image of God and who relate to Jesus, who is God in the form of a man, in a similar relationship of worship and dependence. The same is true at all levels of the incarnation. It can even be seen extending into the scriptures where there are many other inspired books written, and other creative expressions, always relating back to the foundational and complete expression of God in the scriptures[333].

In view of this repeated progression of creation – incarnation – creation – incarnation etc. we can see and appreciate why God the Father, Son and Spirit can be three forms and yet one God, with each as a full expression of God within their relevant domain. We don't see a hierarchy, but we do see a progressive cascade of expression where God is seen perfectly expressed in forms and sub-forms, within domains and sub-domains. We have every reason to believe this stretches on and on, whereby God is in all, and all is in God in unfathomable ways. We see this creative

---

[331] Rom 1:20 Ps 19:1-3
[332] Gen 1:26-27
[333] 2 Tim 3:16 2 Pet 1:20

expression of God stretching through many dimensions, domains, and forms, and into the ages of ages to come where no doubt God's creativity extends to an infinite extent, and is perfect in each and every form as an expression of the being of God.

What is spirit?

So, the spiritual domain is a domain of existence designed by God specifically so that he could give full, complete and perfect expression of himself in it. In the spiritual domain we know fully, and are fully known[334], so it is appropriate that this is also true for the form of God as spirit. A spirit is simply a being in this domain. God himself took the form of a spirit as the central being of this whole domain, on which all other spiritual beings created within this domain depend for their existence. For this domain to reflect God in his fullness, the spiritual domain had to be truly glorious, allowing for the widest possible expression of love and goodness as expressions of the being of God.

The demand that this domain fully express God as he actually is, required that it should contain other free-willed beings like himself so that love and goodness could be fully expressed in their relationship to him and each other.

Levels of incarnation

At every level that God creates a domain or sub-domain we see an act of incarnation as God expresses himself within each domain by taking form in it. We see this in God becoming spirit in the created spiritual domain, and God becoming man in the created physical domain.

None of these forms of God can be said to be created because they are the eternal element of each domain. It is only correct to say that for each created domain, God's form in that domain is begotten. Therefore, though Jesus was born after Abraham, he said *'before Abraham was born, I AM'*[335]. We are told that he is one *'whose goings forth have been from of old, from everlasting'*[336]. He is seen throughout the history of the physical creation taking physical form and thereby reflecting the eternal nature of his being as God. We almost certainly see him as Melchizedek *'king of*

---

[334] 1 Cor 13:12
[335] John 8:58
[336] Micah 5:2

Salem' and *'priest of God Most High'*, who received tribute from Abraham, and whose name means *'Prince of Peace'* and *'king of righteousness'*[337]. He was around at the time of creation and the fall of angels[338]. All domains see the eternal existence of God in their respective form in the same way; with his form always truthfully reflecting God as the eternal one who even pre-exists that very domain.

Similarly, regarding the scriptures, Jesus said that heaven and earth would pass away but his words would never pass away[339]. We therefore see that the expressed and written word of God has a permanence that is even beyond the domain to which it is given.

As man we often express creativity in our work and activities in the earth. As God is expressed in and through the angels in their domain, so God is able to express himself through us in our physical beings and in our creative expressions. We therefore often see a form of incarnation even in our own creative expressions – art, science, technology. When such expressions come from God and are inspired by him, they are often among the highest delights of men in this age, because they reveal something of God. We cannot fathom the depth of this any more than we can know the extents of God's love. These things are simply there as a true expression of the reality of God, and it is for us to wonder and marvel at, and enjoy into the eternity of ages to come.

The manifestation of God in the spiritual domain

The representation of God in the spiritual domain as the Spirit of God, is a full, perfect and complete expression of God in all that he is as the God of love and goodness. As seen in the book of Revelation, this form in heaven comes in the glorious combination of two aspects.

The first is as a God of incredible glory and splendour. In this aspect his form is beautiful beyond description, and his glory is truly breath-taking to us and any created being.

In his second aspect, the form of God is seen as the Lamb that was slain. Here he displays the full horror and cruelty of the scars of his incredible sacrifice and suffering on the cross. In this form he has been

---

[337] Heb 7:1-3
[338] Luke 10:18
[339] Matt 24:35 Mark 13:31 Luke 21:33

referred to as the God of terrible aspect[340]. To see God in this aspect alone invokes shear fear and dread.

It is these two aspects of God, combined and integrated into one, that gives him a form and expression that is captivating and awe inspiring beyond description. Only with the two aspects together is the effect of fear and dread mitigated by the aspect of incomprehensible love and goodness. Only together can any dare to view him. We see him as both fearful and dreadful, together with unlimited love all in one view. All of this expresses his holiness, and only the holy can bear the view of him. We see incomprehensible beauty, together with marks of unimaginable suffering[341]. He is both awful and awesome. He transfixes every eye that beholds him. His form invokes such a response in all that see him that no man can see his face and bear to live on in the physical[342]. To merely glimpse such a view of God would immediately alter us, and bring us into a place where we yearn for heaven as our deepest need and desire, as the apostle Paul discovered through his revelations. Angels are irresistibly compelled to cry '*Holy, Holy, Holy*'[343] at the very sight of him. None of us have yet comprehended the impact that seeing him will have on us. Having seen him, none will ever be satisfied to leave his presence, or to lose sight of this vision of him in all aspects of his being.

This view of God is the full and perfect representation of his being. It is not some modification of God. This is what he truly is and always has been. Jesus is the same yesterday today and forever[344]. God does not change form, he is eternally the same. The fearful, and even terrible aspect of the slain Lamb is as much a vital and eternal part of him as his glorious splendour. For God to be fully expressed, all of this had to be included in the form of the expression in which he is seen and represented. He is both a vision of unlimited love, and at the same time he is a fearful and truly scary sight. One description of him in scripture is as a '*consuming fire*'[345]. The Lamb is both a vital part of the representation of

---

[340] Ps 47:2
[341] Rev 4:6b, 5:1,6-7,13
[342] Ex 33:20
[343] Rev 4:8 Is 6:3
[344] Heb 13:8
[345] Heb 12:29

the being of God, and the eternal testimony of what God has done to secure the purposes of love for all the ages.

The blood of the Lamb

We now see that the slain Lamb is not just an event in history, he is an eternal feature of heaven as part of the very being of God. Nothing impure will enter heaven; it is a place where there is no corruption. The Lamb is therefore pure and holy throughout. What we see in him is not sin, but the counterpart and equivalent thing that obliterated sin that reflects the full truth of it[346]. We see the blood of the Lamb. This blood and the image of the slain Lamb is a horrific scene, and as such it bears a full testimony to the horror of sin that it has replaced. But in itself it is pure, and his blood has cleansed from all sin by becoming a perfect and pure replacement for it, and representation of it in heaven.

C. S. Lewis points out that though time seems to erode our guilt over the sins we have committed in our lives, it is an illusion that comes from living within time, as we do in this age[347]. In the eternal and heavenly view, in the tapestry of time, the sins we have committed are ever present as blots on the landscape of this age. Time is not able to erase them. The only thing that cleanses and completely obliterates them from the eternal record is the blood of Christ[348]. However this is not God simply covering up the events of history and pretending they never happened. There is no concealment of the truth on God's behalf. This would be against his nature and purpose. Rather what he has done is put in place an eternal record of these things in the form of a substitute or replacement that fully reflects the truth of it, and that will bear a true and valid record of the horror of sin, though not the sin itself. Rather it comes in a form that is pure and holy, and fitted for heaven, whilst at the same time bearing an accurate witness to the truth of the horrors of sin and evil.

This is what the scripture means when it says that *for those who repent and confess their sin, and come to walk in the light the blood of Christ has cleansed them from all sin*[349]. In this way – in the blood – God has set in place an eternal record of the horror of sin, and the cost of

---

[346] John 1:29 Heb 9:14 1 Pet 1:19
[347] The Problem of Pain – C. S. Lewis
[348] Rev 7:14
[349] 1 John 1:7,9

redemption from it that will become a source of eternal security from there ever being another fall.

Another eternal testimony – hell

While we are on the subject of the eternal testimony and the scary aspects of God; I must mention yet another testimony of this age that will be carried forward in heaven. It is a principle of God to use several different testimonies of truth in all things, especially things that have eternal significance[350]. In the context of this study we must mention it because the Bible bears a true and faithful record to it, though many find it hard to bear. In God's economy of purpose nothing is wasted, not even the waste product of the process and purpose of love. I speak of the testimony of hell and eternal damnation. How do we view these things?

In the ages to come God will not have left no trace or record of all those fallen beings that were in this age. This record is an important part of the testimony of this age that is needed to protect all creation for eternity from ever falling into such a thing again. There is a consuming lake of fire where these lives came to their final end and they were finally consumed[351], but where something like their fossilised record persists – *their worm does not die and their fire is not quenched*[352].

To use an analogy – in eternity, when we walk the shores of that lake, its fire will no longer have any power over us, but it will be like walking the shores of our oceans on earth and picking up shells that are the only record of creatures that once were, but are now no more than an empty and lifeless relic that bears a record of their existence. When we put the shell to our ear we hear a faint and eerie echo of the ocean that is before us, together with the distinct sound of emptiness and nothingness that now persists there. The whisper and echo is of what once was but is no longer, and is now washed and cleansed by the ocean and by fire.

The shells vary in size and shape, and each shell bears a record of that life and self that once was, in its form and its markings, but nothing of that life now persists. It is now only the shell of a self that was consumed that bears the record. It is the record of a self that is now gone; no longer able to scavenge for its life, or deal for its self in corruption and death as it

---

[350] Heb 10:28 2 Cor 13:1 Matt 18:16 1 Tim 5:19 John 8:17-18
[351] Rev 20:14-15 Matt 25:41
[352] Is 66:24 Mark 9:48

once did. Its only connection to life is through the impact that remains as only a shell and record that persists to the living who live eternally in love, and hear the echo of the eternal testimony of what it once was.

Among them are the record of the fallen spiritual beings of angels and men, but most scary of all is that here somewhere among them is the very shell and record of the old fallen spirit that was once I, my life of death, but who became corrupt and wretched, and who through the mercy of God was separated from me by the cross. Here on my final separation from the mortal earthly body it met its final end, and here its memory lies. We may search for it along the shores, and should we by chance happen upon its shell, the faint echo of its once pitiful life may cause a shiver through the depths of our being as the distant memories of a bygone age wash over us, but it will no longer persist to have any power over us, or be able to cast any shadow of a former life. It is only the shell and record of a former self. Its existence and its tyranny are ended. No longer does it hurt or impact my being, or spoil the fellowship of love that is now and forever the eternal inheritance of all those that live forever in Christ.

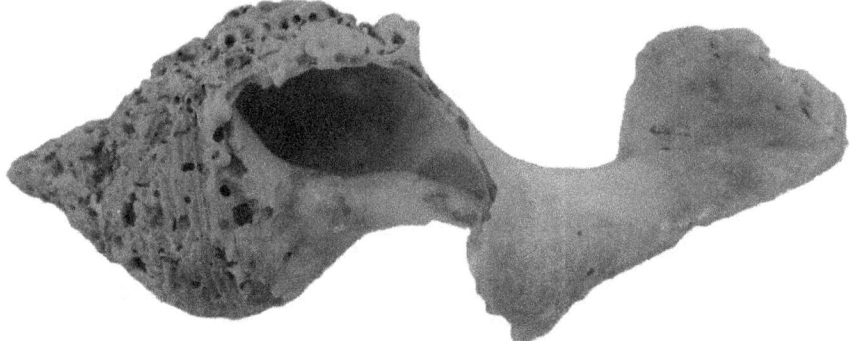

The sea of bronze – The temple of Solomon was built according to a specific pattern revealed to him as part of the wisdom God gave him. The temple and its artefacts were a larger and more permanent version of the tabernacle of the Ark of the Covenant. All of its structure, and the artefacts associated with it, are made to reflect the reality of heaven[353]. One of these artefacts is the cast of a huge circular bronze sea, like a disc or cylinder

---

[353] Heb 8:5

that sat on the back of twelve cast bronze bulls. The sea was 15 feet (4.5metres) in diameter and 7½ feet (2.25metres) high. It formed a huge laver, or washbasin, for washing utensils and things for the temple service.[354] This structure would possibly have weighed hundreds of tonnes. It would therefore be immoveable and must have been cast in position in its place outside the temple at the south east corner[355].

This sea depicts the reality of the lake of fire. Bronze is used as a symbol of fire both by its colour, and by the way it tarnishes and blackens over time like charcoal. Fire as well as water was used in the tabernacle and the temple as a means of cleansing, and bronze is therefore used to symbolise that. The same is true of all the basins used for washing, the altar, and all the utensils associated with the rituals of washing. In the same way that water was used in baptism for cleansing by John the Baptist, so he declared Jesus to be the one who baptises with fire[356], and so the use of water with bronze instruments is used in the tabernacle to reflect heavenly fire and its cleansing power in the spiritual realm.

Bulls were the animals of sacrifice. Here with the sea over the bulls we see a permanent image of sacrifice with fire over the bulls. The twelve bulls are configured with three facing each point of the compass indicating their relevance to all of this earth. Its location outside of the temple indicates that this is something outside, and on the outskirts of heaven, not within it, as Jesus described for the lake of fire[357]. Similarly with the Ark of the Covenant, the bulls were always burnt outside the camp as an offering for sin[358].

The message is clear: that for heaven sin has another permanent record in a sacrificial scene on the outskirts of heaven in the lake of fire. It depicts the cost of this age of sin and evil as a permanent record and reminder to all. The fire becomes part of the repository of the knowledge of God that forms the foundation of faith that God has designed to keep eternity secure from any repeat of the fall for all ages. The use of the sea of bronze for washing depicts the fact that all that enters heaven is first proved and cleansed by fire. Nothing that is corrupt or unclean can enter.

---

[354] 1 Ki 7
[355] 1 Ki 7:39
[356] Matt 3:11 Luke 3:16
[357] Matt 8:12, 13:42
[358] Ex 29:14

This is not the sacrifice for the redeemed; that sacrifice is seen in the Lamb at the very centre of heaven in the being of God. This is the sacrifice of the destruction of some that must be lost through the events of this age; the objects of God's wrath, in order that objects of his mercy may have a part in eternity[359].

Jesus likened hell to Gehenna; the place outside Jerusalem where rubbish and filth was burned, and the dead bodies of animals and criminals were often thrown. Such images may depict a hard truth, but the reality of it is clear in the biblical record.

The anatomy of man and the death of the soul

As a final word on this difficult topic, and before we move on to focus on the realities of life rather than death, we should draw this whole subject out of the realm of symbol, simile, and metaphor, and put it all in real terms. To do this we should have a good understanding of the anatomy of the being of man – body, soul, and spirit – but this is a whole subject in itself so we can only cover it here in terms of the conclusions of what we have been discussing.

The soul of man is the frame of his being. The physical body is a sensory organ having senses that connect him to the physical domain. Equally the spirit of man is also a body; a spiritual body, and as such it is a sensory organ connecting him to the spiritual domain. However for the soul there is no corresponding domain as there is for body and spirit. The soul is therefore entirely dependent on the bodies it is in union with for it to have any form or expression of life. Without these bodies – physical and/or spiritual – the man would have no connection to any domain. We may therefore think of the soul as the frame of the being of man; a frame on which his sensory organs are carried that connect him to the real world(s). We may therefore regard the soul, in relation to the being of man, as we would the skeleton to the physical body of man. It is the solid and permanent part of his being, but it has no life without the living tissues that it is designed to carry.

The soul is mind, will, and emotion; but what are these if there is no source of stimulus or object of desire.

---

[359] Rom 9:22

Descartes' famous maxim 'I think therefore I am' suggests that as long as a man thinks he has proof of his existence. However, as the study of man's anatomy highlights; intellectual thought is a process of the physical body, not of the soul. The mind of the soul is only a repository of values and beliefs, and therefore a product of the stimulus that came from body and/or spirit while these parts of his being were intact and in union with his soul. Once the soul loses these connections through the death of its bodies – physical and spiritual – the soul itself can truly be seen as dead. It is no longer active, sensitive, or responsive, but is dead to all worlds. Such a creature is then no more than a skeleton. And, like a skeleton, though it continues to exist, it is nevertheless dead.

What it is important to understand is that fallen man has already died spiritually. His spirit died when it lost all connection to God, because for a spirit, God is the sustaining source of life. He is therefore left only with a body that is connected to the physical world. But as the physical domain is temporal, and the life of any physical body is even more fleeting, man's soul stands in the precarious position of clinging to life only through a body that is destined to soon pass away; something that can happen at any moment. If man's soul loses that physical connection before he is spiritually reborn, and thereby equipped with a new spiritual body, he then becomes a 'lost soul'; unreachable by any means. Therefore all men that have only a physical existence will pass away with the physical world, and continue to exist only as a kind of skeleton of their former being. The record of their life and existence is there, but there is no life remaining.

In the process of evangelism the Spirit of God speaks to the soul of man through the only active sensory organ his soul has; the intellect and the emotions, via the constitution of the physical body, and through that channel persuades him to receive spiritual rebirth. For this to happen the soul must reject and discard the old dead spirit that clings to him, and receive the new spirit God is offering. This awakens his soul again to the reality of the whole of the spiritual domain, and God himself becomes the highest delight of his soul that had formerly become so focused on the physical world. It takes some time for the soul to fully learn and switch its focus back to the spirit, having been so long dead in that department, but this is the way in which the soul is reformed and progresses back the original life God intended for it.

CHAPTER 8: The Incarnation of God in Creation

This leads us to an important and pivotal understanding of our self once we are born again. The spirit is completely restored at rebirth, but the soul has to catch up and learn to live from the new spirit, rather than focusing on the flesh as it has for some time before its spiritual rebirth.

This process of reform is something we discuss in more detail in a later section on the reform of man, but before we get into that we must go on to a whole section in which, having been spiritually awakened, we study the spiritual realities of the being of God; the highest desire and delight of the renewed spirit of man.

PART II:
THE BEING OF GOD

CHAPTER 9: Coming Face to Face With God

Moses – Moses was a man who met with God face to face. When he came down the mountain from such encounters his face shone with the glory of God; the Shekinah glory. Those that saw him found they were unable to look steadily on the face of Moses and they compelled him to put a veil over his face, at least until it faded, to enable them to face him.

Moses came to be known as the meekest man that ever lived; something that it seems we must attribute to his encounters with God. Moses only ever came into these encounters after being humbled by God, first by falling from the status of prince of Egypt to a shepherd, and then by wandering the desert with sheep, that were not even his own, for no less than 40 years.

When his first direct encounter with God came, it took the form of a burning bush and holy ground; the holiness of God. Moses first came to know God as a consuming fire, as the writer of the book of Hebrew describes him.

What we find throughout scripture is that sin and all that is unholy cannot stand in the presence of God. All that is unholy is consumed and driven off in such an encounter. Why would any of our fallen sinful race desire such an encounter? Yet we find that there are men and women throughout the history of our race who have passionately and fervently sought the face of God – Why?

The next time we see this kind of glory described in scripture, manifest in a man, was in Stephen, a deacon (server) of the early church. He was a man who showed great wisdom, and worked many miracles in the days of the early church in Jerusalem; even beyond the apostles.

As one who preached and demonstrated Christ in the earth this led him into direct conflict with those that had crucified the Lord, and refused to repent of their deeds. The scripture says his hearers looked on him and saw that his face shone like that of an angel. This glory that Stephen carried was a result of him spending time seeking the face of God and entering, on the spiritual plane, beyond the veil and into direct encounter with God and Christ in all his glory; a way that has now been made open for all through the crucifixion and resurrection of Jesus. This glory that was upon Stephen, and the words that he spoke, had the effect of exposing the depth of sin and depravity of those that looked on. They reacted in the same way they had with Jesus; they sought to kill him and rid themselves of the torment it caused them as it exposed all that existed in them beyond their religious veneer, showing their true state.

As they took up stones and began to stone Stephen he looked up to heaven. As he did so his face brightened with the glory that was upon him and he said: *'I see heaven open and the Son of Man standing at the right hand of God'*. Here was the risen glorified Christ standing to receive the first martyr for the faith.

It is said in scripture that no man can see the face of God and live. All that do not belong to God shrink from his presence because it reveals all. To be forced into an encounter is like being put through fire, where all that is impure is burned up. But to those that have received Christ, they are filled with treasure that is impervious to fire and is eternal – depicted as gold, silver, and costly stones. For these ones the effect of facing God is to strip off all that is reviled by them and reveal them as they really are in all their purity before God. For them, the face of God will satisfy them to their very core, and upon such an experience there is no way that any will cling to a fleshly life any longer. To see God is to come home to all that one's heart has ever truly desired.

There was no way that Stephen, on seeing this vision of God, would have wished to stay on this earth a moment longer. If his martyrdom hadn't released him, his overwhelming desire to be released from his mortal body would have, and he would have gone to be with the Lord; the very source of the glory that was already upon him.

Isaiah – There are occasions in scripture where we get a glimpse of heaven and the glory of God that is seen by all that are there. Not least of these is the vision of Isaiah when he is irresistibly compelled to cry out: *'I see the Lord high and lifted up, and the train of his robe fills the temple. And the angels cry holy, holy, holy is the Lord'*.

Isaiah's first response to this vision is not only awe, but in his own words: *'Woe is me, I am undone. I am a man of unclean lips and I live among a people of unclean lips and my eyes have seen the King'*. We see in him unimaginable awe as he looks at God in heaven, followed by unimaginable horror as he looks back at himself and the exposure of his own sinfulness. The experience shook him, even unhinged him, to the very core of his being.

We are again led to ask: Who of us would wish for such an encounter? And yet from the deep heart of every born again believer comes the unmistakable response: 'I Lord, please let it be me!'

There are some that have walked (and do walk) this planet that have known this kind of direct encounter. Not many; only a few. Perhaps more than we may realise because not all have been public figures. When we look at their lives and their outlook we see a distinct common thread; their passion and overwhelming desire in life is to get back there!

Paul – Among these, one of the most prominent is the apostle Paul. He was a man who had surpassing revelation, and had been caught up to the third heaven and heard inexpressible things; things that man is not permitted to tell. The effects of such revelation were, for Paul, radical. It made him almost fearless in the face of death and ready to hold his life on earth to be of little value, seeing it merely as the barrier to him permanently returning to that glory he had encountered. He was ready and willing, even hopeful, that at any moment he may shed his earthly body and go to be with the Lord whom he loved so passionately, and desired to be with above all things. He saw his life above as his only home. All that compelled him to stay was his realisation that his work for his Lord on the earth was not yet complete, and his self-sacrificial love for those with whom he desired to share all that he had received and been blessed with.

Sundar Singh – Of those who had these 'close encounters' there are also some more modern examples. I recently came across one such individual; an Indian Sadhu by the name of 'Sundar Singh' who became known to the world through his travels in the 1920's.

He was a Sikh from Northern India; an aristocratic son of a Maharajah. The Sikh religion believes in one God and as such is somewhat at odds with the polytheism of Hinduism, as it has become, and that is practised across most of India.

His mother was a devout follower of the Sikh religion and raised her son to develop the same spiritual sensibilities. When Sundar was twelve years old his mother died, leaving him bitter and vulnerable. He soon after encountered Christian missionaries from the west who were preaching the gospel, but also bringing western culture and values as part of their package, rather than embracing the culture of the Sikhs to which they came. This led him into conflict with them because it offended much that he loved. The conflict led to personal bitterness, and then to outright anger; to the point that at the age of fifteen he undertook some acts of violence in opposition to Christianity, culminating in him taking a Bible, tearing out each page and burning it in the fire.

Within three days of this act of opposition he came to face his inner state, and recognised that his Sikhism had not brought the peace and fulfilment that he had hoped for, but quite the opposite. He then decided to lay down an ultimatum to God; that he should reveal himself before a certain time, and he committed himself to commit suicide under the 5pm train three days hence if God did not meet his demand, intending thereby to continue to seek the peace he craved beyond the grave.

At 4.30pm on the day of his intended departure from this world, Jesus revealed himself to him in a vision in a similar way to the apostle Paul on the road to Damascus. Sundar Singh then surrendered his life to Christ and began a remarkable life of intimacy with God that was characterised by ongoing encounters in the same vein as he had begun his new life.

The presence of God that was with him was a phenomenon that many observed, and for a while in his later life he swept across the globe carrying a unique testimony, and giving some clear and profound insights that he gained from his close relationship with the Lord.

He was fully grounded in scripture, but was able to give some very profound insights into other religions, and into heaven and spiritual realities beyond this world that came to him through direct encounters with the Lord.

He often walked on missions across India, even through parts of the Himalayas, carrying the message of the gospel, living by faith, and visiting remote regions, sharing the love of Christ with those that received him. He was even observed interacting with nature; at one time in the cool of an evening he was seen stroking a tiger that had emerged from the bush.

Sundar was once asked why he should receive such special encounters with God when most men seem to have no such experience or testimony. His answer was that he had forced God to reveal himself by his determination to otherwise end his life. In his case God had condescended to his demand, and given him an experience and revelation of himself that was above the norm. However Sundar suggested that this was no special blessing, but reminded us of the words of Jesus that '*more blessed are they that have not seen and yet believe*'.

What this leads us to understand is that all that are spiritually reborn can come to see God clearly through faith, with the eyes of the heart, and that this kind of seeing is a far greater blessing than any other kind of revelation we can receive. Seeing in this way is true sight. The phrase 'blind faith' is a profoundly unbiblical idea, and is in fact a contradiction in terms because faith is itself sight; spiritual sight. Through it we perceive spiritual realities that are more real than any of the temporal physical realities we acknowledge in this world. In this way the scripture turns the tables on the idea of blind faith by showing how, in fact, our materialistic faculty of natural/physical sight can take our focus away from the spiritual, and blind us to the greater realities beyond. We then see that our physical eyes have become our blind sight, not our faith.

Agnes Sanford – To give one further, and more modern example of those that find remarkable intimacy and revelation of God, let me share something related by one of my favourite modern Christian authors – Leanne Payne. I have received considerable blessing through Leanne's unique ministry and writings, and her genuine spirituality was confirmed to me by once visiting one of her pastoral care conferences with a friend, and meeting her first hand.

What was most confirming was the impact that these meetings had on my friend who had not read her books, and probably would not have appreciated them as much as I did, but who had a keen spiritual sense that discerns God without the intellectual trapping that sometimes cloud the issue. We came out of each conference session aware of the deep spiritual impact these sessions were having on us, that was simply too deep for words. Inner healing was and is the focus of her message, and we undoubtedly came away from these occasions with some measure of deep inner healing.

However, though I regard Leanne as a deeply spiritual woman of God, what I want to share is an encounter that she writes about herself with someone that she herself regarded as a deeply spiritual woman; a lady called Agnes Sanford [360]. This lady is reckoned to have been one of the four most influential Christian writers of the 20th century, and one of the greatest influences on modern day Christian thinking. From the 1950's onward she led the way in a new move of the spirit that focused on inner healing.

Leanne was privileged to visit Agnes at the age of eighty, though her age had forced her to cut back and become selective on the amount of time she spent with visitors.

Agnes's life had shifted, in her later years, into a focus on intercession and prayer, and a deep walk of intimacy with God. She had been led by God to live in a house in California, deliberately chosen over the San Andreas Fault so she could pray and intercede that the fault pressure would release itself slowly without loss of life. Having long since learnt her authority over sickness, evil, nature, and death; as demonstrated by Christ, here we see one whose realisation of the authority of man over their domain extended even to the very earth itself.

Leanne remarks about Agnes's extraordinary interaction with nature, including birds that visited her garden, and her ongoing dialog about boundaries with a rattlesnake that lived down her garden; where it was allowed to go and not go. While Leanne was with Agnes, in high summer, fires were breaking out in the surrounding forest in the dry heat of the summer. This reached a point where there was fire visible on all four sides of the house, and Leanne was seriously thinking it was time to evacuate. However Agnes's response was simply 'Oh I wouldn't worry dear' and she turned her eyes to the distance pacific ocean and prayed for rain, commanding it to come. In Leanne's words she says 'and yes folks the rain came and put out the fires'.

They then engaged in a conversation about when Agnes was to die. God had said to Agnes that he would like her to stay until she was 88 years old and then come home (she was 80 at this point). But she had said she didn't want to wait that long and was asking to come home at 82. Leanne suggested a compromise of 84, which after some thought Agnes agreed with after raising it with the Lord, and she subsequently went on to die at 84 without any disease on her body. She simply went home.

---

[360] Heaven's Call – Leanne Payne

I realise for some this kind of thing is really off their page, and many are sceptical. But for myself, though I would so far not claim to have found quite such a place in God, yet I have enough experience of God's power in healing and miracles, and in my interactions with nature to know and believe these things to be perfectly authentic and real. Nor is it the only time I have heard of this kind of thing in mature believers that have an intimate walk with the Lord.

Our appetites are whetted for God, and we have cast iron promises that if we want this kind of relationship with God we can have it. So, above and beyond ministry, or anything else we get up to in this world, in it all we are, and ever shall be, primarily in pursuit of God as the highest priority of our lives. Everything else is subsidiary to that.

But: What about the fear? What about the fire? Should we not be reticent of such encounters, at the very least? How can any that still partake of flesh not feel a tinge of fear that would make them flee such an encounter? These are the questions that arise for many.

My answer to these questions for myself, and all that are born again, comes from an understanding of myself as a born again believer; an understanding that it took me some time as a Christian to reach due to my unwitting excursions into legalism, and other mistakes that came along and led me off track. But having eventually come to receive the truth about myself, I find I am liberated from any reserve I had from encountering God in these ways, and even greater ways than I have described in the lives of others.

This understanding of myself is something I have written more extensively about in the last section of the book – *The Reformation of Man* – but I mention it here because desiring God is a vital key to encounters with him, and until we resolve the things that prevent us from desiring it *now,* we will not press on towards it. While ever we feel unready for such an encounter we will not desire it. But for every born again believer, a true understanding of themselves as a new creature is actually all that is needed to release them from their reticence.

Too often the immature believer is focused upon their experience, believing that to be the reality about themselves; not realising that it is this very focus that is inhibiting the reality and truth of their new life coming through into their experience. They are caught in a vicious circle that can only be broken by grace and a revelation of truth regarding themselves and their standing with God. I therefore devote the first chapters of this section to dealing with these issues with a view to clearing the way for the rest of the book that focuses not on us, but on God.

Once we manage to get beyond the issues of ourselves, then all that is needed is some revelation of God as he really is to spark us off on an eternal pursuit of passion towards him. Many, even among those that have found spiritual rebirth, have a vague view of God. Enough for them to have fled this world to cling to him for security, but not enough to make him such an object of their desire that the things of this world grow dim and unappealing by comparison.

For many the truth of him as Father has been revealed, but then for many, or even most, this can be clouded considerably by our earthly experience of Fathers, which are often no more than a shadow of what this means, and sometimes are diametrically opposite to the truth.
     Others have a revelation of the Trinity and its members – Father, Son, and Holy Spirit, and relate to one of these more than another according to their revelation. Like most truths regarding the being of God, all of these representations have infinite depth and are ripe for exploration. But there is far more revealed to us of God by the Spirit and through the scriptures than this. The object of this section is to chart a course deep enough into that truth that it will gain a momentum of its own. Something that I assure you God desires for us far more than we even desire it for ourselves.

It has been said of the scriptures that we should not as much read them, as let them read us. This prevents our learning from becoming a merely intellectual exercise. In truth we should always allow the Spirit of God to be the interpreter of his own word. I would strongly advocate the same kind of dependency with this and any other spiritual book. All that is here is based on scripture. Only God can take it and impress it upon us in a way that will increase the measure of his glory that shines through us.
     As God said to Abraham: '*I am your shield, your very great reward*'. Beyond anything that God can give us, the thing that eclipses it all is the gift of God himself. Like the pearl of great price we should cast

CHAPTER 9: Coming Face to Face With God

all else aside, if that is what it takes, so that this may be ours. Please reveal yourself to us Lord Jesus.

CHAPTER 10: Clearing the Way for Encounter

As already mentioned, the subject of this chapter is a pre-requisite for some to come to even develop a desire to encounter God. It is a subject in itself, and those that come to understand the truth about themselves, as born again believers, are not only free to seek God in an unhindered way, but are also on their road to experiential victory in life.

As mentioned earlier: I have given a fuller treatment of this subject in the last section of the book – *The Reformation of Man* – but my goal in this chapter is to deliver a preview containing the keys of that teaching in a nutshell, so that you may be ready for what follows. However, it is well to be aware that if we have the kind of barriers to encountering God that I will describe, such truths take a revelation of ourselves from God to release us, and then the revelation must mature in our thinking to truly become a part of us. On the other hand, we should always be expectant because God works to no man's rules and he often surprises us by bypassing the normal channels. The vision of Isaiah can be seen as just such an experience, radically impacting him to the core of his being, and then very quickly shifting him onto a higher spiritual plane.

For many this chapter will be superfluous as you have already grown beyond these matters into a firm security in your identity, and are already hungry for a *now* encounter with the living God. But it may serve as a good reminder of the truth of who you are, and how God sees you, before we change gear by turning our attention to God and beginning to explore and encounter him.

Talk of holy fire

The talk of the holy fire of God is extremely unnerving to some, especially young Christians that are profoundly more aware of their sinful inner condition than of what the Spirit of God is telling them. It is not that these ones don't desire an encounter with God, they do, especially in their hidden depths, but it's just that they feel unready, inadequate, and unprepared, and they feel they should wait until they are more secure and have overcome some of their nagging problems with sinful behaviour patterns, so that when they meet God there will be no need to be ashamed before him.

The first thing to say here is that God is profoundly sympathetic toward these ones, and desires to bring them to the place where they are ready to encounter him, but the way to it is almost invariably very different from the way they imagine. It is a way of grace through faith alone, in exactly the same way as it was for their initial step into salvation.

This means they must come into a place of understanding the truth about themselves by pure revelation of God, and this must come even before and apart from any experience of victory over their experience of sinfulness. Why must this be? Because it is this very revelation of themselves that is needed to bring them into the experience of such victory.

So what is the truth about myself as a born again believer?

The truth is this: that which is born in me is perfectly holy! The biggest mistake Christians make is to fail to draw the proper distinction that the scripture draws between the old nature of flesh and the new nature of the Spirit. Instead either the two become fudged together in their thinking, as if they were all one entity, or they make the classic mistake a owning both of them as if both of these natures define their true identity.

However, the truth, the real truth, is that the old nature has no part whatsoever in defining our true identity once we are born again. This stands true regardless of the constant failure with sinful behaviour patterns that some experience, and recognise as distinctly un-Christlike.

To put this in other terms – the real truth about ourselves is not necessarily what we see, but what God sees when he looks at us. What does he see? He sees nothing but the new nature of Christ in us; and absolutely nothing else. It's not that he is not aware of that old nature that continues to attack us, and even (often) gains control of our mind. It's just that he in no way identifies that as part of who we are; he sees it only as an oppressing entity that is now external to our being, and he sees and treats it like any other evil spirit that would and does attack us in the same way.

It is only we ourselves that are continuing to believe these cunning deceptions of the old nature, and in our minds acknowledge the lie it wants us to believe; that this old nature still forms at least part of our true identity. This is a lie, but accepting the lie brings the mind; the control centre of all our behaviour, under its control, so we are no longer able to live out our true inner identity that is in fact entirely holy, but we are instead controlled by this sinful imposter. The state of our mind does not in truth define who we are; that comes from a deeper level. The mind is simply a servant or slave of the nature it acknowledges as its true centre.

When the mind becomes controlled by the old nature it is being subdued by something now external to our being; not something internal. This old nature was expelled on spiritual rebirth and has no legitimate claim. But it still continues to harp back to its old pre-rebirth position as part of our former identity to try to stake its claim. The only way to overcome it, and see experiential victory, is to come to see ourselves through our spiritual eyesight of faith and agree with God on the way he sees us; which is defined entirely by the new nature of the Spirit of Christ within.

These truths will be continually challenged and pounded by attacks from the old nature and the Devil until we come to the point of maintaining our position by positive declarations, by faith alone, of who we really are regardless of continued ongoing failure and the onslaught of accusations.

It is not that we should fail to recognise it when we are experiencing defeat, and are enacting sinful patterns – i.e. sinning. No we must continue to admit to what is happening and face the truth, never entering into denial. But even while it is happening we must come to maintain and stand by the belief that this is not an expression of our true inner self, but is an imposter that has temporarily gained control of our mind. When we come to fully believe this, even against the ongoing onslaught of accusation, we are close to experiencing victory over everything that has hitherto controlled our behaviour.

Once again let me reiterate that this is not the main subject of this book and it has been covered more thoroughly elsewhere, but it is foundational, and key to us coming to desire encounters with God here and now that will so radically fulfil us. Only when we realise how God sees us in our true being – entirely holy and Christlike – and we come to see ourselves in the same terms, will we desire with all of our heart, mind, soul, and strength to encounter the living God who loves us.

What does God see in us – he sees 'Christ in us, our hope of glory'. Now believe it.

CHAPTER 11: A Vision of a God Encounter

As a final word of preparation before we begin to turn our attention to study the being of God, let me share a prophetic vision I once had that has led me and others to seek these encounters with God. It shows something of the impact these experiences can have, and the resistance that is often encountered when we begin to seek it:

A vision of an eagle

I saw an eagle flying just below a dark blanket of cloud cover. The cloud cover was only a few feet thick, but was very dark and it put the whole of the ground below in dark shadow. Equally the eagle looked no more than a dark shadow, with its brown feathers, as it flew in the shadow of the cloud. I then saw the eagle respond to a call and begin to rise higher, and fly up through the cloud cover and up into glorious warm sunshine above. Above the clouds the eagle became weightless, as if it no longer even needed to make an effort to fly. As it flew it rolled over and over, basking in the sunshine, soaking up the warmth. As it did so its feathers slowly changed from dark brown to golden, and began to glow shiny bright gold until the whole eagle was lit up like the sun – a true Golden Eagle. Then, at just the right moment it flew back down through the cloud cover, and as it came once again below the dark clouds the glow of its feathers lit up the ground below. I sensed the joy of the eagle as the illumination and glory of its bright feathers lit up the ground below, and brought the glory of the sunshine above to the inhabitants on the ground below.

Interpretation of the vision

The eagle is the mature Christian who is flying as high as they are able in their spiritual life within the realm of this world. The call and urge to rise higher is a call from above, and as they do so they find themselves moving through a period of darkness. Without the call in their hearts to rise they would normally have dropped down again to regain visibility and vision, as they have done sometimes before. But this time the call they hear from above is strong enough to carry them through the dark experience and they continue to rise, very quickly coming through out of this brief darkness into God's glory. The glory of the sunshine is an experience of pure waves of Love. In this place they become weightless and experience awesome rest. The sun, which is God, shines on them and through them, and they are filled with Love and begin to glow with his love. This is the 'Shekinah' glory of God that Moses's face shone with when he came down the mountain having come face to face with God[361].

I believe God is saying he is drawing those that are already flying high with him in this world into a heavenly experience that will even transform their very demeanour. He will then send them back to the people of the world below to bring the glory from above down to the earth below, and show them something of what is above.

I believe for the mature Christian there will be an irreversible change in their lives. They will no longer have any desire for this world other than to bring God's glory to those below. They will always be filled with a yearning and desire to return to the glory above, and God will draw them back frequently to be filled again and again for all of their remaining time on the earth.

I believe that in this experience they have reached the place that Peter spoke of when the morning star (the sun) rises in their hearts[362] and they come out from all inner darkness into glorious Light.

The darkness

I feel I should add a word of explanation about the layer of darkness represented by the cloud cover. This represents the oppressive resistance and opposition that the enemy of our souls continually puts up towards those who seek to transcend it into the full light and presence of God above, because they know the magnitude of the impact and the damage to their cause that will come from those that have had such an encounter. The darkness is designed to keep the saint away from a full revelation and appreciation of the magnitude of this experience. The move to rise above the dark clouds can only therefore be sustained by faith in the value of the ascent received by those that hear the call to it, or see a revelation of the glory above.

When the saint seeks to make this ascent, the enemy exploits all remaining areas of weakness, including pockets of emotional damage and areas of deception or wrong thinking, together with his entire diabolical

---

[361] 2 Cor 3:7-11
[362] 2 Peter 1:19b

arsenal of: temptations, lies, half-truths, flattery, distractions, deflections, obstructions, counterfeits, falsehoods, evil suggestions, harassments, oppressions, slander, and accusations. These weapons of darkness are used to discourage the saints and force them to abandon the ascent, dropping back to the lesser and more shadowy place beneath the darkness with its worldly emphasis. Most have to attempt the ascent more than once, and on each occasion that they experience the attack and temporary setback, they are purified further through it until they ultimately overcome and break through[363]. The saint should be encouraged that this resistance may be dark and fierce, but it is surprisingly and deceptively thin. Few realise before the breakthrough how close they really are to this heavenly experience, and how desperately the opposition is working to conceal it.

We are now ready to look upwards and study the being of God with a view to encountering him in a greater way!

---

[363] Eph 6:12

CHAPTER 12: The Seven Spirits of God

The seven-fold spirit of God

The vision of the throne in heaven in the book of Revelation shows God to be a truly magnificent spiritual being, as he is seen in the spiritual domain.

We have said that the spiritual domain was specifically designed to be able to fully express God as he is. The Spirit of God, as a full and complete expression of him as spirit, must be glorious in the extreme.

We have said earlier that the fact that he is uncreated is one way in which he differs from all other created spirits in this domain. Another way that the book of Revelation shows us that the Spirit of God differs from created spirits, is that he is in fact seven spirits; or a seven-fold spirit[364]. We could not parallel this by imagining a seven-fold man, but spirits are different in that they can form union, and become greater by their union. Perhaps the nearest to this in human terms are a unified team that know each other so well they function 'as one man'. Of course in this world such a team is still a unity of separate beings, but with God the seven spirits together form the same being in the perfect unity of love.

When we, as men, spiritually unite with God we take on everything he is within our capacity to contain it; we are filled with the Spirit of God. We find ourselves enlightened with his mind, speaking his words, and doing his deeds.

So in the spiritual domain God is represented as the Spirit of God, who is a union of seven spirits. This is truly mysterious, even to angels who are themselves a singular spirit. These seven spirits are not seven separate beings, they are the same being. It appears that angels are therefore subject to the same kind of mystery in seeing God in the form of the Spirit, as we are when we think of the doctrine of the trinity – Father, Son and Holy Spirit. In this case the mystery is even greater as a union of seven rather than three.

To comprehend the nature of this union further is probably a stretch of the imagination beyond us. Many have decided the same for the doctrine of

---

[364] Rev 1:5

the trinity. However we can explore God further by looking at each of the spirits that make up his seven-fold spirit. Fortunately God has revealed some details of himself in this regard in his revelations to the prophet Isaiah (See Isaiah chapter 11:1-3).

The seven spirits of God are listed as:
1. The spirit of **The Lord**
2. The spirit of **Wisdom**
3. The spirit of **Understanding**
4. The spirit of **Counsel**
5. The spirit of **Power**
6. The spirit of **Knowledge**
7. The spirit of **The Fear of the Lord**

We have previously spoken of the New Jerusalem and the glory and splendour of that heavenly city, who is the mother of all that are spiritually reborn. We have discussed the fact that we are part of its very fabric. What we are now discussing is the very centre of all that is seen in her, and even eclipses her in splendour and glory. In fact God is the very glory of her. All her radiance and magnificence comes from him as he inhabits her[365]. This is the being of God, seen on the throne.

Angels are transfixed by the very sight of him. The uproar of 'Holy, Holy, Holy' is spontaneous, irresistible and inexpressible[366]. We only know a glimpse of it in the very best of our music and singing of praise and worship. When one angel sets off the worship, the others move in unison, compelled by the sight of the being of God. This is what God meant when he said to Abraham: '*I am your shield, your very great reward*'[367]. This is true for us too as the spiritual children of Abraham. God himself is our great reward, and no matter how glorious everything he has created is, even in heaven, he eclipses it all in glory.

There are many things in the physical creation that are truly beautiful – we see landscapes, mountains, creatures. Much is made of the human form and our appreciation of beauty in it. Space is continually revealing new wonders, apart from the very vastness of it. The same is true

---

[365] Rev 21:11,23,25
[366] Rev 4:8 Is 6:3
[367] Gen 15:1

CHAPTER 12: The Seven Spirits of God

if we look into a microscope and see how deep the creativity goes. We are then further impacted by wisdom and philosophy, and the characters of men with their words and deeds. Even the creativity of man is a fascinating thing. We see great expressions of power in many forms from the natural; such as volcanoes; to the man-made – buildings, rockets, computers etc. All of this is the wonder of earthly things, but heaven eclipses it all by far in every aspect. This is an amazing fact, but what is more amazing still is that the Spirit of God, as seen on the throne by the angels of heaven, completely eclipses heaven itself. He is by far the most glorious thing there. At the moment this vision of God is above us and is a mystery to us, but we may well ask – What do the angels see?

In the vision of Revelation the spirits of God are seen before the throne, first as seven lamps representing the light of all creation, and then as the seven spirits[368]. Let's look at each of them in turn.

God the spirit of the Lord

Here we see God as the spirit of the Lord. Within this spirit we see all his attributes of majesty and authority. We see him as King of kings, Lord of lords, and Prince of peace[369]. The disciples recognised this aspect of God in Jesus as Lord and Master, often addressing him in this way. His right and authority to rule are seen here in the spirit of the Lord. Of the increase of his government there will be no end[370].

The disciples thought he was here on earth to establish an earthly kingdom as the Pharisees had taught them to expect. It was only on his resurrection the full import and extent of his authority began to dawn on them. When Thomas saw him he fell on his knees addressing him with reverence and awe as '*my Lord and my God*'[371].

We are assured that one day every knee will bow before him and call him Lord[372]. He is the Lord of glory[373]. He is Lord of time. He is Lord of history and the future; the ages of ages to come[374]. All things are his, and he is Lord of all things[375].

---

[368] Rev 4:5-6
[369] Rev 19:16 Is 9:6
[370] Is 9:7
[371] John 20:28
[372] Is 45:23 Rom 14:11 Phil 2:10
[373] 1 Cor 2:8

Lordship is fundamental to who and what God is, but he is no tyrant. All of his knowledge and power are committed to raising a people that are freely committed to him as a decision of their own will, as a product of faith alone, and not in any way as an expression of forced submission. This state of submission is seen perfectly modelled in the very being of God himself, and in the way he relates to the other spirits that make up his seven-fold being. In the description of Isaiah we therefore see the spirit of the Lord presented as the one of the seven within whom all the others exist. It is as if the Spirit of the Lord has a cloak within which all the others that follow abide.

We are instructed by Jesus to abide in him, and here within the being of the manifold Spirit of God himself we see that very abiding state perfectly modelled.

God the spirits of Wisdom, Understanding & Knowledge

Here we see three of the spirits of God together: God the spirit of Wisdom; God the spirit of Understanding; and God the spirit of Knowledge. These three all bring different offices, powers, and attributes into the being of God. These spirits of God are all in perfect unity, and together these three make up the omniscience of God; he knows and understands all. All that he has done is infinitely wise.

One remarkable aspect of these three is the gender assigned to them. The book of Proverbs unequivocally identifies Wisdom and Understanding as female, declaring they were present at creation. Through them the design of all creation was completed and accomplished. Here we see the much disputed but unequivocal feminine aspect of God. The scriptures affirm it.[376]

God the spirit of Wisdom – Her handiwork is magnificent and perfect. She is beautiful. The wisdom of Solomon impacted the queen of Sheba to such a degree that he far exceeded even the stories that were told of him[377]. This was the gift of God's spirit of Wisdom upon him, working through him, displaying her glory.

---

[374] Rev 22:13
[375] Col 1:16
[376] Prov 4:6 Ps 104:24 Jer 10:12, 51:15 Prov 3:19
[377] 1 Ki 10:6-7

CHAPTER 12: The Seven Spirits of God

Some have misunderstood true wisdom, coming to see it as an attribute of themselves, but it is of God alone expressing himself through man. When we hear wisdom expounded we continue to be profoundly impacted by her. Her touch can be soft and delicate, yet more powerful than might. We are told to sell everything to find her because she is more precious than rubies. She will watch over, exalt, and honour those that find her. She will be a crown of splendour on our head[378].

To see her there among the seven spirits of God, with all the masculinity of God the spirit of the Lord, and God the spirit of Power, she is perfectly in place, and her grace and beauty are exemplified by her company. The sight of her alone would invoke the angels to cry 'Holy, Holy, Holy' but among the seven her glory is magnified beyond all of creation itself.

She is bonded to the seven in love, and to the spirit of Understanding and the spirit of Knowledge as her beloved female companions in their exquisite work of creation. As one they diligently care for all that they have created. Never for a moment are her children out of her sight. Together she watches over them; watching over the weakest with care and protection, and encouraging the strong ones that they may reach for all that she has designed and desired for them[379]. She glories in her sons as they mature and flourish. Her daughters are beautiful, and are raised to emulate her in all her graces, with crafts and skills that are magnificently sublime.

God the spirit of Understanding – Her skills and her handiwork are the marvels of the ages. She is the companion of Wisdom and Knowledge. She is the architect and implementer of all the laws of the universe. She knows how to perfectly control every star and every atom. She is highly skilled in design. It is she who knows how all can be accomplished. She is the inventor of all mathematics, physics and chemistry. She is the designer and originator of DNA and all physical and spiritual life. She constantly draws on the advice of her sister spirit, the spirit of Wisdom, to decide what should be done, but it is she who then determines how it is done, and the natural laws that govern it. She designed and delights in the beauty of nature, and is the one who determines how it all functions together. She

---

[378] Prov 4:6-11
[379] Phil 3:12

can explain every secret of the physical and spiritual universe. All things conform to the laws she created for them. She is the one that has fearfully and wonderfully designed and made us, and who determined how the bodies of men and all creatures should be knit together as they are developed. She is the solution to every problem, because every problem is of her design. It is she who has ensured that all things work together in the purpose of love for those that love God. Nothing escapes her attention, and nothing surprises her. In all of this she and her sister Spirits are delighted with all she has done. She is the aspect of God that has designed and understands all that is made, and ensures it works together in his purpose of love.

God the spirit of Knowledge – She sees and knows all. She knows even the thoughts of all her creatures from afar. She knows the plans for the ages of ages to come. Before a word is spoken she knows it completely. Her knowledge is too lofty and wonderful for any to attain[380]. She knows the end from the beginning, right out into the infinite reaches of eternity. Nothing escapes her attention. She is the cosmic librarian of the ages.

Together – Together these 3 are the omniscience of God. Their feminine beauty is beyond description. They care for all that is made, as a mother cares for her young[381]. The New Jerusalem is the pinnacle of their creation, and as the mother of all that is spiritual she is made to reflect them, including the seven in every detail. The New Jerusalem is founded and built on wisdom, understanding, and knowledge[382]. They are her architect and they designed her to reflect all their feminine grace and beauty.

These three stand among the seven with all the honour, respect, and love they deserve, as they are to the seven their female companions in the unity of love. Their work and their beauty are highly cherished by the seven. They know, for each one of the three, that her care and compassion for her offspring extends beyond her very self.

---

[380] Ps 139:2,4,6
[381] Matt 23:37
[382] Rev 21:21

It was Wisdom that first saw and delighted in the great prospect and prize of creation; that God should make free-willed beings. Man, made in the image of God, and angels, created to serve him and them.

When she revealed her design for creation to the spirit of Understanding, they rejoiced in it together with tears of joy and delight that the purpose of love should be so worthily served, but it was the spirit of Understanding that first saw the awesome cost. Together they wept that it should be so costly, but the plan was so great they could not forget or relinquish it. It was their highest creative idea.

They saw together that through the spirit of Knowledge the purpose of love could be served in a way that nothing else could fulfil. It was she, the spirit of Knowledge that would be able to keep the seven in the most intimate relationship with every creature of free will, knowing every detail of their ways and thoughts.

Together these three worked through the plan, right down to the finest detail, seeing the intricacies of every being that they would create in all the ages in this most perfect plan.

To fulfil the plan the spirit of Understanding designed the places and times in which each and every member of the race of men should live[383]. It was she, the spirit of Understanding that accepted and devised the age of the fall, knowing it to be incredibly costly, yet the path of least suffering and distress for the plan to be fulfilled.

When the plan was complete, God the spirits of Wisdom and Understanding laughed and wept together, all at the same time. They desired its fulfilment with all of their being, but it was too great a plan to decide on it alone. When the design was complete they went to the spirit of the Lord and showed him the plan. He looked into their eyes and saw the anguish and distress they suffered, and yet they had great joy and anticipation that they may have sons and daughters after their own heart, but yet that there must be a Lamb.

It was these three, with their caring feminine heart, that felt the burden of care more than any for the Lamb. They loved him dearly. It was they who wept the most at the knowledge, and wisdom, and understanding that he must be slain. It was they who cried out to the Father '*if any other way be found please let this cup pass from me*'[384]. But it was they who

---

[383] Acts 17:26
[384] Luke 22:42

could only confirm to the Father that there was no other way, it must be done.

The decision rested with the spirit of the Lord and it was he that made it. So through the zeal of the Lord, and with the spirit of Power he carried it through[385]. But it was the feminine heart of the three, the spirits of Wisdom, Knowledge, and Understanding that felt the grief and the loss most keenly. They could not bear to leave the Lamb to suffer, but they had to look away[386]. Their sorrow was deep and they wept together, but they were consoled by the others, led by the spirit of Counsel, who comforted them, reminding them of their wisdom, and knowledge, and understanding that they must endure it for the joy set before them[387] that their sons will be delivered and saved for ever and ever, and for all the ages to come.

Like a child is before its mother it was these three I asked to help me to write these things about them, to tell the world of their love and their beauty. With care and love and patience they taught me how to write, so I have written the best way I knew how. I showed them my work and they read what I had written, but it was not very good. Their beauty is too marvellous for me to describe. How could I tell my companions with only words? They looked at me with care and compassion and told me how good it was, that they loved it just the way it is because it came from my heart.

Faith in Omniscience – We have mentioned previously that faith in the omniscience of God is a vitally important asset for the security of the ages. Through all that God has done in creation, and his handling of the fall of all free-willed beings, he has shown for all the ages that his wisdom, knowledge, and understanding is unlimited. He is truly omniscient, and by faith we and all creation say with David *'his works are too wonderful for me, I know that full well'*[388].

---

[385] Is 9:7
[386] Matt 27:46
[387] Heb 12:2
[388] Ps 139:14

God the spirit of Counsel

Here we see God as the spirit of Counsel – the Counselor[389]. Within this spirit of God we see him giving us the gift of himself. Remarkably we can assign this spirit neither to one gender or another, but here we see both genders at work. Here is the one in whom both male and female appear together, bonding the male and female attributes of God's being together.

We therefore see that the three spirits of Wisdom, Knowledge, and Understanding, are depicted as female in form, whereas the three spirits of the Lord, Power, and the Fear of the Lord, are depicted as male. Given that God the spirit of Counsel has both genders we see that the male and female attributes of God are in perfect balance (3 Female–The Counselor–3 Male).

God the spirit of Counsel is the one that comes near to us when we come near to him[390]. Of course he brings with him the whole Spirit of God, but it is he that leads the approach of God into intimacy with us.

He introduces the other spirits of God to us when we are ready to encounter him in these ways and forms. Jesus therefore says that part of the ministry of the Counselor is *'to take from what is mine and make them known to you'*[391]. He reveals God to us in all his glory, as we are ready and able to receive it[392].

We see him working through the apostle Paul when he said: *'I become all things to all men'*[393]. God the spirit of Counsel is able to approach us in a way that we can receive him. He can be gentle or bold. He can be soft or direct. He is the one who is able to adapt to us, whoever and whatever we are. Every individual in the universe has a unique relationship to their creator. He made them all, and within the spirit of Counsel gave himself the capacity to relate to them all on perfect individual terms. It is the spirits of Counsel and Knowledge that work so closely with us to keep us in intimate fellowship with the Lord.

As a clearly masculine expression of him we see in the Spirit of Counsel the relationship to us of a father, and as a mentor that instructs and guides us. We see Jesus as our elder brother[394], protecting us and

---

[389] Is 9:6 John 14:16,26
[390] Jam 4:8
[391] John 16:15
[392] John 16:12
[393] 1 Cor 9:22

showing us the way. He is to us a friend, sharing his business with us[395], in all cases taking a form and gender that is perfectly suited to us as individuals.

In the female aspects of his expression, we see him as a comforter and protector. In him the mother's heart is revealed. We are told that God would have gathered his children to him *'as a hen gathers her chicks'*[396]. In this role God protects us, weans us, and trains us for life.

To the young girl *he* can be as a sister, to the old man as a lifelong trusted companion and confidant. He is the one who we need him to be at all times; counsellor, comforter or friend[397]. I believe it is for this reason; in the multiplicity of way he approaches us, that whenever people see the Holy Spirit, the Counsellor, in vision, they never see his face.

God the spirit of Counsel is our constant companion[398]. Jesus promised *'never will I leave you or forsake you'*[399]. Many have learnt the secret of 'practising his presence'; being always conscious that he is there with us and for us wherever we are, or in whatever we are doing.

We see him as our teacher, leading us into all truth. Within God the spirit of Counsel we see him as our advocate, defender, and intercessor[400]. In these roles he becomes our legal counsellor, repelling the attacks of our accuser who demands judgement for our sin[401]. He reveals to us God's forgiveness and points our accuser to the cross where all our debt was paid for in full.

In all of this he draws alongside us, caring for us and leading us to all that is good for us.

God the spirit of Power

Here we see God as the spirit of Power. This is God Almighty, the omnipotent, all powerful God. He is the God with whom all things are possible. He is the one through whom the whole universe was made.

---

[394] Heb 2:11
[395] John 15:15
[396] Matt 23:37 also Ps 91:4
[397] John 14:26, 15:15
[398] Matt 28:20
[399] Heb 13:5
[400] Heb 7:25 Rom 8:27
[401] Rev 12:10

Together with God the spirit of the Lord, and God the spirit of the Fear of the Lord, the spirit of Power is the truly masculine expression of God.

When the female expression of God, the spirits of Wisdom, Understanding and Knowledge, designed the plan of the ages, they did it knowing full well the unlimited energy and skill there is in the spirit of Power. They knew the limitlessness of his craftsmanship and the plan was devised to fully display his glory with perfection through creation.

As God, the spirit of Power went ahead and created everything that is made. The spirits of Wisdom, Understanding and Knowledge stood around him, guiding him as it was all brought into being[402]. They saw him fling the stars into space[403], and observed as he created every living thing. They watched as he created the daisy, the Horsehead Nebula, and the constellation of Orion. When God the spirit of Power completed the work of creation he and they were satisfied; it was perfect[404].

In God the spirit of Power we see the omnipotence of God. Together with his omniscience, his omnipotence forms part of the basis of our faith in him. Through creation his power has been displayed and proven beyond doubt. Through his power he made the physical and spiritual universe.

In our age we see only his first act of creation and we marvel, but in the ages of ages we can anticipate there is far more yet to come and we can expect that, like the angels saw the physical creation, we will yet see him at work. We, his created beings, are satisfied that his Power is limitless and he can do all things to perfection. How awesome he is.

God the spirit of the Fear of the Lord

Here we see the last of the seven spirits of God, the spirit of the Fear of the Lord. Within this spirit we see a frightening aspect of God. We see the God of justice and judgement. We see his hatred of sin and all that is opposed to the purposes of love and goodness. Here we see the scars and horror of the slain Lamb and the evidence of the suffering of the sacrifice in all its shocking detail. Paradoxically horror, fear, and dread combine here with a Lamb! His aspect is terrible[405], yet we see nothing of the tyrant

---

[402] Jer 51:15
[403] Is 45:12 Job 38-39
[404] Deut 32:4

or the despot of this world. As the Lamb of God, all judgement has been given[406] to him because his sufferings have proven his love for those he must judge[407].

In the book of Revelation we read of the wrath of the Lamb[408]. In any other context this would be comic – wrath – a Lamb, but here it carries the gravity of all the sin of the world and there is no laughing matter in it. Fortunately those that are spiritually reborn will not experience the wrath of the Lamb[409], only his judgement[410]. But we will undoubtedly see it administered on the earth and the demonic realms. A key to the interpretation of the book of Revelation is that the church must be evacuated (raptured) before wrath falls. Those who are forgiven cannot possibly suffer it. We therefore see a clear point of evacuation of the church in Revelation 6:12-17 as the sixth seal is broken and the wrath of the Lamb comes on the earth[411].

Though it was the whole being of God that went to the cross and suffered, it is here in God the spirit of the Fear of the Lord that we see the eternal consequences of that event fully displayed before us and all creation for all the ages to come.

When Christ was slain the whole of the being of God was assaulted, insulted, and abused. For a time God the spirit of the Lord was cast from his throne of majesty and glory to the humiliation of a criminal. God the spirit of Wisdom, Understanding and Knowledge were derided and insulted by the whole evil realm of demons and men as the ultimate folly. The spirit of Counsel was despised and rejected of men; treated as an enemy, all while seeking to save the souls that scorned him. In Christ the spirit of Power took the form of weakness, receiving the abuse of wickedness without a murmur or complaint, or any hint of retaliation. But it was God the spirit of the Fear of the Lord that bore the eternal marks of it all.

---

[405] Heb 10:31 Ps 47:2
[406] John 5:22,27
[407] Rom 5:8
[408] Rev 6:16, 14:10
[409] Rom 5:9 1 Thes 1:10, 5:9
[410] Heb 9:27 Jam 2:12 2:Tim 4:8 2 Cor 5:10 1 Cor 4:5 Rev 11:18 1 Cor 3:13
[411] Rev 6:17 Rom 5:9 1 Thes 1:10, 5:9

Together the seven spirits of God were subjected to the cross and suffered for a time, but it is God the spirit of the Fear of the Lord that is assigned to carry the scars and evidence of the suffering for all eternity to come[412]. When angels and men see God they also see this truly remarkable and fearful aspect of his being. All the others recovered after the event and were restored to their former glory, but in the spirit of the Fear of the Lord is the eternal record. Here we see the eternally bruised heel that crushed the head of the serpent[413]. It is here also that we see the mercy of God, but only in association with the tremendous cost God paid to secure it.

David says of God *'with you there is forgiveness; therefore you are feared'*[414]. In eternity the very realisation and memory that once we were lost will always evoke the most fearful emotion when we see what it took to redeem us from that condition. The Lamb on the throne, and God the spirit of the Fear of the Lord, will always keep this reality before us. It is now part of God's glory.

The contrast of this aspect of his being is in perfect balance with the other spirits of God. It amounts to just one seventh of his full spiritual being, but together with the glory and splendour of the spirits of the Lord, Wisdom, Knowledge, Understanding, Counsel and Power; the spirit of the Fear of the Lord and his effect completely balance in him to make the vision of God bearable to all that are holy, and truly awesome beyond description with unique form in all of God's creation.

In God the spirit of the Lord, and the spirit of the Fear of the Lord, we see the opposite sides of the same coin. This coin bears the Lord; the head of the universal state, on one side, as the symbol of the authority of his benevolent government. Whilst on the other, in contrast, it bears the emblems of justice and judgement. These spirits of God; the Lord and the Fear of the Lord, are like book ends containing everything that the being of God is between them. All that are between – the spirits of Wisdom, Understanding, Knowledge, Counsel and Power, are there to serve the purpose of both ends of this spectrum. They serve the Lord and the Fear of the Lord equally, all in unity of the purpose of love, which is what God is from end to end.

---

[412] Rev 5:6
[413] Gen 3:15
[414] Ps 130:4

In Isaiah 11:3, at the end of the list of the seven spirits of God, we read *'and he will delight in the fear of the Lord'*[415]. Here we see the special regard that all the other spirits of God have in this part of his being – the Fear of the Lord and the Lamb. The picture is one of the other six spirits of God gathered around the Spirit of the Fear of the Lord and delighting in him, and his part in their one being, above all else in the intimacy of their fellowship. We see that God delights more in this than is his lordship, his wisdom, or his power, because this part of himself has been the most costly to reveal through the wisdom of the cross, and it shows more than any other part of his being the truth of his sacrificial heart of love.

Demons tremble – In the book of James it says: *'the demons believe in God and they tremble'*[416]. The sight of God's holiness is unbearable to them because it exposes the depravity of their wretched condition. As for fallen man he prefers to remain in spiritual darkness, hidden from view[417]. Of all that makes evil tremble, God the spirit of the Fear of the Lord invokes the greatest response. They react partly because they are responsible for what they see before them; partly because it exposes the extent of the hatred of God toward all the destructiveness of evil; partly because it was they that smote him and crushed him; and partly because it is a permanent reminder of judgement upon them. No wonder that evil shrinks from God's presence. C. S. Lewis made the point that hell is locked from the inside[418]. We see the reason why.

It is the mercy of God that has allowed us to be 'covered' as we pass through this present evil age[419]. The truth of our present being is for the moment veiled in flesh, and our struggles to overcome wickedness and evil assails us daily. Only when we are ready, when faith has overcome, does God plan to unveil us, and unveil himself fully to us.

When we are perfected and ready he will give us our new spiritual bodies that will be glorious, perfect, and holy; able and ready to stand in the presence of God and his holiness[420]. In these immortal bodies we will

---

[415] Is 11:3
[416] Jam 2:19
[417] John 3:19 Jam 1:6
[418] C .S. Lewis – The Problem of Pain
[419] 1 Cor 13:12 1 John 3:2
[420] 1 Cor 15:35-58, 52

then have eyes to see with perfection all that is glorious in God and in everything he has made, including ourselves. Maranatha!

The masculine and feminine nature of God

We have seen how we can recognise in God both masculine and feminine attributes and qualities in equal measure. Rather than see God as somehow reflecting earthly reality in this, we should understand that in fact God created and configured the earthly reality of gender to truly and accurately reflect himself as he really is. This is categorically expressed in Gen 1:27 at the very creation of man – '*God created mankind in his own image, in the image of God he created them; male and female he created them*'[421]. God is not just reflected in both genders but also in the mystery of union and partnership of marriage where the two become one flesh[422]. This reflects that which exists within his manifold spirit, the Spirit of God.

Some time ago I read of a case of a man donating a kidney to his wife even though the tests proved it would be incompatible. However she experienced no rejection of the kidney, which was an anomaly that the surgeons put down to their long term physical interaction and union. The physical union of sexual relationships are a true mystery where two become one flesh.

Man is made in God's image. It is unfortunate that in the English language we use the same term 'man' for mankind, as we do for the male gender. This is a limitation of English language. God is reflected through both the genders together. Neither of them alone fully reflects the image of God. They are in perfect balance. Only at the fall did that reflection become imbalanced[423]. The fact that man/male and woman/female form such a partnership is itself a reflection of God.

The God of relationship

Relationship and partnership is a recurring theme within the one being of God with the various expressions of his manifold form. This is a deep and profound mystery.

---

[421] Gen 1:27 – Gender specific terms (man, him) are sometimes used incorrectly.
[422] Matt 19:5 1 Cor 6:16 Eph 5:31
[423] Gen 3:16

First we see the trinity of Father, Son, and Holy Spirit with all three in a perfect relationship of unity and love. Then we have God as the seven-fold spirit.

In studying this we have to keep reminding ourselves that God is one being, not three, or seven, or many. What is clear is that even though he is a single *being,* yet a single *person* expression of his being would not have fully represented God to his creation as he really is.

God is Love, and within God there is the fellowship of love. God is more mysterious and awesome than we can possibly imagine. We see that God is able to express himself through all his created beings[424]. It should not therefore be surprising that within his own created domains he should have a manifold form with its own intrinsic unity of love.

How he can do this and yet be one being is beyond us, but this is an essential part of the mystery of God that should and must transcend us in every way, even transcending the limits of our imagination. As our creator, God is necessarily mysterious and complex to us. We should not expect him to be anything less. If he were we would be suitably disappointed. The remarkable thing is that despite his complexity we have been invited into relationship with him. How can this be? What will it be like?

We have already explored God as the spirit of Counsel and seen what diversity of form that can take, allowing him to enter into the closest intimacy with us. But we will see much more than this. We will discover God within the fellowship that there is in himself. In the trinity of Father, Son and Holy Spirit we have three persons all fully expressing his one being. In the seven-fold Spirit of God there are seven, together giving a full spiritual expression of his being. The permutations of relationships within God himself are numerous and we can expect to witness and participate in this with him. It will be by far our highest delight in heaven[425].

When I was a boy I sometimes had the privilege of sitting in on the conversation and fellowship of some very mature and wonderful godly men of God. As a developing young life this was at times almost a healing

---

[424] Eph 1:23
[425] Ps 17:15

experience as I saw, heard and experienced the fellowship of the Spirit in action between these men of God.

Now imagine sitting in on some combination of fellowship within the manifold person of God. We may observe and experience God the spirit of Wisdom, and God the spirit of Power, working through the person of God the Son. Or we may witness and experience the Father in fellowship with God the spirit of Counsel, and the God the spirit of the Fear of the Lord.

Here we are not talking of the fellowship of men; we are talking of the fellowship of God himself. If the shared experience among mere men can be so profound, how incredible it will be to share an encounter of God himself in this way. To the discovery of such relationship in God there will be no end. We will know God personally and intimately, and yet at the same time we will discover all this together as we sometimes do now so relatively faintly when we worship together. How profound will that be?

God is infinite, and our joy and delight of going deeper into him will forever impact us profoundly until we grow through each age and become greater by it, and become ready for yet another age where we may discover God in even higher dimensions of glory, of which we have not yet even conceived, and for which we are not yet ready, even in the next age of heaven.

The eternal family of God

In all that we have explored there have been many uses made of the symbols of family. We have seen there are the Father and the Son. We have seen that the symbol of Mother is used to represent the New Jerusalem of heaven[426]. The Bible also uses the symbol of the Bride of Christ[427] to represent the church and the New Jerusalem, who is soon to be the daughter through her union with the Son in this eternal family of God. Once again we see in this both the male and female attributes of God fully represented.

It is probably a little early now before the wedding or the honeymoon to speculate on the offspring that may be ahead, but we have already acknowledged that God may not have finished creating. In fact he

---

[426] Gal 4:26
[427] Rev 21:2

may have hardly begun. We have the ages of ages to find out, but we can be sure beyond doubt that God intends the fairy-tale to come true, that they do live happily ever after, wherever that is leading them.

The colour spectrum of the Spirit

Light – Jesus said '*I am the light of the world*'[428]. When God created the universe he made light as one of his first acts as a vital and significant part of the creation[429]. The scriptures tell us that the creation pours forth speech[430]. Creation itself is made to reflect God and all that he is. Light is therefore something significant in creation as a reflection of God, and worthy of some study. It is notable that in the scene of the throne in the book of Revelation there is a rainbow encircling the throne[431]. The rainbow is a continuously changing spectrum of colour, but it is traditionally divided (quantised) it into seven distinct colour bands. It is interesting to try to align these colours with the seven-fold spirits of God, represented by the seven lamps that are before the throne, blazing with the light of God[432]. Colour is an important feature of the Bible, used clearly in the symbolism of the tabernacle of the Ark of the Covenant, and in several books from both Old and New Testaments in the form of jewels. In turn jewels are clearly identified by Paul as symbols of reward[433], so the meaning of colour is highly relevant to our heavenly destiny, and worthy of some study:

The seven colour spectrum of God from the rainbow, inside to outside:
1. **Violet** – The spirit of **The Lord**
2. **Indigo** – The spirit of **Wisdom**
3. **Blue** – The spirit of **Understanding**
4. **Green** – The spirit of **Counsel**
5. **Yellow** – The spirit of **Power**
6. **Orange** – The spirit of **Knowledge**
7. **Red** – The spirit of **The Fear of the Lord**

---

[428] John 9:5
[429] Gen 1:3
[430] Ps 19:1-3
[431] Rev 4:3
[432] Rev 4:5
[433] 1 Cor 3:12

The rainbow encircles the throne with the violet/purple at the innermost circle nearest to the throne depicting the spirit of the Lord, and ranging out to red as the outermost circle at the opposite end of the spectrum, depicting the spirit of the Fear of the Lord. All of these colours have significance and meaning which we cannot explore fully here, but we can highlight a few *speculative* observations.

Violet – Signifies the spirit of the Lord. As a shade of purple, violet and indigo together are symbolic of royalty and represent the spirit of the Lord. Blue is also typically used as a royal symbol, both in the tabernacle of the Ark of the Covenant and in many cultures. As we move towards the blue sections of the spectrum these too contribute to the constitution of royalty.

Indigo – Signifies the spirit of Wisdom. Indigo is positioned on the spectrum between violet and blue. She stands alongside the spirit of the Lord assisting him in his rule and reign of the Kingdom. Together with the violet they form shades of purple that together form a symbol of royalty with the authority of government. We see in this the symbol of Solomon in his glorious reign with the wisdom of God establishing his kingdom and authority.

Blue – Signifies the spirit of Understanding. In nature blue is significantly the colour of both the sky that in creation is above and higher than us, and the sea that is on our level. There are both higher and lower understanding and wisdom – of the earth and of heaven.

The lower wisdom depicts the principles of this world that is based around self. Within this is what has been secularly called 'the law of the jungle', and 'the survival of the fittest'. Here the principle of law maintains order. In the world 'there is no such thing as a free lunch'. We only get what we can wreak from the earth by the sweat of the brow. The world is a competitive place where self-interest prevails. Domination is the norm. It is the world of the predator and the parasite, where one species sustains itself at the expense of another. Tennyson famously expressed this observation in the words: '*Nature, red in tooth and claw*'. A branch of philosophers known as the 'pessimists' observed that in this world, even in the beautiful and idyllic scenes of nature, beneath every crevice and blade of grass, there is an immense and cruel struggle for survival among its creatures. These philosophers were pessimists because they saw no further than this world and its principles. This earth is a temporal domain that God has used to fully elucidate the evils of a world based on the principle of self.

At times in history men have considered and embraced these laws of nature and used them as a justification for the worst atrocities of our age. Elitism and racism has often characterised these descents into the brute nature, which has been one of man's forms for expressing these principles. At other times men and nations have risen above these principles, recognising that as man we are made in the image of God, destined for higher things. At these times men have recognised that for us to behave and become as brute beasts is a total corruption of all that God intended for us, and for a few brief moments of history, amid the clamour of self, we have seen men rise up to demonstrate a higher order of life that reflects more the age to come than this present age of evil.

By contrast heavenly principles are based on freedom, given that all are committed to the same shared cause of love. The weak are valued and cared for with special honour by the strong[434]. The strong serve the weak and prefer them to themselves. There is harmony in all things, with each committed to the other as a valued and cherished part of a unified creation. The pinnacle and precedent of heavenly wisdom is seen in God himself in the self-sacrifice of the cross.

With a little effort we could imagine a creation teeming with living creatures like our own, but where the principles on which it works, and the order of life on which it is based, are the laws of heaven. What would such a system look like? Rather than one species preying on and competing with another, all creatures would be committed to the welfare and survival of the others, even above their own! This is a stretch of the imagination, but we are given tantalising hints that even before this age is complete there will be an era where Christ reigns over this present earth, and the predatory aspects of this present system are suppressed and superseded in reflection of the principles of the age to come[435].

Green – Signifies the spirit of Counsel. Green is the basic colour of the earth's vegetation forming a carpet of grass and other plants. This depicts

---

[434] 1 Cor 12:23-24
[435] Is 11:4-9, 65:25

the spirit of Counsel who is at ground level with us, through whom we interact most closely with God, and through whom we obtain our spiritual sustenance. The fact that the plants generally have a base and background of green, but also have representation of every imaginable colour is a significant reflection of the fact that the Holy Spirit, the Counselor, brings to us every aspect of God in all his forms, ministries, and offices. He brings to us wisdom, understanding, power and every other aspect of God.

Yellow – Signifies the spirit of Power. Yellow is the brightest colour that lights up the rainbow more than any other, representing the spirit of Power. It is the colour of the Sun that is pure energy and that sustains the earth. Without the sun the earth's surface would freeze and all life would die. In the same way the Son is the radiance of God's glory sustaining all things by his powerful word.

Yellow is also the colour of sulphur, another substance that is used in biblical symbolism, probably in relation to its presence in volcanic fire and its corrosive qualities. In this case it signifies the application of the power of God in implementing judgement.

As with all the central colours of the rainbow spectrum; power is seen to serve both the spirit of the Lord, and the spirit of the Fear of the Lord at each of the opposite ends of the spectrum.

Orange – Signifies the spirit of Knowledge. Orange is the combination of Red and Yellow – Power and the Fear of the Lord – that are on either side of it in the spectrum. It must therefore be understood in the context of both Yellow and Red, so some further discussion of them are given in the following section.

The colour of orange naturally occurs in our world in several significant places. These are firstly the sunrise and sunset, and secondly in fire. Both of these we will cover in the discussion of the colour red because both examples also involve red.

A third significant place is in the colour of metals, particularly gold and bronze, which are biblically symbolic materials, as we have already discussed. Gold is sometimes referred to as a yellow metal, but in fact its shine can give it a darker or lighter appearance depending on the lighting, but refined gold has a colour that is between orange and yellow on the spectrum. As a symbol of faith in God this seems quite significant given that faith is based on knowledge (orange), and it is the means by which we implement the power (yellow) of God through speaking words of authority.

Similarly bronze is also used as a biblical symbol of strength, fire, and cleansing. The pillars of the temple were made of bronze. This is a picture of a heavenly reality. We are promised in the book of Revelation that those who overcome will be made a pillar in the temple of the New Jerusalem. As the same author; the apostle John, points out, this overcoming is by faith, and as we have already discussed; faith is based on the sure and firm knowledge of God. Through our development and learning in this age we see that our knowledge of God becomes a strong and fixed repository that acts as a pillar of the heavenly kingdom.

Red – Signifies the spirit of the Fear of the Lord. Red is the colour of blood and highly significant in that within the spirit of the Fear of the Lord is the slain Lamb, and the sacrifice of the cross. Within him are the office of judge and the function of judgement.

Just as the spirit of the Lord at the other end of the spectrum stands together with Wisdom in support, so the spirit of Knowledge, signified by the colour orange, stands in support of the spirit of the Fear of the Lord. At the judgement at the end of the age, we read that books were opened along with the book of life[436]. The books are the records of the age; the repository of knowledge concerning all men and their deeds. All of this knowledge becomes part of the process of judgement. We therefore see the spirit of Knowledge in support of the spirit of the Fear of the Lord, together with the Spirit of Power that executes the judgement.

These colours of yellow, orange, and red most naturally occur in two places; the sunrise/sunset and fire. As the sunset marks the end of the day we see reflected in these colours the fact that all knowledge, including all the deeds of men, are complete, and that at the end of the age judgment will show everything for what it really is. The sunrise forewarns of the same; that all the deeds of the day will come under judgement at the end. It reminds us that the knowledge of God includes his foreknowledge. Fire is both a manmade and naturally occurring phenomenon. As such it symbolises the same thing; judgement, but we will discuss the phenomenon and symbol of fire both in the context of the physical, and the spiritual in a later chapter.

---

[436] Rev 20:12

Judgement is a scary idea for many, but should be seen as a solemn essential at the completion of this age, as we move into the next. For a Christian it is a profoundly good thing, and an essential to release him into the next age. We will say more on the subject of judgement later, but we can hold to the assurance that all those whose names are written in the Lamb's book of life have an eternal future, and will carry forward all that is of any real value to them and to the ages to come.

White – When we see any two or more of the spirits of God together in some context, it has the spiritual effect of combining light to produce a wide spectrum of secondary, tertiary, and more complex and unusual shades of colour. All the colours of the spectrum together combine to make white light. This reflects the way that the seven spirits of God combine as one to become a single indescribable expression of pure and perfect glory. The phenomenon of colours reflects the spiritual truth of this. Only the holy can bear to look upon him. Those that see him are satisfied completely to the very depths of their being – so they cry 'Holy, Holy, Holy!' What else can they do?

These 'speculations' on the meaning of colour are only suggestions at their symbolic meaning, but this does at least show there is some significant correlation between them and the being of God. Clearly colour does have some real parallel spiritual meaning as a part of a creation that is designed by God to speak to us of its creator. This is also significant for us because a primary attribute of jewels is colour, and jewels are constantly used as symbols of heaven. The basic premise here is that colour symbolises the various aspects of the being of God.

The royal procession

In the scripture Isaiah 11:1-3 that lists the seven spirits of God, there is an order that shows a 'procession' of the spirits of God. Earlier, in Isaiah chapter 6, the prophet had already seen an awesome vision of the Lord on the throne in the temple, where the train of his robe filled the temple. We can be sure that the whole seven-fold spirit of God was present in this vision.

The list from Isaiah chapter 11 shows the procession with the Spirit of the Lord alone at the head – *violet*. Behind him are the spirits of Wisdom and Understanding side by side in total support of the Lord –

indigo–blue. Behind them, side by side, are the spirits of Counsel and of Power – *green–yellow*, and behind them are the spirits of Knowledge and the Fear of the Lord – *orange–red*. These pairings have significance.

Wisdom and understanding are together the complete vision of omniscience. The spirits of Counsel and Power are a partnership that defines the gift of the Spirit to us. The disciples were told to wait in Jerusalem until they were clothed with power from on high, which came in the form of the Holy Spirit, the Counsellor. We then see the pairing of the spirits of Knowledge and the Fear of the Lord, which is a partnership we have already discussed in terms of the process of judgement and the opening of books, the repository of knowledge.

The order of the procession therefore shows us something more of the unity of relationship and function that exists in the multiform expression of the being of God.

Most interestingly, here too is the gender arrangement and pairing that we have already discussed. At the head of the procession is the Lord, who is the head and is represented as the singular male – the King. Behind him is the female-female pairing of the spirits of Wisdom and Understanding, like the attending bridesmaids at a wedding. This represents the special relationship, friendship, and union that we see among females as God has created them. Behind them is the male-male/female pairing and union of the spirit of Power and the Counsellor. This expresses and includes all working relationships that includes both genders as they work together to fulfil their purpose and destiny in the service of love. Last but not least we see the male-female pairing of the spirit of the Fear of Lord and the spirit of Knowledge. Within this pairing we see the much celebrated union of male and female, including the special union of marriage; of which we will say more.

Together this procession represents the multiplicity of relationships we see active in the race of men and how it is all created in the image of God, reflecting the fellowship of love and relationship that exists within him, even though he is one.

The significance of marriage

The relationship of union of man and woman is the most highly celebrated relationship in our race, and it is almost universally recognised as something profound and sacred. Marriage has therefore been created to preserve its intimacy so that it can reach its full glory. This relationship is made to reflect something within God that we have already discussed in a measure, but in the light of the relationships we have now explored we should take this a little further.

At the rear of the procession of God seen in the temple by the prophet Isaiah is the pairing of the male spirit of the Fear of the Lord, which we have said includes the Lamb, and the female spirit of Knowledge. This is the wedding couple of the Lamb and his bride, represented as knowledge that is the basis of the faith of the true church who is the bride. As we have previously said; Paul and his life of *'Christ in me'* is shown to be a part of this union by his passion and desire expressed as *'I want to know Christ and the power of his resurrection and the fellowship of sharing in his suffering'*[437]. We see here that Paul's faith is him partaking in the spirit of Knowledge as he takes his place in the bride of Christ, with his overwhelming desire to know Christ more. That is the desire of every bride; to come into the full knowledge of union through the intimacy of consummation.

It has been said that marriages are made in heaven. Though marriage is a commitment until death, nevertheless within marriage an eternal love relationship is often forged that will persist long after the union of flesh, that happens in marriage, is discarded. As we move into the next age, that union of flesh will become obsolete and will be cast off as it is totally eclipsed by the universal intimacy of the age to come. However the true love that is formed within marriage will persist into eternity, and will be celebrated among the jewels of heaven. In other words every marriage contains something eternal, and as for the individual and every other relationship of love, it is designed to bear fruit that will last.

It is therefore not surprising that in this world marriage comes under such vicious and malicious attack. Satan's malice towards it is immense as he jealously tries to destroy that which he and his cohorts once tried to take for themselves and make their own in defiance of God[438].

It is remarkable that though Paul was unmarried and celibate, he nevertheless has a part – even a special part – in the marriage of the Lamb and his bride. Jesus said there are some in this world that have relinquished the opportunity for marriage for the sake of the kingdom[439]. I

---

[437] Phil 3:10
[438] Gen 6:4
[439] Matt 19:12

personally know some that have done this, and I am often astonished to see how their relationship with the Lord has a greater dimension that on inspection seems like that of a marriage relationship. Such sacrifices will not go unrewarded, and we can be sure they will bear fruit for eternity, though we should realise that the same is true of marriages in this world[440].

With this heavenly perspective of marriage we should do all we can to guard and preserve it, treating is as sacred, and seriously heeding the warning that 'what God has joined together let no man separate'. There is a great reward in the love of marriage that reaches eternal consummation. Any attempt to destroy it is a direct assault on the kingdom of God and of heaven[441].

The vision of the throne

As we have explored God and the vision of his multi-spirit being, together with the throne, we have come to see how the form, colour, and relationships of God will all be displayed before us in heaven, and any part of that vision is breath-taking. We now see that it is an incredibly colourful scene, but we should remember that colour itself, though it enriches our lives on earth incredibly, is only a faint reflection of something vastly more glorious in the spiritual form. It is the spectrum of the glory of heaven. When the scriptures speak of being glorified, we can translate it into the nearest earthly symbols by thinking of it as something that is made to be magnificently resplendent and colourful.

We should also consider that Isaiah saw the Lord and the throne, with multitudes of angels in attendance, all worshipping God. These angels themselves are separate individual beings from God, but all life comes from God, and as such the life of God is reflected through them in a vast array of colour, showing all that God is. It is fascinating to think that some angels have a purpose to attend more to one spirit of God than another, and through that they become more of a display of one colour than another.

To take this further, and without wanting to be controversial; this may therefore mean that though angels do not have gender[442], they may manifest more of what we would recognise here as the masculine or

---

[440] 1 Cor 7:38
[441] Matt 19:7-9 Mark 10:12 Luke 16:8
[442] Matt 22:30

feminine attributes of God, depending on how they relate to the gender specific qualities and roles evident in God, as we have discussed them. An angel attending the spirit of Wisdom will appear more with the indigo colouring. One that attends the spirit of Power has a bright yellow appearance. In reality they will probably not exclusively attend one of the seven, but in varying degrees they will attend them all. They are therefore multi-coloured, but with emphasis on one expression or another with the relevant appearance of colour and gender to match.

As no two humans are the same, so no two angels in heaven are the same. They each have unique expression, with gifts and purpose that reflect through them. Imagine the scene in heaven that is filled with myriads of unique angelic beings, all with their unique form and colours[443]. We can anticipate that in their new bodies multitudes of men will also have the same variety of colouring according to their ministry, role, service, and constitution. The scene is beyond description.

Race and colour have often been made grounds for division and even oppression in this world. But here we see that the shades of skin colour we see in our age are only a faint shadow of the plethora of colour that we will see in heaven. There this diversity is celebrated and cherished in total contrast to the way it has been abused here.

The treasures of heaven

In the book of Revelation, among the splendour of the rainbow and other things around the throne, we see many jewels reflecting the whole spectrum of the colours of the spirits of God[444]. As we have previously discussed: jewels are used to represent the fruit of the Spirit that we are forming in this age, and that will last for eternity as an eternal reward to those in whom they are formed[445]. However jewels also have the attribute of colour, which is significant in the context of the spectrum of the Spirit of God as we have discussed it. As with many biblical symbols, we have a twofold representation that together give us a perfect image of a heavenly reality.

---

[443] Rev 5:11 Dan 7:10 Heb 12:22
[444] Rev 4:3, 21;11,18-19 Ez 1:26, 28:13 Ex 24:10,28:17-21, 39:10-14
[445] 1 Cor 3:12 John 15:16

Jewels are primarily defined by their twofold attributes of colour and form. The colours embody the spirits of God as seen in the spectrum, whereas the form of the jewel that is cut and shaped represents the various fruits of the Spirit that are formed within us[446]. This dual image of fruit/jewels shows that these jewels will be more than showpieces in heaven. They will be enjoyed by all of our spiritual senses in the spiritual realm.

Here once again we see some of the remarkable treasures of heaven that we will enjoy as a reward together[447]. They are living things that become part of our very constitution and being, as both expressions of Christ in us, and the fruit of the Spirit that forms in us. The jewels therefore specifically show that the rewards we receive in heaven are a combination of the fruit of the Spirit, together with the being and Spirit of God in us. These things of us form part of the structure and highlights of the living City, the New Jerusalem who is our mother, and the bride of the Lamb[448].

By combining the 7 spirits of God with the 9 fruits of the Spirit we have 63 primary paired jewel combinations of colour and form – spirit and fruit. All of these become areas of exploration into the being of God that will be among our highest delights in heaven[449]. All of these combinations provide rich food for meditation and revelation of God.

We can imagine for example, exploring the fruit of gentleness expressed in the spirit of the Lord – power, authority and gentleness combined. How about the fruit of peace expressed through the Spirit of the fear of the Lord – yet another paradoxical view of God.

Every combination is fascinating, and worthy of a whole study and exploration in itself. Then consider that within each fruit there are many variations of form, as in the varieties of different apples, or grapes. Also within each of the spirits of God are many forms, attributes of character, and aspects. Consider, for example, all the forms that the spirit of Counsel takes to reach intimacy with us on our level as an individual. All of these can be combined with the various fruits of the spirit to form

---

[446] Gal 5:22, 1 Cor 13 2 Pet 1:5-7
[447] I Cor 3:14
[448] Gal 4:26 Rev 21:2
[449] Ps 36:11, 37:4 Is 61:10

jewels that are entirely unique. No two jewels in the New Jerusalem are the same. Each has its own beauty and characteristics of glory.

There is much to explore, and all of this will delight us to the depths of our being as we move into the fellowship of heaven. But it is by no means all reserved for then. Here while on this earth, we are able to get a foretaste of heaven[450], which is enough to thrill and delight us ready for us coming into the fullness of what is yet to come. These are the true riches of wisdom and knowledge[451]. When we have them, our worship moves into levels of appreciation of God that becomes exquisite and delightful beyond description. Every worship leader should seek to explore these depths of the beauty and glory of God.

Judgement

At the end of the age all are appointed to be judged[452]. We are told by Paul that fire will test the quality of each man's work. Anything of worth will survive, but everything else will be burned up. The precious things that will resist the fire are symbolised as gold, silver, and precious stones[453]. We are now in a position to understand these. The gold is faith, the silver is purity, and the precious stones are the fruits of the spirit, combined with the attributes and character of all the seven spirits of God that are ours as beings in whom the life of Christ is formed within[454].

The simple idea that we work and receive wages for our labour in heaven is not enough. The true reward is in the very state of our being as we come through the age. Though our reward is related to our labour[455] this is only because our works reflect the truth of whom and what we have become. The truth is that as we work for the Kingdom through the power of the Spirit, we bear spiritual fruit[456]. It is only work done in the Spirit that has that effect. The fruit of the Spirit comes only through walking and working in the light by the Spirit[457]. When we apply ourselves as the Spirit

---

[450] Eph 1:14 2 Cor 1:22 Heb 6:4
[451] Col 2:3
[452] Heb 9:27
[453] 1 Cor 13:12
[454] 1 Pet 1:7 Ps 66:10 Is 48:10 Mal 3:3 1 Cor 3:12 2 Pet 1:8
[455] 1 Cor 3:8
[456] Col 1:10
[457] John 3:21

leads us, we and others are spiritually formed. When we work for others through the Spirit, they are spiritually enriched, but according to the spiritual laws of giving and receiving; we cannot enrich others without it enriching us too[458]. It is a profound thing that the rewards for what we do are what we become. We are our own reward; our very being and constitution. We are not working for the treasure of possessions, as this world would define it; the treasure is in our very being. The treasure is not like some trinket that can be lost or taken away[459]. It is the glorious and permanent features of our very being.

Those that see the reward for their work as some kind of wage that is unrelated to their own constitution and character, tend to develop a worldly materialistic view of these things. We may then see the values and evils of the world manifesting themselves in a religious form, where God becomes secondary to one's own purpose of earning a heavenly reward. The results may include competition, and the pursuit of roles and position that we often see in religion, as we do in the world[460]. None of this grasping and posturing serves to develop the character that is the real eternal treasure and reward; though it may develop character indirectly in those that are forced to tolerate it with grace. Instead it will develop bad character that will be seen as combustible wood, hay, and straw when it comes to the fire of judgement[461]. When we genuinely serve others and put them first,[462] as the spirit guides and enables us, we will ourselves bear good fruit for the Kingdom that will become an eternal reward.

For some the foundation of the gold of faith in Christ for salvation is laid, but there has been no walk of the spirit and as a consequence nothing, or very little, is built upon it. They will come through the fire of judgement with just the foundation.[463] This is part of the New Jerusalem and they have eternal life, but there may also be a sense of loss over what might have been. For those that did not have even the foundation of Christ, all will be lost. They will have no part in eternity.

---

[458] Gal 6:7 2 Cor 9:6 Mal 3:8-10
[459] Matt 6:19-20 2 Cor 5:10
[460] 1 John 2:15-17
[461] 1 Cor 3:12-13
[462] Phil 2:3
[463] 1 Cor 3:14-15

For a Christian the fire is not a threat but a liberation from all that is hated and despised. This includes all that belongs to the sinful nature that dogs us throughout life, seeking to live its own life through us[464]. The sinful nature is like the shadow of death to us, but the cleansing of fire brings shear relief and a joyful homecoming to light and freedom.

The meaning, purpose, and function of the symbol of fire are something that needs further discussion, but the subject requires a fuller treatment and so it is dealt with in a later section.

Our role in heaven

God's plan for us in the coming ages is not simply to display his glory as a kind of exhibition[465]. There are many indications in scripture that show us we will have a significant role to play in heaven and the future ages that includes the authority and responsibility to guide, manage, direct and rule as a form of service[466]. This age and its challenges are uniquely fitting us for those purposes. It is clear that this will include considerable responsibilities, allowing us to even guide and serve the angels almost as a reversal of the roles of men and angels, as we move into the coming ages[467]. No doubt we will work together with them in ways and for purposes that are presently inconceivable to us.

We will have new bodies that are vastly superior to these fragile bodies we now have[468], and we are likely to have vastly greater resources of energy and creativity to draw on that we will be eager to express.

Given that intelligence is a feature of our physical body; when we receive our new bodies we can also expect to have a much higher intelligence to work with that will enable us to understand what is presently beyond us. All of this will seem like an incredible release from the tight constraints of this age[469]. Even in this age we are told that '*if the same Spirit that raised Christ from the dead dwells in us then he will quicken the mortal body*'[470]. So even the presence of God within these

---

[464] Rom 7:24
[465] Eph 2:7
[466] 1 Cor 6:2-3 Luke 19:17
[467] 1 Cor 6:3
[468] 1 Cor 15:42-44
[469] 2 Cor 5:2 Mal 4:2
[470] Rom 8:11

earthly bodies can have a profoundly energising effect. How much more when we come into our heavenly bodies, and God begins to express himself through us there.

When Lucifer fell and became Satan he left a vacancy. It seems he was among a number of angelic beings known as the *'morning stars'*[471]. We don't know how many of them there were, perhaps seven as a reflection of the seven spirits of God[472], but together they clearly had a role that was and is specifically related to serving us and our world in some significant way. As with all angels, they are messengers of God, delivering not just messages, but impartations of God himself[473]. All of God's ministry to the world seems to be through, or accompanied by, angels. This is their role and purpose[474].

It was the morning stars that sang, and the other angels shouted with joy, as they witnessed God create the physical universe[475]. It is incredible to think that Lucifer sang with them, and in his pre-fallen state experienced genuine joy and delight at what God had done.

As with all angels, they are created to be a form of expression of God, therefore we see that Jesus identifies himself as *the* morning star[476]. The morning star in the physical realm is the sun which brings the morning. It is the light of the world; one of the many things Jesus revealed himself to be both in the gospels[477] and also in the Old Testament, where, speaking of heaven it says *'the sun of righteousness will rise with healing in his wings'*[478]. These angels together would have fully expressed this morning star ministry and revelation of God's glory to the world, but what is it?

When we think in terms of the ages, and the future of God's creation passing from age to age, it is clear that each age will have a dawning. It seems that the role of the morning stars may be as some kind of herald of the age, in some ways like John the Baptist was to the coming

---

[471] Job 38:7 Is 14:12, 9-15 Ez 28:14,16, 13-17
[472] Rev 1:16, 1:5, 3:1
[473] Luke 22:43
[474] Heb 1:14
[475] Job 38:4-7
[476] Rev 22:16
[477] John 9:5
[478] Mal 4:2

CHAPTER 12: The Seven Spirits of God

of Jesus, the Christ[479]. They are like the announcers at a prestigious event where the dignitaries are introduced as they enter. Their role is to herald God's incarnation as it is revealed at the dawning of each new and emerging age, revealing something of his identity and glory before he emerges into the fullness of that glory like the midday sun. One aspect of this role of the morning star is to proclaim and show forth God's righteousness, almost as a kind of preparation and preview of it before he himself emerges into a full revelation of himself to the age. The morning stars are to the age what the doorkeepers were to the temple, and as for the role of all angels it carries with it immense authority and responsibility to fully and accurately represent God in this way. As such they themselves are the most glorious beings, adorned for their role with something of God's magnificent splendour.

When we consider Lucifer from this perspective, we begin to realise just how great his betrayal was in the Garden of Eden, where at the dawn of the age he so misrepresented God to man. He exploited his incredibly glorious position of trust that God had given him, and used all of the authority[480] and responsibility it carried to exalt himself in God's place. This would be like John the Baptist proclaiming himself to be the Christ, as many others have done, and will do before his second coming[481]. Lucifer's fall was from a place that showed forth the light of God's righteousness and glory, into a state of complete wickedness and depravity. Instead of heralding God's light he has now become a spirit of darkness, the prince of this dark world[482].

God's plan is now made clear: that this vacant role as a morning star that Lucifer abandoned will be one of the positions and roles that the redeemed of men will go on to fulfil in his place in the ages to come. We are explicitly promised that to those that overcome, he will give us the morning star[483].

Imagine the grief that the other morning stars suffered when one from their own number fell and led both mankind and a host of angels into corruption and rebellion. Imagine also how their grief must have been

---

[479] Luke 3:1-6, 7:26-28
[480] Jude 1:6
[481] Matt 24:5
[482] John 14:30
[483] Rev 2:28

turned to joy as God not only redeemed man, but as they realised that we, mankind, will be their companions and co-workers in the kingdom of God in the ages to come, heralding his righteousness and glory to each age[484]. Here we see the very purpose of God in placing upon us the righteousness of Christ[485]. It is the very clothing and glory of the morning stars.

The morning star is something that rises in our hearts as we grow into maturity, and progress towards completion, as God does his work in us, and with us in this world[486]. When we consider the formidable power that Satan has; in relation to our present capabilities, we can anticipate that our replacement of him in this heavenly role will include similar, or even greater responsibility for immense power in the coming ages[487].

When God places us in this position, our experience of this age, and our faith in God that we have developed here in this world, will become the foundation of security for this power in our hands. God is raising us as ones that he can fully trust with this role. Equally for the other morning star angels, it is likely that we will find in them powerful and glorious companions as we come to work together with them in the ages to come. Equally, for them their experience of seeing one of their own kind fall, then God's handling of the rebellion in this world right through to judgement, and his raising up of us to fulfil that role with them, will also give them faith that will make sure that such power is equally secure with them, as it is with us who have been redeemed from this age.

All of this will constitute part of the reward God has for us in heaven. Our beings will manifest God's Spirit in us, together with all the fruits of the Spirit. These are the jewels with which Lucifer was adorned, and which he cast off when he fell[488], and which now God is developing in us. These jewels, as they are described in the prophesy, seem to cover the whole spectrum of colour representing the whole being of God, showing that as a morning star herald he really was adorned with a full representation of the whole spectrum of God's glory. Lucifer lost his place because he became enamoured with these jewels and his own beauty – vanity. Forgetting that they were a reflection of God, he came to see them

---

[484] Luke 15:10
[485] Gal 3:27 2 Cor 5:21
[486] 2 Pet 1:9
[487] Heb 6:5
[488] Ez 2:13-14

as something of himself, independently of God. He lost sight of the fact that in the same way that jewels need light to display their glory, and in this sense are completely dependent on the light, so he was completely dependent on God for the glory he came to see as his own, independently of God.

Lucifer's jewels were set in the gold of faith that was too weak to retain them[489], but we will rise from the experience of this age to fill his role with much greater faith that has the strength and security that will stand for eternity, and will never fall or fail. Here we see that God has used Lucifer's deficiency to develop what he lacked in us, who will come to fulfil his role in his place. We therefore see that God's plan for the ages continues to forge ahead, regardless of the temporary opposition that is raised against it.

In each age to come we will herald God's coming, but like John the Baptist, and unlike Lucifer, we will be ever ready and willing that he should become greater, and we shall become less[490]. Even now in this age, our challenge is to relinquish our self-life and let Christ in us rise to his full glory. As such we are in training for our morning star role in the coming ages.

The fruit we bear will be applied to our roles and service to all of God's creation for the ages. We can expect that these roles and responsibilities will demand the application of all the lasting fruit that we have developed – *faith, knowledge, patience, tolerance, forgiveness, self-control, perseverance, humility, sensitivity, truthfulness, protectiveness, goodness, godliness, brotherly kindness, compassion, hopefulness, peace, joy* and *love*, all of which are expressions of our God who is Love. All of the rewards of power, role, and responsibility come to those that, in preparation for the coming ages, overcome through faith in this age[491], and when the scripture says '*the sun of righteousness will rise with healing in his wings*'[492] it is speaking of both Christ, and us, with Christ in us, and clothing us with his righteousness and glory[493] as will be seen clearly at the dawn of the coming age; a righteousness that is by faith[494].

---

[489] Ez 28:13 – Your settings and mounting were made of gold
[490] John 3:30
[491] Rev 2:26 3:21
[492] Mal 4:2
[493] 1 Cor 2:7 2 Cor 3:18, 4:17 Col 1:27 2 Thes 2:14 1 Pet 4:14, 5:4

Our attitude to this present age

Some of these things are abstract to us who are only accustomed to the order of this age. We need to become comfortable with the abstract and unknown; it will always be present with us, even through the ages to come. This is part of the reason faith is so important. If we could at any time fully understand either the present universe, or the future plans God has made, then it would probably be disappointing, and would show God to be finite like us. As it is we can't understand, we can only anticipate a little of what is to come next. Thank God it will always be true that God is always as much greater than we are, as the next age is above the present one. Hope is a permanent feature of eternity[495]. The mystery aspect of God will always exist, and will always leave much to be explored. It leaves us open to see there are infinite opportunities for greater and greater things as we personally and collectively grow through each age, becoming ready for the next, together with all God's other created beings that we will enjoy them with.

We may have realised that God is in no rush to move us on from age to age. Each age lasts for an age. So far we have only experienced the present age, which is just the first. Our best approach is always to value, appreciate, and celebrate the 'now' of what God is doing, whilst holding the next in patient anticipation. Even in this age, which is evil and is no place to stay[496], we should realise that it is a unique and valuable experience. God is our security in it. There is no need to rush it. It is designed to bring forth unique fruit that will last into all of the coming ages[497]. We should therefore be patient and allow God to accomplish everything in us that he desires, making the maximum of the eternally unique opportunity of this age that comes to us at such great cost.

We should make no plans to stay here, but at the same time we should remain in a place of personal inner peace, rest, and trust, as we wait patiently for what is to come[498]. This was the attitude and perspective of the apostle Paul in his work on earth.

---

[494] Rom 3:21-25
[495] 1 Cor 13:13
[496] 1 Cor 15:19
[497] John 15:16
[498] Rom 8:25 Heb 11:10

CHAPTER 12: The Seven Spirits of God

If we ask God, he will give us enough revelation of the coming age to keep us in the same frame of mind while we are here, and keep us from the ignorance of living only for the present age. Our treasure will then truly be in heaven. Our lives will then be lived in anticipation and expectation of what is coming, and we will avoid the trap of coming to live in this world as if it were the extent of God's plan for us.

CHAPTER 13: The Wisdom of the Cross

The doctrine of substitution – the problem

That Jesus died on the cross to save all men from their sins is not in question[499]. However there are often problems with some of the explanations that are given on how this act of God's grace in going to the cross, in the form of the Son, can serve to provide men with the opportunity for forgiveness.

The idea that is sometimes presented in gospel preaching, is that Jesus had to die to satisfy the anger of the Father against our sin. This idea may in some sense be true, but if that is the extent of our understanding, it has some real problems associated with it. It presents an understanding of the Father as vengeful and merciless, while Jesus, the Son of God, is shown to be full of mercy and grace. It suggests some disunity between the desires and actions of the Father and the Son. This in turn challenges the understanding of Father, Son, and Holy Spirit as one, and that they are in unity and of the same mind and purpose.

With this kind of thinking we end up with a view of God the Father that is much like Shakespeare's Merchant of Venice. In this story Shylock, a moneylender, demands his 'pound of flesh' from his debtor, the merchant, as his right according to the letter of the law as agreed in a contract between him and his debtor. Though genuine grounds for mercy were offered, including full repayment of the debt, the hatred of Shylock towards his debtor led him to lean on a strict interpretation of their contract that permitted him to make his morbid claim simply on the grounds of the late payment. In the end the mercilessness of Shylock is turned against him by permitting him his legal right to use the knife, and take his 'pound of flesh', but then denying him the right to spill a drop of blood in the process because this was not explicitly permitted in the letter of the contract. When Shylock realised he had been outwitted, he withdrew his claim and sought to take the offered repayment. The defence lawyer then withdrew the offer of payment on the same grounds; that it was not permitted in the letter of the contract. He demanded that Shylock

---

[499] John 12:32 Rom 5:18 1 Tim 2:4,6, 4:10 Ti 2:11 2 Pet 3:9

execute his claim and take his pound of flesh, according to the letter of the law; yet without shedding blood. Should Shylock have chosen to go ahead and use the knife on the body of his debtor, he then stood to be charged with murder for taking blood against any contractual right or agreement to do so. On the other hand to refuse to do so would mean a breach of contract. His punishment for murder would mean Shylock would lose his own life for the crime. Shylock was then forced to breach the contract and seek mercy for himself, which he was granted, though at a considerable cost to his freedom and his estate.

This is a great story that explores the function of a system of law. We are led to see Shylock as a villain for his refusal to grant mercy when he is given every opportunity and reason to give it. The brilliance and irony of the story are that we are then gratified with justice against his mercilessness, as he is outwitted at his own game.

The lesson is that the strict interpretation of the letter of the law is not necessarily the grounds of morality, but it is always the spirit of the law, that the letter seeks to interpret, that is the true moral authority. Had Shylock been more in touch with his cultural heritage he would have known that mercy is a fundamental part of it.

The story illustrates an important point – that where it is possible to show mercy morality demands it, even against the letter of the law. How does this work?

The demand for mercy

We have discussed the fact that love and morality do not just demand a commitment to good, but it must commit to the highest good. To opt for the second highest good would therefore be an immoral act.

This principle is hard to illustrate because we can nearly always think of possible reasons why an action may be thought to be for the highest good in the mind of another.

Imagine a hungry traveller asking a countryman for food. In response the countryman asks if he would like some cold porridge. When the traveller accepts with great relief, the countryman tells him to come back tomorrow because the porridge was still hot.

Assuming the porridge was better served hot than cold, and there was no reason why the countryman should not give it there and then, this would have been a cruel and immoral act. Morality demands the highest good. Even the second highest option is immoral.

CHAPTER 13: The Wisdom of the Cross   215

On this basis it was an imperative that God's creation should be established and secured with a minimum of suffering, without compromising the supreme goodness of his purpose of love in creation. If God could have fulfilled his purpose in creation through a path with less suffering, then his own nature of love would have demanded that he take that course. On the same reasoning; if it was in any way possible that God should be able to redeem fallen beings, without his actions thwarting his supremely valuable and eternal purpose, then he would have been obliged by his own nature to take it. This is true for the redemption of both men and angels; where it is possible.

In the case of fallen angels, it is clear that no way could be found for them to be forgiven or redeemed, even though according to apocryphal writings they appealed to God for mercy[500]. For them justice had to prevail first by their permanent expulsion from heaven, and last by the lake of fire. This does not diminish the fact that had infinite wisdom been able to find a way for redemption, without compromising the purpose of love, then God would have taken it without hesitation, whatever the cost.

On the other hand, in the case of man, the infinite wisdom of God saw a way for his redemption, and although it was at incredible cost to himself, what God saw was that even the very cost of this way could be made to serve an even higher purpose of love, without compromising the supreme plan of God. In God's mind therefore, this way had to be taken. To refuse mercy, having found that it was possible, would have been against his very nature. The radical cost did not even make him hesitate because in his plan even the cost would be made to serve his purpose.

We should not be under any illusions about the cost of redemption for men. There are few things in scripture that are declared to be difficult for God, but the salvation of the righteous is stated to be exactly that – hard for even God to accomplish[501]. For that reason alone we should not be surprised that there are eternal costs associated with it, and that the cost is immense.

The problem with the costs we are talking about is that they are eternal. As we have previously discussed: it is only when we have the eternal perspective of the cost and its effects in all the ages of ages to come, that we come to appreciate why a compromise cannot be accepted.

---

[500] Enoch 13-14, 2 Pet 2:4 – The book of Enoch was probably Peter's source.
[501] 1 Pet 4:18

Eternity is an extreme. So is God's love. His handling of creation must reflect that.

This way of redemption for man had to be something extraordinary, because mercy in the face of sin would leave doubts about God that would threaten to undermine the eternal security for all ages, and this would be an eternal cost. The way God saw to accomplish man's redemption had to redeem man without in any way compromising eternal security or the purpose of love. We will explore this further, but the way God saw for man's redemption was of course through the extreme action of the cross.

Government and the demands of law

The story of the Merchant of Venice treats the letter of the law as the supreme authority. The story of the Father demanding vengeance for sin by the death of the Son, can be interpreted as the same; as if the letter of the law were dictating to God. In actual fact this is a perversion of the purpose of the law, because the letter of the law is being used to displace God, rather than to serve him. In other words, the law is placing itself above the supreme principle of love, goodness, and the moral demand, which is immoral.

The only 'law' that God conforms to is the law of his own nature, which is love. Even this is a voluntary thing; he chooses it, always. It would be against his own nature for him to choose any other, but it is still a free choice. It is what James called 'the *perfect law of freedom*'[502] which seems to be a contradiction in terms, but simply means it is a natural choice for an uncorrupted moral being.

There was in fact no legal demand upon God to provide a substitute because he is the highest authority, and none can make such a demand of him. The only demand upon God came from his own nature. He was simply unwilling to go against his own nature with his commitment to the highest good and purpose of love. If he was able to find a way of redemption that required a substitute, then his reason for taking that course would be a reason of love, not some self-imposed demand that every debt be paid in full, whether it served the highest good purpose or not.

---

[502] Jam 1:5, 2:12

In modern democracies the government makes the law, and the law courts administer it. In such states there are many instances where individual subjects of the realm have appealed to the government against a decision of the law courts, who are simply applying the letter of the law. The appeal is made on the grounds that the decision is unjust. This either implies that the law in question is universally unjust, or it may mean that for some special reason the law is unjust when applied to the particular case in question that was probably not considered when the law was made. In any case the claim against the law in question is based on its non-conformity to the moral principle; it must serve the highest good of the community it serves.

In such cases a moral government is obliged to look at the case and weigh it, not against the letter of the law but against the original spirit and purpose of the law; to fulfil the highest good. If the law is proved not to conform to the moral principle, then a legitimate demand can be made to override the decision, and even repeal or modify the law. If for some reason the application of this law to this particular case can be shown to be against the original spirit and purpose of the law, then the government can make a safe decision to grant an exception. In fact in these cases the government must act to show its commitment to the moral principle. Any use of law to serve a purpose other than the highest good is an immoral act. The law is therefore subject to the moral principle.

In any such case, when the government overturns a decision of the law courts, they are careful to publicly restate the purpose of the law in question, and show why the case in question is an exception against the letter. In other words they have to show how the purposes of the highest good are served by overturning the decision, in order to keep their authority and maintain the faith of the people in their government and its laws.

This shows that the law is subject to the government, and not the other way around. The government is accountable to the moral principle. Equally when God the Father sent the Son to the cross, it was not to fulfil some legal demand upon him because he himself is the principle of the law; he is Love. It was simply because his own nature and purpose of love demanded it. The godhead was united in this purpose. All three persons of the godhead understood the cost of fulfilling the highest good purpose of all creation. The Son went to the cross in full agreement, knowing that it was the only way that the highest good purposes of love could be accomplished for all creation, for all ages.

In the case of man, he is guilty of sin. He has broken the letter of the law. There is no fault in the law, so there is no way to overturn the transgression by proving the law to be at fault; so what grounds did God have to forgive man for his sin? Simply this: that by going through with the plan to send Jesus to the cross, mercy could be shown to men and the highest good could still be served – period. This is all that the love, morality, and good nature of God required. This alone needed to be proved. There is no legal demand higher than this. The letter of the law has to submit to it. If a way to show mercy was possible, and the highest good could still be served, then that way had to be taken.

What did it take to redeem man with mercy?

When created beings fell, God could have simply administered justice on all fallen creatures, and gone ahead with his eternal plans for the ages with those that remained faithful to him. No doubt all that remained in his company would have been happy forever, but the wisdom of God saw a far greater opportunity in the fall. That opportunity came in the form of the opportunity to show mercy as an aspect of love[503], but that option brought massive complications with it. The plan of God had to have a way of mitigating or reversing the effects of those complications for the mercy option to be possible in the purposes of love. The issues that had to be considered, and the problems that had to be answered, were considerable. They are:

Faith that God is committed to the highest good – The faith of all created beings in the fact that God is Love, and that his commitment is to the highest good must remain beyond question. Anything less would undermine the eternal security that comes from all free-willed beings having faith in God's goodness.

Appreciation of the horrors of sin and evil – Through the experience of sin and evil, all created beings, including men and angels, must be led to an appreciation of faith regarding the horrors of a fall to the extent that there will never be a repeat of the fall.

---

[503] Rom 11:32 Eph 2:4 1 Tim 1:16 Jam 5:11

CHAPTER 13: The Wisdom of the Cross

Faith in God's Justice – Faith in God's commitment to the highest good includes faith in all free willed beings towards God's commitment to justice as a necessary part of his commitment to the highest good. The justice of God would therefore have to be known, understood, and believed in by all. Faith in justice is faith that God is ready and willing to make whatever hard decisions are demanded by the principle of love, even when they are clearly a source of great pain and unimaginable heartache to him.

The reformation of man's nature – For fallen man to be redeemed to have a place in the eternal plan of God, the fallen nature of man must be reformed. This is vitally important. Man's corruption must be completely overturned, and his wholesale commitment to the purposes of love restored. To release man into eternity in a corrupted state would clearly undermine the eternal security God was seeking to establish for his creation in eternity. We will discuss how this is accomplished later, and its relationship to the work on the cross.

Faith in the Mercy of God – Mercy, where possible, is an aspect of God and of the principle of love. The opportunity for the great mercy of God to be seen and appreciated towards the redeemed was a great prize that God could not refuse to reach for. However the danger of God offering mercy is that it threatens faith in the uncompromising justice of God as an essential expression of love; the highest good of all. This leads free-willed beings to believe that a future fall may be met by the same 'leniency' and compromise. It would therefore have the effect of undermining the eternal security of creation derived from the faith of all free-willed beings towards God's justice. The justice executed on fallen angels, and a large proportion of fallen men, go some way to alleviating this problem, but not nearly far enough in God's mind to serve the purposes of the highest good for all creation through all the future ages that God has planned. If nothing else was done this problem would have removed any possibility of redemption for any. Other measures are therefore needed to make sure all of creation appreciates the enormity of the cost and sacrifice that is needed to deliver mercy, while at the same time delivering justice. This demand for awareness by all of the cost is fulfilled in the cross, as we will see.

Faith in man's total dependence on God – Man was never intended to become independent of God. He was born into fellowship and dependence on him as his very source of life and strength. For God to show mercy to man he must not only come back into the place of dependence on God, but he must come to believe in his dependence on him as his very source. He must know that without God he cannot continue to be a being of love, and he must understand the full implications of that fact.

Faith in the Omnipotence of God – Faith in God's omnipotence is established in his creatures most of all by them witnessing his handling of the fall. He is seen dealing with highly intelligent beings that fell beyond redemption, and that then attempted to achieve their own selfish purposes in opposition to God's purposes. God's complete victory over these events, even down to the last discernible detail,[504] results in a far greater faith among created beings in the omnipotence of God than there would have been had there been no fall. Without the fall there would have been no such demonstration of his infinite power and ability to bring about the purposes of love, no matter how extreme the situation, or the opposition.

Appreciation of the Humility of God – Through the cross the great humility and servant heartedness of God is seen by all creatures[505]. The principles of heaven that demands that the strong value, serve, and defend the weak are seen in action in a supreme way. This demonstration of profound humility in God most high reveals the truth of God in ways that nothing else could, and it serves to nullify for all eternity the dangers of the pride that led to the fall. Any that ever after aspire to compare themselves with God again will have to assess themselves in the light of such humility.

Why God is worshipped?

Omniscience, omnipotence, justice, mercy, love, and humility – all of these attributes of God are the things that angels behold before them when they see him. All such things are clearly visible in the spiritual realm. In the spiritual realm they are glorious beyond description and are

---

[504] Rom 8:28
[505] Matt 11:29 Phil 2:7 John 13:12-17

CHAPTER 13: The Wisdom of the Cross

expressions of his holiness. They invoke worship, and cause all that see them to cry 'Holy, Holy, Holy' from the very depths of their beings.

Seraphim dwell in the presence of God. They cannot stand to be away from it for long. They are worshipping angels ministering directly to God. When Isaiah saw the throne room, the exposure of his depravity and need in relation to what he saw overwhelmed him. The Seraphim had to come and minister to him with cleansing in the vision, by pressing a hot coal to his lips. He felt the transgressions of his mouth to the very depths of his soul[506].

God is the highest pleasure and delight of all his creatures. David speaks his faith when he anticipates what is coming as he reaches the end of his life on earth – *'in the morning I shall see his face and be satisfied'*[507]. God has destined this for us. As it is for Abraham; he (God) is our very great reward[508]. We really have no idea of it yet. Indeed for most of us we are not yet ready for it. As we progress through life we begin to perceive it more and more, until we come to the place where we know our work on earth is done, and his work is done in us.

Throughout life God intends that the vision of heaven and his throne should become clearer and clearer, enough to make our hearts yearn more and more for our heavenly home[509].

Celebrating heaven – I got my first glimpses of these truths in times when my deepest trials converged: financial pressures, work pressure, health issues, relationship troubles, and the ongoing battle with self and temptation. At such times my life seemed to lose its value, but God drew near and heaven became clearer. I think I understand just a little of what grace the martyrs knew that made them even despise their very lives on earth, and sent them looking for, and seeking, the exit God had called them to. The revelation of these things is often dulled by comfort on this earth[510]. Perhaps we should despise that even more.

If you realise your need of heavenly vision, and you want to expand your view on life and destiny, simply ask God in faith to open to

---

[506] Is 6:1-7
[507] Ps 17:5
[508] Gen 15:1
[509] 2 Cor 5:2-4
[510] Mark 4:19 Jam 5:5

you some heavenly revelation. He is happy to give it to any ready heart, but be warned – don't expect to ever be the same again. Expect, like Isaiah, for your life on this earth to be ruined[511], and God himself thereafter to be your only pursuit, and the only satisfaction for your soul.

In Tolkien's *Lord of the Rings,* though he was always evasive about the symbolism in his novels, he seems to use the Elves as an image of the higher life of the Spirit and of those that have found rebirth. They are seen leaving Middle Earth as they respond to an inner call to set sail from the Grey Havens to a higher life beyond the sea. In one of the many simple details, that make no appearance in the films, he says of the Elves that if they ever see the sea their hearts are forever filled with yearning and desire to move on from Middle Earth to that which awaits them beyond. Even if they hear the sound of a seagull they feel the draw to their destiny beyond.

This is a great picture of what it is like for those that have glimpsed the reality of heaven. If you don't believe me ask the apostle Paul.[512]

For me these revelations have sustained me in my darkest times, but even after and since the trials passed these revelations have remained deep in my spirit and occasionally things come along that invoke them and remind me of my eternal destiny.

I have been, and continue to be inspired particularly by certain songs, drawn directly from scripture, that speak to me of the reality of the heavenly city[513]. These songs are like Tolkien's poetic Elvish songs that populate his books, the only difference being that whilst Tolkien's writings are fiction, these psalms and songs speak of eternal realities that exist right now, and are more factual and real than anything in the physical world we live in, which is so temporal[514].

These songs are best heard sung from the heart by one that has the revelation of their reality, but it may be helpful to share one such song here, that is a celebration of that city, drawn from Psalm 46 that, as for

---

[511] Is 6:5
[512] 2 Cor 12:4 2 Cor 5:2-4
[513] Heb 11:10,16
[514] 2 Cor 4:18

many of the Psalms, was composed in times of great anguish when only the help and salvation of God could ensure the survival of Israel:

> *There is a river,*
> *Whose streams make glad,*
> *The city of God,*
> *The city of God.*
>
> *The holy habitation,*
> *Of the most high,*
> *The city of God,*
> *The city of God.*
>
> *God is in the midst of her,*
> *She shall not be moved,*
> *The Lord of hosts is with her.*
>
> *There is a river,*
> *Whose streams make glad,*
> *The city of God,*
> *The city of God.*

The cost of mercy

The great opportunity for God in the fall was to show mercy to some. It was never possible for all to find it, but for some it could be done. This act of God would not only redeem some of the creatures that would otherwise be lost, but would illuminate his character more than anything else he could ever have done in all eternity, and it would therefore serve all the more to secure his free-willed creatures by faith towards God in all the coming ages.

However, given that God must consider the vast implications of such actions to myriads of created beings, and for the infinity of ages to come, there was no room to leave any doubt in the mind of any being of the depth of his hatred towards sin[515]. This hatred is the inevitable reverse side of his love. As much as he is committed to the highest good of all

---
[515] Rom 12:9

creation in his love, so he is committed to oppose all that opposes the purposes of love in the same measure.

Paul tells us of the inestimable extents of the love of God, but his hatred for all that opposes it is essentially as great. It was essential that the action God took to mitigate the mere suggestion that he can compromise the purposes of love, was extreme. The extremity of it had to reflect the extremity of God as a being, and the extremity of eternity itself. Anything less would not have reflected the truth about him.

It was also essential that in taking action, the cost of it should be entirely borne by him alone, and no other. The cross was his alone to bear. To allow another, such as an archangel, to take his place would have made the eternal declaration that redemption could be achieved by the action of a finite created being, such as Lucifer. This would essentially have taken the issue of eternal security out of God's hands, and would therefore have been drastically inadequate in the mind of God to fulfil the eternal purpose.

To ensure the security of the ages beyond, it was essential for all creatures to realise that the action demanded for mercy and redemption would be so far beyond them that no created being could ever possibly meet the demand. The possibility of redemption therefore only ever resides in the hands of God, and its cost is way beyond anything any creature can meet. For this reason God chose to put forth an action that was even extreme for an infinite God, and way beyond the bounds of any creature.

The Son of God was tested to the limit, and the effects of his actions in becoming the Lamb that was slain were set to be carried into all the ages of ages of eternity, and held thereafter in full view before all creatures forever[516]. It was vitally important for God's purposes, that the remote possibility of redemption was in his hands alone, and that the cost of it is radical, in proportion to God himself. This was God's solution to the problems associated with showing mercy, together with the universal understanding among all his creatures that the act of redemption in this age is a once only event. It cannot be repeated because for all ages to come, all creatures will be well informed of the horror and cost of a fall through the testimony of this age, and the evidence of suffering before them in the Lamb that was slain. To fall in the face of this evidence would

---

[516] Rev 5:13

CHAPTER 13: The Wisdom of the Cross

be worse than even the original fall of angels that brought this evil age about. For them there was no president to show them the cost of their actions, yet there was no way back for them[517].

Yes, the fall must be a once only event. That is why God must secure the created universe in this very first age so it is done once and for all ages. By doing so the suffering it demands is kept to an absolute minimum, without in any way compromising the purposes of God. It was extreme in the extreme, but for God there was simply no other choice. Only the cross would express him as he truly is; as the God of infinite Love.

We should at this point realise that God personally knew and loved every angel that fell, and every man that will not receive salvation or see any part of eternity. His love for them was as boundless as for any other being in his creation. We marvel that he still created and accepted the fact that he must bear this unimaginable cost. As we have discussed before, we cannot appreciate the balance of the costs and returns to the purpose of love. We can only accept by faith that according to the infinite wisdom and love of God, that this had to happen, and there was no other choice that love could make.

To not create at all was not an option for God. Neither was it an option to redeem all in the event of a fall. The cost of losing some, and God's personal suffering at the prospect of it, was more than matched by the cost to him personally in becoming the slain Lamb. This is what is abundantly visible in the slain Lamb when angels see him on the throne[518]. As we have described before now; the sight of this scene of the evidence of immense suffering, together with infinite glory and splendour, only serves to reveal God in all his glorious fullness.

Words are running out at this point. Nothing can describe it. We see no more than the faintest of reflections when we try to see it in earthly terms. One day we will see him and know beyond doubt that what God has done is nothing other than an expression of infinite love.

---

[517] 2 Pet 2:4 Enoch 13-14
[518] Rev 5:12

PART III:
THE REFORMATION OF MAN

CHAPTER 14: The Reformation of Man by Spiritual Rebirth

Reformation and the Cross
Our central theme is an exploration of the cross and all it means. We have so far explored in detail God's big plan of creation, and the central part that the cross has played in that. We now come to consider the impact of the cross on man from an individual point of view. This includes its place in the redemption and development of man, particularly in the light of the eternal plan and big picture of the ages to come, that we have discussed. What we will see is that God has utilised the event, and subsequent situation of the fall, and especially the cross, in the process of reform to the very maximum for developing the faith that is so essential for the security of our eternal future, as we have discussed.

God's big plan of creation – review
God has planned an eternal future of ever advancing ages of ages to come for men and angels to enjoy with him forever[519]. This plan is immense because it is eternal, and it was devised as the highest creative idea in the purposes of love, by a God of infinite wisdom and power. Only this would reflect God in all his fullness.

Central to this highest of all ideas for creation, is the inclusion of men and angels as truly free-willed beings, that are as free in their will as God is in his, and as able to serve the purpose of love in their capacity as God is in his. However there was a weakness in the plan that must be overcome; the risk that free-willed beings would use their free will to corrupt God's creation by deviating from the purpose of love.

For this idea to remain God's highest idea, God had to set in place a plan to overcome and remove this risk. The plan of God therefore had to include a provision, in the event of a fall into corruption, for God to utilise an evil age of pre-history, right at the beginning of creation, as a once only event, to once and for all eliminate the vulnerability and risk of any further fall ever taking place in all eternity.

---

[519] Eph 2:7 1 Thes 4:7 Rev 21:3

The provision of this pre-age of evil is an unavoidable essential for God to have the eternal fellowship of true free-willed beings, as his love passionately desires, without compromising the sovereignty of their free-will in any way.

An unavoidable cost of this plan would be the eternal loss of some of these beings, in order that the rest may go forward into an eternal future that is completely secure and invulnerable to any repeat of the fall into corruption. However for God to go ahead with such a creation plan, the only way he could ensure this invulnerability was by developing faith in all his beings towards himself, so that they will always hereafter adhere to the purpose of love.

To secure such faith in view of these unavoidable eternal losses, it was essential that God himself bear an even greater cost that would be evident to all of his beings in heaven and for eternity. Only in this way would they gain the necessary faith, through an appreciation of the extremes to which the love of God extends, in order to fulfil and secure the purposes of Love. This loss took the form of the suffering of God himself on the cross in the form of the Son, and the eternal view of the Lamb that was slain standing in full view of all beings at the centre of creation, in the form of the very being of God[520].

The unavoidable losses of this age of pre-history would include both the loss of a proportion of men, and a proportion of angels. However another essential part of the plan is, that God is seen to extend mercy to redeem as many as possible in the purpose of love. Sadly the plan is too great for it to be possible to redeem all, and the eternal purpose of Love could not be served by reducing the plan so that they could all be saved. However for some it was possible for them to be redeemed, and therefore to God it was essential that they were, providing that the purpose of the highest good – love, be served and not compromised by it.

It was not possible for any fallen angels to be redeemed, but it was possible for some of the race of men. This may be due to the fact that men were deceived into sin and corruption from a place of relative moral naivety; not knowing good and evil, by another being of higher intelligence. Prior to this, man's knowledge of good and evil extended no further than to a single command that instructed him not to take of such knowledge. However, having taken it in disobedience, man became

---

[520] Rev 5:13

CHAPTER 14: The Reformation of Man by Spiritual Rebirth

morally enlightened but spiritually dead, having been spiritually cut off from God, the source of love, and therefore became selfish and corrupt.

This completes our review of what has been argued so far. We can now use this as a foundation as we look at the subject of the reformation of man.

Man's need for reformation

Having become morally enlightened in the process of the fall[521], the reformation of man demands much more than simply restoring him to his former condition, as Adam and Eve were in before the fall. It was never in God's plan that should man fall by independently grasping for moral enlightenment, that God should reform him by then removing his increased moral knowledge. Rather, what we see is that in response to the fall God's plan for man has shifted into a still higher plane where man keeps this level of enlightenment, knowing good and evil in a way he never did before the fall. The plan is higher because from this enlightened position the potential for man to know God intimately is much greater, and therefore the purpose of love could be served by a radically increased opportunity for intimate fellowship with him throughout the ages.

We cannot be sure whether God could have somehow led man into this place of enlightenment sometime in the future ages had he not fallen. All we can be sure of is that for man to have true free will, he had to have a way to express it, and therefore there had to be a risk of the fall in the original creation. This is what the creation story of Genesis is about. In all of these events, God guaranteed that the purpose of love would be served, regardless of man's free choice, by having a plan in place for any of the possible eventualities.

So the question arises – What does man need to be reformed and made fit for heaven and eternity? Man needs two things:
- Love
- Faith

Love – Man must have his whole being restored to be intrinsically, eternally, and securely committed to the purposes of love in the whole of his capacity as God is in his.

---

[521] Gen 2:17, 3:5

Faith – Man must develop unshakeable faith in God that will render him invulnerable to another fall from God, in his now morally and spiritually enlightened condition, for all eternity.

Love and Faith – It is essential that man is not simply reformed in either faith or love. He must be reformed in both.

To be reformed in love without faith would leave him vulnerable to another fall somewhere in the vastness of eternity, as it did for Lucifer.

Also the demands of love on God, to choose the path of minimum suffering, means that the possibility of a second fall must be eliminated right from the start.

To be reformed in faith without love would mean admitting a corrupted being into eternity, thereby corrupting the eternal domain right from the beginning. A commitment to love is a basic essential for a moral being to have an eternal destiny, because the extension of love is the fundamental reason for God creating in the first place[522], and anything else is corruption.

Man's reformation to Love

We defined love as the commitment to the highest good of all things. The Bible says that God is Love[523]. It follows that man's commitment to love is solely derived from God. It flows from his relationship with God; from God in and through him; from his spiritual union with God. When man fell he was cut off from God. In doing so he was cut off from love. This reduced him from a commitment to God, and all that is in God, to a commitment to just himself. Though he may have continued to exist in a creation of many beings, he was reduced to self-love where, at the deepest and most fundamental level of his being, his only commitment to the highest good was to the highest good of self.

Having lost the place of love by being cut off from God, it follows that the way for man to be reformed is to regain his relationship with God, so that once again through unity with God, love should become his motivational force and purpose in life. Somehow the connection between him and God had to be remade.

---

[522] 1 John 4:12
[523] 1 John 4:16

CHAPTER 14: The Reformation of Man by Spiritual Rebirth

The death of man's spirit – Man's original connection with God was primarily through his spirit. Spirits know and relate through union. They communicate through communion; which we can think of as a community of man and God in a communication union[524]. When man was cut off from God in the fall, it was his spirit that was cut off. For a spirit to be cut off from God is death. God is life. He is the source of life. To be cut off from God is to be cut off from the source of light and life, which is death. We can therefore truly say that when man fell, his spirit died[525].

Restoration to Love – This places the original spirit of man in exactly the same position as the fallen angels who are also spirits; they are cut off from God and have become thoroughly selfish and corrupt. There is no way of redemption for fallen angels. They are eternally lost. They cannot be restored to a relationship with God. In exactly the same way the spirit of fallen man is eternally lost and beyond redemption. This is true for all men. It is not God's plan to restore man by *fixing* his dead and corrupted spirit[526]. I repeat; the fallen spirit of man is beyond redemption. God has therefore turned his attention to the soul of man, which is the only part of fallen man that can be saved and restored.

For this to happen the soul must once again be brought back into fellowship and union with God, but the problem is the soul of man had fellowship with God through his spirit; this was the purpose of his spirit. As a result the death of his spirit had thereby also severed the soul from contact with God, and his soul had become *lost*.

How is this problem resolved?

As the spirit of man is beyond repair and is dead, there is only one option left for man to be reformed and returned to fellowship with God in the purpose of love; *the spirit of man must be **replaced**[527]* so that his soul may be saved, and only in this sense – by replacement – can his spirit be saved[528].

---

[524] 1 Cor 6:17, 12:13
[525] Rom 5:12
[526] Rom 7:18 Ps 51:5
[527] Gal 2:20 Rom 6:2 Col 3:3-4
[528] 1 Cor 5:5

The soul defines the person, but the spirit defines the life that flows through that person. We therefore see that the soul is saved by finding new life – a new spirit – all familiar terms to the informed Christian.

We will explore this further, but beyond this there is a second demand; that man must also be reformed by the development of faith that will always serve to prevent another fall from ever happening.

Man's reformation of Faith

God's answer to establishing invulnerability to another fall in all of eternity is that all his free-willed creatures should have developed faith in him. This faith will always serve to protect them against another fall, and will therefore guarantee the security of God's creation in love for all of eternity to come. This faith must take a number of forms which we can briefly reiterate as:

- Faith in the love of God.
- Faith in the horrors of evil and separation from God.
- Faith in the justice of God.
- Faith in the mercy of God.
- Faith in man's total dependence on God.
- Faith in the omnipotence of God.
- Faith in the omniscience of God.
- Faith in the selfless humility of God.

Observation – In God's eternal scheme, much of this essential faith is developed through observing and understanding the events of this pre-age of history. By far the greatest and most central event of all this is the cross of Christ, and that is the very cornerstone of faith. Beyond this, all the events we witness of God's dealings in this evil age serve to develop in us the faith we need to provide the eternal security God intends for us for all the ages to come.

Eternal Testimony – Faith in eternity has not been limited to observations from a memory of a bygone age. God has placed the full evidence of the sufferings of the cross at the focal centre of all eternity in his own being in the form of the Lamb that was slain[529]. This awesome

CHAPTER 14: The Reformation of Man by Spiritual Rebirth

view of God in heaven, together with the eternal testimony of those that experienced this age, will always serve to secure the faith of all beings in eternity.

Participation of Faith – An old Chinese proverb says: '*I hear I forget, I see I remember, I do I understand*'. So important is the development of faith in this age, that God has not left it to either observation of his dealings, or the eternal testimony alone. He has gone further by fully utilising this age to bring us into the participation and exercise of faith. Every man that has an eternal destiny has an appointed and completely individual pre-season experience in this age, designed above all to develop faith in them that will be utterly and completely unshakeable in all of the eternity of ages to come[530]. As the constitution of every person is unique, so the circumstances and challenges that have been crafted by God for them are totally unique, and designed down to the fine detail[531]. None of this overrules free-will, which would be self-defeating. Instead God works with our free-will to develop the faith that will ultimately be the thing that defines and controls the way we live.

It is not always appreciated that the implications of the combined teachings of the apostle Paul, and the apostle James, on faith, are that faith and behaviour are tightly coupled; they cannot be separated[532]. One is the unavoidable expression of the other. Provided the heart is renewed in the purpose of love, faith is all that is required to align the behaviour with the same purpose. This confirms that the development of faith is the primary issue of this age to prevent a further fall into sin in all eternity.

The way God has configured things, in order to bring redeemed men into the participation of faith, is profound. It will therefore form a major topic as we continue to explore these truths.

Man's reformation of love by faith

Given that man must be reformed by both returning to a total commitment to love, and by the development of faith, in order to have an eternal destiny; we now find that God's plan for the reformation of man has keyed

---

[529] Rev 5:6,13
[530] 1 Cor 13:13,3:12 Re 2:21 1 Pe 1:7 Ja 2:5 Ep 6:6 1 Tim 6:12 2 Tim 4:7 1 Jn 5:4
[531] Acts 17:26 Rom 8:28 1 Cor 10:13 1 Pet 1:6,5:10
[532] Rom 4:4-5 Jam 2:24

these two things together so that man can only be reformed back to a nature and spirit of love by the action of faith[533]. Faith and love have therefore become inseparable, so that any man that is reformed in love, must have also found faith. It follows that no man can find reformation in love without also finding the essential faith that allows him into a secure eternal future.

What we will come to see is that the reformation of the whole being of man to love, is at one level instantaneous and absolute, and at another level progressive. To be more specific, the spirit of man is replaced absolutely and instantaneously on rebirth, but it is the mind and soul of a man that is subsequently only changed progressively[534]. What we will see is that the development of faith is the key factor in this. Not only is faith instrumental in the initial instantaneous change of the spirit of the man – his rebirth – but it is also instrumental in the progressive changes to the mind and soul thereafter through his daily application and appropriation of faith.

Two kinds of faith

It is sometimes said that fear is the opposite of faith. This is only true in the sense that fear is the result of the absence of faith. However we should be clear that when we speak of faith, unless otherwise stated, we are referring to faith in God. The truth is there is more than one kind of faith in the world, and with this in view the real opposite of faith in God is in fact faith in self – or self-belief. By faith in self we mean; faith that is independent of God and that believes in its own self sufficiency without the need for God's help or supply. Fear therefore becomes the middle ground between faith in God, and faith in self, where faith is absent, and there is nothing for the man to cling to or trust.

Faith in self is an expression of independence of God, and is the fundamental state of the fallen sinful condition[535]. Having been cut off from God, the being is plunged into selfishness, which means it puts itself first, but also means it seeks to be self-dependent and self-sustaining in all things[536]. When both Satan and Adam fell, they both did so as a step from

---

[533] Eph 3:17
[534] 2 Co 5:17 Rom 12:2
[535] Gen 3:5
[536] Rom 5:12

CHAPTER 14: The Reformation of Man by Spiritual Rebirth

total dependence on God, to a place of independence of God. Satan sought to become 'as the Most High'[537]. He then tempted Eve with the offer that she could become like God. Independence is the fundamental corruption of the fallen condition, and as such must be reversed in the process of reformation. By contrast faith in God is an expression of total dependence on God, and is therefore the reverse step away from faith in self, and back to faith in God[538].

Transitions of faith

As we have said: fear is the absence of faith. It is therefore the middle ground between faith in God, and faith in self. It is the place where one is not able to believe or trust in anything. It is therefore a very insecure place to be. In both the initial and the progressive parts of the process of reform, God leads man to take steps from self-dependence, to dependence on him in numerous areas of his life. As such, in each case, he often passes through the place of fear and anxiety where faith in self is lost, and faith in God is not yet fully established. When in such a transition, man is like a child trying to cross a stream with only a hand offered from the other side to hold on to and guide him.

Faith in God is first established in the initial step into spiritual rebirth. It then progressively expands into every needed area of trust in God where man has fallen into self-dependence. God's ongoing methods in dealing with man must therefore have a double edge. On the one hand they must challenge the man's faith in himself, and on the other hand they must offer him the alternative of faith in God for each aspect of his life. The transition is always difficult for the man. It feels precarious, and seems fraught with anxiety and danger, but God provides all the assistance needed[539] for these steps to be taken.

Failure – For a man to take the step of laying down his faith in self in any given area of his life, it is often necessary for him to come to a point of recognising failure in that area in his trying to achieve things, or improve himself, by using his own independent resources. God therefore sets him up to test the truth of his perceived independence – his faith in himself. In

---

[537] Isaiah 14:14
[538] John 14:1
[539] 2 Cor 1:9 1 Cor 10:13

each of these areas of failure that the Holy Spirit reveals to him, God offers him the alternative which always comes in the form of some new application of faith in God. The process of maturing in faith is therefore often difficult, because in each area of reform the truth of the man's condition of self-belief must be revealed and exposed to him, in order to motivate him to abandon it, and to then seek and receive the alternative answer of faith in God that God is offering[540].

The function of law

We are now able to understand the function of law, as the apostle Paul so brilliantly expressed it. The law holds out a noble standard, but in itself provides no means by which one may attain to it[541]. On encountering the law, and recognising the nobility of its standard, many have assumed that all that was required for them to secure an eternal future was to keep it. This is the fundamental concept of most religions, and for many the fundamental misconception of the Christian religion. True Christian teaching actually presents something very different.

The reality is that the law is designed to lead us into a head on collision with the truth about the fundamental corruption of our own nature in the form of failure to keep it[542].

We see this depicted in the story of Moses, who represents the law. First in the way he received the law; written by the finger of God on tablets of stone. As he came down the mountain with them he found the Israelites in the middle of an orgy and worshipping false gods. At this he threw the tablets down and broke them; demonstrating the fact that no sooner than the law is given, it is broken. He then went about remaking the tablets, but this time by chiselling them out manually, by hand. This depicts the way that having broken the law, man then sets about trying to fulfil it, and reform himself, by his own effort[543].

We then see another similar parallel in the failure of Moses to enter the Promised Land, despite twice coming to the point of entry. In each case he failed through the disobedience of himself or the people; the inevitable result of law without faith[544].

---

[540] Gal 3:24 Heb 4:2 Rom 10:3 Gal 3:11
[541] Gal 2:16 Gal 3:10 1 Tim 1:9
[542] Gal 2:16
[543] Ex 31:18, 32:16,19 34:1,4

Instead, entry to the Promised Land was accomplished through Joshua, who is the namesake and representation of Jesus; who is 'the Way'. The Promised Land depicts the life in the Spirit where the Israelites lived on the fruit of the land, rather than depending on the daily provision of God in the trials of a desert, which parallels a life under the law, as described in Romans chapter 7[545]. It is only a life lived in the Spirit that can bear spiritual fruit,[546] rather than the arid and difficult life under the rule of law. Though God sustains us through the experience of the desert of the law, his plan and purpose is to lead us into the fruitfulness of the life of the Spirit.

It is at this point that the path forks into either life by the Spirit, or life under the law. One path leads to real nobility, and the other to ignobility[547].

The first path starts with honesty and humility, where one faces up to the failure, and allows the law to exact its penalty of condemnation. But then this road leads us on to seek another answer which is ultimately found in faith in Christ, based on grace, through the fundamental inner transformation of rebirth, then on to life in the Spirit[548]. This is the true path to nobility.

The other path is one of hypocrisy where one denies the failure and seeks to cover it up, both to oneself and before men[549]. This path is fundamentally dishonest, and leads to total ignobility of character that in the end cannot be denied because its 'fruit' eventually makes it all too obvious[550].

The teacher of the law – A teacher of the law approached Jesus and asked him an honest question about the law regarding which is the greatest commandment. Jesus gave him an answer that he recognised to be scripture and truth – to love God with all of ones being, and to love ones neighbour as oneself. In honesty and humility the teacher of the law

---

[544] Num 14, 14:30 Deaut 3:21-26
[545] Rom 7:7-25
[546] John 15:5
[547] 2 Tim 2:20 1 Tim 1:9
[548] Rom 3:22-24
[549] John 3:20
[550] Luke 6:44

accepted and acknowledged the answer. In response Jesus said he was '*not far from the kingdom of God*'. So what is clear is that this man was close, but not yet in[551].

What did Jesus mean by '*not far*'? What did he still have to do to complete the journey? The teacher of the law would have assumed that what Jesus meant was, he now had to go away and obey these laws; however it is not quite so simple. There were in fact still two or three steps this man had to take to find his way to heaven. The first may have been to try to keep the law. The second would be to admit his failure to accomplish it. The third would be to seek another answer, and put his faith in Jesus that he would receive salvation as an undeserved gift – by grace[552].

He was close to heaven because he was on the path of honesty and humility. He had shown some humility already by both coming to Jesus, and by asking him to answer an important question. He therefore acknowledged he did not have all the answers. What Jesus was saying was that if this man continued on this path of honesty and humility, then when it came to the critical point of realising that he was not going to make it on his own merit by keeping the law, then the same honesty would lead him to admit it, and the same humility would sooner or later lead him to come back and accept the answer as undeserved favour by grace alone[553]. It was not the fact that he was successfully obeying the law that meant he was not far from the kingdom of God, as Jesus said, but the fact that he was ready to be honest and humble in the way he would need to be to take the remaining steps.

Jesus said that all must come to God as a little child[554]; in total dependence on their father. The problem is not getting people to obey the law; their condition is sinful so they can't possibly do it. The problem is getting them to lay down their self-belief and independence to become totally dependent on God. It is the reverse of the step man took at the fall. This surrender is itself salvation, and the receiving of a heavenly heart[555].

---

[551] Mark 12:28-34, 34
[552] Eph 2:8-9
[553] John 1;17 Rom 3:24, 4:16 Eph 2:8 2 Tim 1;9 Jam 4:6
[554] Mat 18:2
[555] 2 Cor 4:6 Gal 4:6 Eph 1:18 Col 3:1 1 Pet 1:19

The true place of faith is a place of total dependence on God. If this is achieved, then for this individual the kingdom of heaven has come.

The law and self-dependence – We therefore see that the true purpose of the law is to challenge the root problem of the self-dependence of man, leading him through honesty and humility to lay his independence aside, and move into total dependence on God. This is a move from self-sufficiency, and therefore faith in self, to a place of faith in God based entirely on grace – undeserved favour. Such a change is not possible for the fallen spirit of man to make. As we have said: the fallen spirit of man is entirely cut off from God, and has become corrupt and beyond redemption. It is proudly self-sufficient and cannot change. The only possible way for the man to move to this place of total dependence on God, is to have this broken part of his being – his spirit, replaced. He must be reborn by exchanging his broken spirit for one that is completely new.

Grace – We begin to see now how grace works. Man's problem is independence of God, whereas receiving the undeserved favour of grace is a supreme expression of dependence on God. By God offering man salvation by grace alone, man has to step into the essential place of dependence on God, which is the fundamental step of reform from independence to dependence that is impossible through any means but by spiritual rebirth, which in turn can only come through receiving faith.

Breaking the union of man with his fallen spirit

The bond between the physical body and the soul is strong. It is only broken by the death of the body, sometimes only after prolonged and extreme suffering.

The bond between the soul and the spirit is even stronger. It requires an act of God in the form of the sharp double edged sword of the word of God to separate them[556]. The inner man of soul-spirit must be broken and remade. To break the bond the soul must agree to it being split from the corrupt spirit. It must ask for God to release it from the union, and it must reject the old corrupted spirit as a decision of the will. It must then go on and receive the new union that God offers to it. All these

---

[556] Heb 4:12

elements are accomplished in a single action, and they are all present in the sinner's prayer[557].

The sinner's prayer – Another name for the corrupted spirit is the noun 'Sin'[558]. When a fallen man (a sinner) prays a prayer of repentance for their Sin, this is the act of rejection of the old spirit that is required. By repentance he turns away from his Sin, and the powerful word of God performs the incision that separates his soul from his fallen spirit. The invitation for God to come in then brings the replacement of God's Spirit within to form a new union with the soul.

At the invitation of God, the man has exercised the authority of free will that he has over his own being for this to happen. It is God that does the creative work, implementing the separation, and forming the new union.

Unsurprisingly the soul of man is often profoundly impacted by the event in all areas of mind, will, and emotion. It is amazing to see the difference this act of surrender makes. Suddenly the spiritual light comes on, and often something in the radiance of the demeanour somehow changes. For some it may seem like a gradual process, but there is always a point in that process where a line is crossed, and rebirth occurs.

I have shared my personal experience of the point of my own enlightenment, and I have seen it in many others. I have seen inquirers on Alpha courses go home one week in their darkened, spiritually unenlightened condition, and arrive at the next meeting with their spiritual lights clearly on and bright. I have seen the same with members of my own family. Between meetings they had done business with God, and were spiritually reborn and regenerated. These are real events – no mistake.

The union of the new man – When the fallen spirit is replaced the soul becomes united to the spirit of Christ in a new union. This new union of the soul and the Spirit of Christ forms a whole new man. The scriptures are emphatic on this; that at the point that this new union is made the man is regenerated such that he is a whole new creation; the old has gone and the new has come[559].

---

[557] Eph 2:14-16
[558] Rom 7:17,20

What happens to the old spirit? – There is a simple answer to this. The old corrupted spirit of man is nailed to the cross in Christ. Another name for the old spirit is the noun 'Sin'. This is not referring to 'sins' meaning the wrong things we have done, but it refers to a thing, a noun – Sin, as it is used in the book of Romans from verse 5:18[560] onwards. It refers to the old corrupted, self-dependent spirit. When Christ died on the cross he took our old corrupted spirit down with him, and gave to us his perfect Holy Spirit in its place.

This is a spiritual event that, as with the cross, is an event that exists outside of the limitation of time and space in the physical world[561]. As such our understanding of it is a little abstract, but given what we discussed earlier; that Christ died from the foundation of the world[562], the scriptures can also say that the salvation of grace was given to us from before the beginning of time, but only revealed in time when Christ died on the cross[563]. Equally for us, the personal event itself may not have appeared in time until the point at which we repented and accepted Christ as our saviour, but referring back to the tapestry of time; we can see this does not restrict the fact that, in terms of the spiritual domain, this event was set in place by God right from the beginning of creation. We therefore came into it as a discovery of our God predestined destiny.

The place of the cross of Christ in rebirth

We are now able to see that at the cross of Christ a transaction took place, and that this is true on an individual level for every believer that has experienced rebirth. What happened was an exchange. God led the man to a place where his inner corruption was revealed. Having seen his perilous condition, and seen the offer of forgiveness, he takes a step from sinful independence into total dependence on God as an initial act of faith in a gift of totally unmerited and undeserved grace.

The fact that it is a step into something that is completely unmerited in any way is vitally important, because it is this that makes it a

---

[559] 2 Cor 5:17
[560] See: *The Normal Christian Life* – Watchman Nee
[561] 2 Tim 1:9 Matt 25:34 Eph 1:4 Rev 17:8
[562] Rev 13:8 1 Pet 1:19-21
[563] 2 Tim 1:9-10

step into dependence. Any step that tried to claim salvation on its own merit would be a step of independence, and as such would be an expression of the old independent sinful nature, not the new spirit of Christ which is totally surrendered and dependent on God in everything.

The step is nothing less than a rejection of the old spirit by the soul, breaking the union between them, and the acceptance of the spirit of Christ in its place to form a new union. This is rebirth, and after the event the old corrupted spirit is no longer part of the man's being, but is now *external* to his being, having been expelled from the union it previously had with the soul.

In real spiritual terms, the old nature is taken to the cross and nailed there as the means by which the exchange is made. The corrupt spirit was therefore taken down to death with Christ as he died on the cross. This is an eternal spiritual reality, as viewed from the eternal perspective, as we recall from the illustration of the tapestry of this age. However as we discussed: in the tapestry those things that happen on the eternal level have their counterpart in the events of time. Just as Christ dying on the cross was put in place before anything else, yet it only appeared in time towards the end of the age[564]; so the fact of the death of our old nature on the cross was finished from the foundation of the world in the same way, but still has its outworking in time[565].

This outworking takes the form of first the instantaneous rebirth by faith, and then the progressive defeat of the old nature by faith, together. From the eternal perspective we can see this as a complete and finished work. However from the perspective of time and the unfolding age; these realities only come into full view as the progressive work reaches completion. The actual unfolding therefore includes the initial experience of rebirth, followed by the battles of faith, and every decision of free will that overcomes every aspect of the sinful nature[566].

The eternal is always a little abstract to us, but these two views are actually perfectly compatible; the eternally complete work, and their temporal accomplishment in time.

---

[564] 1 Pet 1:20
[565] Rev 13:8
[566] Rom 8:13 Col 3;5

CHAPTER 14: The Reformation of Man by Spiritual Rebirth

Summary

To summarise our discussion of the reformation of man; we have seen that the fundamental problem of man is his independence of God. The process of reformation is therefore a journey back into total dependence, beginning with initial spiritual rebirth, and followed by a progressive work which we have yet to discuss.

Rebirth was implemented as an exchange of the old corrupt spirit of man, for the spirit of Christ at the centre of the being of the man. This was made possible as an act of God by the man coming into total dependence on God, by faith based entirely on grace. The old spirit was expelled, and in the eternal perspective; nailed to the cross in death with Christ, right from the beginning of time. But this must still be outworked in time by both the initial rebirth, and by the progressive outworking over time, together.

We will go on from this to seek to understand the fallen condition of man, and then the process of the progressive reform of man. But first, having said that spiritual rebirth is the fundamental beginning and foundation of such reform, we will first take a look at the history of this experience in the human race.

CHAPTER 15: The History of Spiritual Rebirth and Religion

The history of spiritual re-birth

There is a common view among Christians that spiritual rebirth only began after Christ came, ascended, and sent his spirit to us. However this is an error.

It is true that Jesus was the first to use the term '*born again*', as seen in that most remarkable chapter of John 3, where Jesus speaks with the Pharisee Nicodemus that came to him by night for fear of his fellow member of his sect, knowing that some would not approve.

Nicodemus came with the most fundamental and basic burning question on his mind: *How may a man be sure to see the kingdom of God? – Heaven*. Though he didn't get chance to even ask the question because Jesus anticipated him, cutting in on his initial gratuities by going straight to the point and answering his question.

Nicodemus was astonished at the answer: *you must be born again*, and he began to ask for clarification. At this point Jesus chided him for aspiring to be a teacher of Israel and yet knowing nothing of this truth. In this one scripture we have proof positive that spiritual rebirth was a reality in the world well before Jesus arrived to reveal it. Otherwise how could Jesus expect Nicodemus to know anything of it if it were a new or immanent phenomenon?

There are many other scriptures that show this to be true, though it had not been openly revealed in such explicit terms. David often spoke of the salvation of God. So did Isaiah. And Job declared his faith, that '*I know my redeemer lives and in the end he will stand upon the earth*'[567], even without the benefit of the scriptures, or God's revelations to the patriarchs and Israel. Both the apostle Paul, and the writer of Hebrews (probably Barnabas) show that the error of the Jews before Christ was that they failed to combine the message of salvation and their pursuit of righteousness, with the essential element of faith[568], and therefore failed to

---

[567] Job 19:25

achieve the righteousness they claimed by their own efforts. Then there is the whole chapter of Hebrews 11 listing those before Christ that were famed by their exploits and endurance that was inspired by their faith, and that gave them a vision beyond this world in anticipation of heaven[569].

Salvation by faith has always been available to men, and prior to Christ it was already a revealed truth in some measure. We see that 2000 years before Christ came, Abraham's faith was *'credited to him as righteousness'*[570]. We also see Old Testament teaching revealing that there was a need for a reformed heart and a *'new spirit'*[571]. Rebirth was an age old reality well before Christ, but the revelation of its truth over the centuries has been gradual, culminating very fittingly in the revelations of the saviour/redeemer himself who the scriptures had long declared would be the one who would reveal ancient mysteries[572].

Despite Job's righteousness that even God acclaimed in him, he knew his need of a redeemer. In fact it was precisely this knowledge/faith that was the basis of his righteousness. Similarly Abraham prophetically proclaimed his faith in his answer to the question of his son Isaac with the answer *'God himself will provide a lamb'*[573], immediately before he, in obedience, prophetically enacted the very event that would 2000 years later secure God's salvation for men for all ages, and he probably did it on the very same mountain on which it ultimately happened for real.

However there are some key differences from the era before Christ came, to the era after his incarnation and mission on earth as a man. First of all, those before Christ had to look forward to God's salvation by faith, not knowing the full details of what to expect, whereas we, together with all those that came after Christ, are able to look back to it as historical fact.

Some Christians would cite the scriptures that declare that there is salvation in no other name under heaven[574], and that it is only those that confess the name of Christ that are saved[575]. However such a confession

---

[568] Rom 9:30-32 Heb 4:2
[569] Heb 11:14-16
[570] Gen 15:6 Rom 4, 4:3
[571] Ez 11:19
[572] Is 46:10
[573] Gen 22:8
[574] Acts 4:12
[575] Rom 10:9-10 Matt 10:32,33

CHAPTER 15: The History of Spiritual Rebirth and Religion

does not need to know either the details of the means, or the specific name of the one that would bring it. Job's confession of faith: that his redeemer would come, was precisely such a confession of faith in his name, even though the actual name or the details of the means had not yet been fully revealed to him. This faith had the same effect on them as it does for us now; they experienced the miracle of spiritual rebirth.

In many ways it took greater faith and spiritual insight to trust God for redemption in the absence of such information, than it now takes for those that hear the full message of the gospel, complete with its historical facts.

What should be remembered is that the cross is an eternal phenomenon, and it was eternally set in place from the very beginning at the very foundation of the cosmos[576]; remember the tapestry of time. As such it has served men from all races and all ages.

Other times, places, peoples, eras and religions

This puts us in a position to understand the many people of other times, peoples, eras, and religions. The way of salvation is, and always has been, the way of faith by grace alone. This way has been open for all men to find, though in times past it came to men primarily through their personal walk and interaction with their creator in this world.

This is not a message of 'all religions lead to heaven'; far from it. The way to salvation is the way of finding faith in God that he will make a way apart from any merit or desert. The religions of the world have served this purpose but only indirectly; by leading men to discover their inability to achieve goodness for themselves, and by their failure to fulfil its demands. All religions have led men to this conclusion, or to hypocrisy.

To those that were humble and honest enough to acknowledge their failure, the way to faith by grace then opened up for them. Their failure would leave them with no other choice than to look to God for help; for a redeemer.

For others it led to hypocrisy, and thereby to corruption, where they chose to conceal and deny their failure, becoming deceitful and corrupt in the process. One path led to faith, and by it to spiritual rebirth. The other led to death and destruction.

---

[576] Rev 13:8 2 Tim 1:9

In contrast therefore to the message of 'all religions lead to God', we see the truth that in fact 'no religions lead to God', not even the Christian 'religion', except indirectly by their inevitable failure to produce good character. Many who take the path of religion discover this truth and come through to this conclusion, at which point they receive new revelation and their faith shifts from their religion, which depends on themselves, to grace that depends entirely on God.

In our day we are able to preach the explicit message and revelation of Christ, and the means by which God has made salvation possible; by grace through faith. However, not all are willing to hear it, but only those that recognise and receive it, and in doing so prove they are those that, in the eternal scheme of things, belong to God[577]. Many that are already aware of their need are able to receive it directly. For others they remain deaf to the true message until they first get to the end of themselves, often through following the path of religion.

This leads us to an understanding of the words of Jesus: *'For wide is the gate and broad is the way that leads to destruction, and many enter by it. But small is the gate and narrow the road that leads to life, and only a few find it'*[578]. The broad road is not just that of unrepentant sin, but also that of the religions of men, which is borne out entirely by Jesus's words and reactions to the religious leaders of his day. Both the path of sin, and the path of religion, are designed to lead men to the same repentance and surrender to God's grace by faith, which is the narrow Way.

The message of faith in God's grace is not a new message, but it is how it has been from ancient times, though it has not always been explicitly preached. It is ignorance to assume that throughout all time and the history of religion in the world, that God has not been active, and that there has been no revelation of truth to men is those eras. God has always reached out to all men on these very same terms. Consider the wise men of the east that attended the birth of Jesus.

C. S. Lewis was a genius, gaining a triple first and professorship at Oxford. His mind and memory were so acute that if someone opened and began to read from any book he had ever read, and stopped at any point,

---

[577] John 8:20,42-44, 10:4,27, 14:7
[578] Matt 7:13-14

CHAPTER 15: The History of Spiritual Rebirth and Religion

he could pick up the thread and recite from memory what followed. He was widely read on history and anthropology, both ancient and modern.

As an atheist in his earlier years, he was challenged by his friend and contemporary J. R. R. Tolkien and others at Oxford to accept that throughout the ages there was a common thread and theme in all of the ancient religions and writings of the past; *that of God becoming man*. He was then challenged to acknowledge that in one unmistakable case in history this story had become fact, and was not fiction. A man came and proved his power over nature, evil, sickness, and death, which covers all that is created in every possible way, and he came with a message more profound than all the philosophers of the ages before or since. In response to this Lewis had two choices: to deny the facts and bury the truth in defiance, or acknowledge it. As a result he described himself as the most reluctant convert in all of England[579].

From his wide knowledge of history and religion, C. S. Lewis was able to go on to write that the one message in all of this that differs from the rest, is the message of grace. Even some of the religious philosophers, like Buddha, declared that there was another yet to come. In this way some even contained acknowledgements of their own inadequacy, and looked forward by faith to something greater to come.

All religions do not lead to God; certainly not directly. But indirectly they lead to failure, and then to faith, and this is the well-worn path of this age to salvation that numerous men have found and trodden from every tribe, language, people, culture, race, and religion. They may not have had the revelation of the New Testament, but the essentials for rebirth were, and always have been, available.

This is not just true for the ancients, but also true for those of different religions and cultures of our day that have not been accessed by the full message of the gospel. Salvation comes through Christ alone, regardless of the specific revelation people have of the means by which God secured it for them.

It is remarkable that often even Christians that have the revelation of these New Testament truths, still have to walk the same path. The errors of legalism have arisen in many churches throughout the centuries since Christ came, both early and modern, and this shows that many follow the

---

[579] Surprised by Joy – by C.S. Lewis

same path in our day as they see the Christian walk in terms of rules, merit, and man's independent effort to reach God – religion. As a result the institutional church has often descended to become nothing more than another religion, and its history in these times has been far from pretty. Even in places where the truth of grace is explicitly taught, the same is often true for many individuals in it. Each person has to have their own personal God given revelation of the truth of grace and faith, and of their need of it, if they are to find the Way[580] of salvation by grace through faith, and spiritual rebirth.

Even more ironic is the fact that there are many since Christ came and in our day that have had the intellectual revelation of these truths, and given intellectual ascent to them, but then assumed that they have thereby found their way to it, yet in reality they have never really come into the place and experience of faith based on underserved grace[581].

If we reflect on all this we may begin to ask: then what did Christ bring that did not exist before? What has changed? And, what is the advantage of living in such enlightened times?

What did Christ bring?

Clearly Jesus did bring new revelation, and there is a great deal of advantage in that to those who also receive spiritual revelation of the truth of rebirth, and find their way to faith through it. However the ancient scriptures, and those that heralded the coming of Christ, foretold of much greater things than just further revelation of truth. We are told that this new era would be marked by the coming of the Spirit of God in unprecedented ways, reaching all people in all walks of life.

John the Baptist declared that he baptised with water, but that Jesus, the Messiah, would baptise with the fire of the Holy Spirit and with power. What was formerly a selective experience of men known to prophets, priests, and kings, would become the gift and experience of all – sons and daughters, young and old – as foretold by the prophet Joel, and confirmed by Peter when it first came[582]. With this deluge there would be given powerful gifts and enabling[583] that would make it possible for

---

[580] John 14:6
[581] John 5:39
[582] Joel 2:28 Acts 2:17

CHAPTER 15: The History of Spiritual Rebirth and Religion

everyone that received it to mutually build up the faith of his brethren[584], and to overcome evil[585] as they shared and moved under the guidance and power of God's Spirit upon them.

As a result we can be found most Saturdays in the market place of my home town of Nottingham bringing God's power of healing and the gospel to those we meet on the street. Before my eyes I have watched bones grow. Finger knuckles that had been sawn through and destroyed by a circular saw, I have seen straighten up, then the knuckle grow back complete with guiders and blood flow, and the grip return. There are constant stories of healings: diabetes, heart failure, ulcers, nervous conditions, and numerous more, and we are delighted when God allows us to show compassion to people who are suffering. We particularly delight in the creative miracles where even solid bone is created because this is something that the counterfeits are unable to emulate.

Beyond this there are even greater gifts of prophesy, and other words that come directly from God that are designed to build up the church and bring it to maturity. All of this is God's power in action, designed to have an eternal impact and outcome.

In this day and age of internet media, I can point atheists and sceptics to view the records of miracles actually happening, and the testimonies that follow with undeniable authenticity. However it is amazing that despite all of this, some of these people often still choose to cling blindly to their faith in atheism, preferring there not to be a God despite such undeniable evidence and testimony. It is remarkable that when we take the scientific approach and offer them the physical evidence they ask for, they often continue to cling to their faith, preferring to believe it to be 'the power of the mind', or some such inexplicable phenomena, despite the testimony of those that administer it that can tell them where the power came from.

Nevertheless the miracles are a sign that points towards Christ, but this frequent unreasonable reluctance to surrender to God only serves to confirm that the only way to God is by direct revelation from him to each individual, and by the honesty and humility that should follow. I am glad to say that amid all this plethora of power in action, there are many that do

---

[583] Eph 4:8 Ps 68:18 1 Cor 12 Acts 2
[584] Eph 4:11-13 1 Thes 5:11
[585] Luke 10:9

find their way to faith and the miracle of spiritual rebirth that comes with it.

Increasing revelation of salvation

Over millennia the revelation of destiny and opportunity beyond this world has been increasing. In a number of instances there has been a step change; as there was when Christ came with his teaching and gift of the Holy Spirit; and prior to that as there was after the flood.

The flood was the first experience of God's judgement since the fall of man. In the 'antediluvian' era (pre-flood) the principle of law had not yet been introduced, and men were left to live their lives without any restraint. At that time their longevity meant that though death was known to be the destiny of all, yet it was rarely encountered in life. Adam, the first man, lived for 930 years to see the ninth generation, and saw the father of Noah – Lamech, with an overlap of 50 years before he died. Adam therefore got to see the full effect of his mistake; what a horror that must have been for him. Many in that era would have trodden the path to his door to hear the message of how he had fallen into sin, dragging the whole race with him.

At that time no-one had any revelation of what came beyond death. There was no concept of human government to systematically enforce the rights of others, and nothing like the flood had ever happened, so the restraint derived from the concept of possible judgement did not come into their thinking. The result was that within a millennium of the fall of the race of men, they almost universally descended into complete godlessness, selfishness, and evil, and through this the effects of the fall of man was seen in its full horror. The earth became a violent place, and murder was a common occurrence, with no repercussions other than the feudal vengeance of tribalism. Men planted, built, and married, and were consumed with their selfish ends without reference to God or others, other than for their own ends[586].

In the end God sent the judgement of the flood both to wipe the earth clean of the corrupt race of men, and to commence a new era where judgment and the principle of law and retribution for sin became the new order of the day.

---

[586] Gen 6:5, 23:24 Luke 17:26-27

CHAPTER 15: The History of Spiritual Rebirth and Religion

This pre-flood age of unrestrained evil was part of the plan of God to allow the effects of evil to be fully exposed in one era of men before beginning to introduce the measures of law, through which they may ultimately be reformed and find salvation, albeit through the experience of exposure of their sinful condition and failure that led to faith based on grace. The testimony of that age is therefore a vital part of the learning and faith building experience in this age that will underpin the security of all ages to come beyond this world and into eternity.

For this reason we now know, by revelation of God through the scriptures, that when Christ died and remained 'beneath the earth' for three days and three nights, he was in fact launched into a mission beyond the grave to the gloomy underworld of Sheol (prison/dungeon) where he reached out to some of those that had lived in that era[587]. It is probably the fact that this era of men was so unenlightened that made this mission possible, but we can assume that by this action, and the work of the cross, God was even able to save a remnant of them from that era, that were being held for judgement, and lead them to salvation by faith and spiritual rebirth, as he has for men of all eras.

If this is so, then what a story these ones will have to tell in heaven and the eternity of ages to come. Through them the full testimony of that era of this evil age, and the power of God and the cross to even reach them, will be carried forward into eternity to secure the purpose of love forever after.

This idea of a rescue mission to the underworld might sound very familiar, even fictional. But the reason for that is that these ancient writings are in fact the source material of many fictional works that have been repeatedly presented in both ancient and modern art and literature. As such these works often have the sanction and approval of the Holy Spirit upon them as presentations based on truth. They therefore have a quality of incarnational reality to them[588].

---

[587] 1 Peter 3:18-20
[588] John 14:6

Sacrifice

This leads us to an understanding of the function and purpose of the practice of sacrifice that has seemed to pervade all cultures from the flood to the coming of Christ.

Before Christ the practice of sacrifice was used as an aid to look forward by faith to the redeemer, and what was yet to come in the sacrifice of the cross for the sins of all men. As such sacrifice was never meant to be pretty. Within its practice were all the elements needed to express faith. These were:

(a) That man is a sinner and needs redemption.
(b) That redemption would be at great cost – death.
(c) Faith that God would provide the answer.
(d) That it would be provided as a substitute for man's sin.

These elements are identical to the necessities of saving faith that we recognise today: recognition of sin; repentance; faith based on grace, and through them men were reborn, even before Christ when they didn't know the details and specifics of how it would be accomplished.

Before Christ the practice of animal sacrifice had the sanction and approval of God, and it was therefore practiced by all men of true righteousness – that is the righteous of faith. It was therefore the nations that fell into wickedness that ceased to practice it, with these nations often descending in feudalism and tribalism that led to violence and murder. Often in these cases sacrifice continued, but became a religious ritual that was often abused and corrupted, even to the point where some cultures began to try to use it to manipulate the 'gods', even turning to human sacrifice; a practice which God never required, and which was heinous to him[589]. In effect these practices reversed the very message of sacrifice: that God would provide a substitute. Instead it turned judgement back on the head of man.

Once Christ came, the practice of sacrifice became obsolete; as the OT scriptures had foretold[590], because the reality that it foreshadowed had been revealed and accomplished. Therefore to persist with sacrifice after

---

[589] Jer 7:31
[590] Is 66:3

the cross was revealed would be to fail to recognise the cross as God's provision for redemption, and would therefore be to turn back to the shadow and away from the reality, which would be a rejection of God and his provision to man.

Faith is spiritual sight, and it is only made possible through spiritual rebirth. Men that found such faith were fully expected to hear and recognise the voice and message of God when they heard it[591]. The value of sacrifice, as used before Christ, became known and understood by the revelation of faith in this way to the men of that era. So also was the fact of its fulfilment in Christ when he came[592]. Sacrifice therefore becomes obsolete to all true men of faith when they discover the message of the cross. Sacrifice should only therefore persist with those in our day that have not yet been accessed and enlightened by the message of the gospel, but when they have it then it should naturally become obsolete.

From our Christian culture, a modern view of sacrifice is that it was a primitive practice from men in more ignorant and degenerate times. However, in our present day, though these days are greater in terms of God's work through his Spirit within, yet the basic need of spiritual renewal has been recognised and fulfilled in many throughout the age.

In the same way that we may, from our current perspective, look at sacrifice as a primitive practice, so those of that day would look at the practice of drinking blood as heinous. Or even the symbolisation of it would have been enough to make them look on us as primitives. In their day they always drained the blood as part of the revealed demand when they sacrificed. To imbibe blood was unacceptable. It is only the fact that the revelation has changed, and that this now symbolises a new reality – of the Spirit of Christ within – that makes this practice acceptable in our day, with the sanction and approval of God upon it. But in that day it was unacceptable because this reality was not for them, and was only foreshadowed in their eras.

We have no record of sacrifice before the flood. The first mention of it comes from Noah after the ark landed[593]. Fittingly, at the same time, the natural fear of man came upon all animals.

---

[591] John 8:47
[592] John 5:36-38
[593] Gen 8:20

In the days before the flood not even the practice of sacrifice had been revealed. They therefore had no vision beyond death, and they became an age where the fallen nature of man was seen for all it is, as we have already discussed. However, even in those days Noah and his family found salvation by faith, with Noah becoming a preacher of righteousness[594], showing that even then men were not devoid of God's help, should they desire and seek it.

This leads us back to the main track of our discussion: the progressive process of the reform of man that follows spiritual rebirth, but first we should seek to understand something of the fallen condition of man.

---

[594] Heb 11:7 2 Pet 2:5

CHAPTER 16: The Fallen Condition of Man

A foundation for studying progressive reform

Having studied rebirth we are approaching a more complex part of our study, which is the question of firstly: Why should ongoing sin continue to be a problem when man's being has been completely spiritually restored with a replaced spirit? Secondly we will come to discuss how this problem of ongoing sin is overcome, and the place of the cross in that process. However before we get into the progressive work, we need to do some foundational work to get a better understanding of the fallen condition of man. This will help us to appreciate what we are up against when it comes to understanding the work of progressive reform.

The definition of sinfulness

The effects of the sinful condition are categorised neatly for us in the letter of 1 John 2:15-17 – using a literal translation:

[15] Do not love the world or the things in the world. If anyone loves the world, the love of the Father is not in him. [16] For all that is in the world—the lust of the flesh, the lust of the eyes, and the pride of life—is not of the Father but is of the world. [17] And the world is passing away, and the lust of it; but he who does the will of God abides forever. (NKJV)

Here we are given a definition of the value systems and full expression of everything in the worldly system. They are:

- Lust of the flesh
- Lust of the eyes
- Pride of life

In these three categories we recognise the root motivation and general categories of expression of all that is sinful and evil in the world of fallen man. As we will see and explore, these are all forms of expression of self, accompanied by their attending aspects of self-belief, and as such they are opposite to faith in God. But first we must distinguish between what are legitimate needs and actions, and what can be identified as sinful.

Maslow's Hierarchy of Needs – Maslow produced a psychological study of man in terms of his needs which is known as 'Maslow's hierarchy of needs'. In it he shows the basic needs to be: hunger, thirst, air, sleep, and warmth etc., basically all the necessities to stay alive and physically comfortable. Beyond that are the need for safety and security. Then it progresses into things like cognitive development – the need to know and understand, the need for self-esteem, and need for companionship. On top of that comes the need for self-actualisation – the need for a meaningful purpose in life. Then beyond that there is an extended form of the hierarchy theory that adds the need for transcendence, which means the need to reach out to others for their good. As these needs progress up the hierarchy they become less vital to life, and move largely into wants rather than needs. At these higher levels they begin to define happiness, and the estimated percentage of people that achieve fulfilment of those needs reduces the further you get up the hierarchy.

The question for us is where does God fit into all of this? And, at what point do legitimate needs get redefined as sinful?

Solomon is a useful character to study to answer these questions. His experience is a valuable part of the history of our fallen race as he, by his own admission, denied himself no pleasure. He says he tested it all by reason. He pushed well up through the hierarchy of needs to achieve for himself great honour and renown. In terms of self-esteem, cognitive fulfilment – wisdom, personal achievements, and the adoration of others, including vast wealth and the acquisition of 700 wives and 300 concubines, there is none to rival him. Yet in the remarkable book of Ecclesiastes, written towards the end of his life, we are given an invaluable view into the state of his inner man when he was drawn away from God as the focus of his life. There, in that partially spiritually blinded state, he placed self-actualisation as the highest thing on offer in life – i.e. work. But he depressingly denounced it all as vanity, and a chasing after the wind, showing the levels of dissatisfaction he experienced were as acute as that of any unfulfilled man. In that state he lost his way completely, even declaring in his depression that there is nothing new under the sun. He lost interest in everything, even food. Having lost God he clearly entered into a place of self-belief that blinded him almost completely. Even on the natural level the potential for new discoveries were clearly lost to him. Our days of computers, space-exploration, and technology actually make his declarations seem incredibly foolish and pathetic. The evidence is therefore that to reach the top of Maslow's hierarchy is no guarantee of happiness or fulfilment in life.

So the question is: When does the pursuit of the fulfilment of personal needs reach the point at which it can be defined as sinful?

The answer to this lies at a deeper and more fundamental level of the person, as has already been discussed in previous chapters at some length. There are two possibilities: Either they are fundamentally driven by love, which includes an unprejudiced commitment to all of creation, or they are committed to self, which is a prejudiced commitment to themselves above all others.

The problem here is that for much of the time personal needs run in the same direction regardless of the fundamental motivator. Therefore the difference only becomes apparent when those interests begin to diverge. That is where these three biblical categories of worldly sin come into play. They each represent the pursuit of one's own needs beyond the limit that love would place on them, into a place where they are destructive either to oneself, and/or another. Lust represents an overindulgence to one's own harm, and pride is something that only defines itself in competition to others, so in each case it clearly gets into the territory of prejudiced selfishness.

What the bible teaches about all this is that if the heart is pure then all things are pure. But if the heart is impure then nothing is pure. In the latter case, therefore, all actions are fundamentally given to the drive of self, and can only therefore be judged as sinful, despite the fact that for much of the time these actions run parallel to those that would come forth from a heart based on love, because love does demand we do the highest good for self, as much as any other, and this is the primary area where we have direct responsibility.

In each case the pursuit of the fulfilment of ones needs that is driven by a selfish root, is always accompanied by some form of self-belief; the belief that we can achieve self-fulfilment in some way by our own independent means.

Lust of the flesh – This is self-belief in the form of the belief that one can find satisfaction and fulfilment through the gratification of appetites independently of God.

Here are all the sensual indulgences of mankind. They are the gratification of appetites without reference to the harm it causes to the being of oneself or others. It is the root and source of many different kinds of perversion. It leads to the exploitation of others where they can be instrumental in gratification. It is hedonism.

God gave many things that he fully intended for us to enjoy and take pleasure in[595], but all of these are intended to serve the same purpose of love, contributing to the highest good. It was always God's intention that we enjoy all he created. However the worldly view is to exploit these things for self-gratification, often even making them the object of worship[596]. Within the context of love they can be received as a form of worship of God[597]. Outside of it they become destructive.

Lust of the eyes – This is self-belief based on what one has. It is based on pride in ones appearance before others. It embodies the whole concepts of status, image, and ego. It includes the elements of competition for value in relation to others. Through it fallen man seeks self-esteem, but only at the cost of and in relation to others[598]. The competitive nature of this sinful expression leads to greed and exploitation. In includes all vanity. It produces all covetousness. It is the foundation of all excessive materialism. It is used widely as the basis of commercial selling. It is the pursuit of the worship from others for the purpose of one's own self esteem. It is self-glorification. It includes all forms of idolatry[599].

Pride of Life – This is self-belief based on what one does. It is the belief in one's own abilities. It is the root of all independence, and the belief in oneself for self-sustenance and self-sufficiency. It therefore rejects any need for God. It embodies the pursuit of power. It is competitive in nature, deriving its self-esteem from its successes and achievements in relation to

---

[595] 1 Tim 6:17
[596] Phil 3:19 Matt 6:24
[597] 1 Cor 10:31
[598] Luke 18:11
[599] Col 3:5

CHAPTER 16: The Fallen Condition of Man 263

others. It produces domination. It exploits others. It is the basis of slavery. It is the most common cause of war. It is ambitious. It is ready to get ahead by overpowering others. It is fundamentally self-belief. It operates by the law of the jungle, the survival of the fittest. It is brute force. It is mercenary and predatory by nature.

Together – Together these three categories cover all the various expressions of sin and evil in the world. They have a common root which is the selfishness of independence. We see in them all the ways that man seeks to find satisfaction and self-worth independently of God.

From a state of dependence on God, satisfaction and personal worth would be derived from him and the gifts he has given. The intrinsic value of man would be revealed directly from God through a relationship with him. As it is, men clamber to extract a sense of value from each other, which has the opposite effect of devaluing them even further.

Law has been added to the worldly system as a means to control and restrain it from the uninhibited expression and exploitation of others. As such the principles of law are often referred to as the '*basic principles of this world*'[600].

Ironically acts of goodness can become part of such a value system, and thereby become part of one's independent claim on self-esteem[601]. However, it is the self-belief and independence of God that identifies it to be 'of the world', and part of the expression of man's fallen and corrupt nature.

Selfishness

Selfishness can be defined as self-love; where man seeks his own interests, giving his own being precedence over all others. He only extends his interests to others for the purpose of self-interest, though he may go to great lengths to disguise his selfish condition by acts that appear on the surface to be charitable and selfless, although in fact they are done in the purposes of self, even if it is only for acceptance.

The root of selfishness is independence. The original temptation of man was to strike out for independence of God. In doing so he fell from love which is the very *principle* and *principal* of heaven, where all other

---

[600] Gal 4:3 Col 2:8,20 1 Tim 1:9
[601] Matt 7:11

beings matter as much as self. Before the fall God was man's source of life and man was totally committed to the good of God and all creation, without any precedence to himself. After the fall he was cut off from God and became an independent being, reduced to having only a fundamental interest in himself, and regarding all others only in relation to that.

Deception

For selfish beings living among other selfish beings, deception and denial of the selfish condition is clearly an expedient thing to do – in terms of the individual's self-interest. As a result fallen man becomes deceitful to the core, denying both its fundamental state, and the selfish root of its behaviour[602].

The selfish nature can be trained in the same way that an animal can be trained to conform to certain codes of behaviour by controlling its self-interest, but this does not diminish the corruption of the root condition. For animals this is not a corruption because they are of this world, and they are given limited understanding. As such this thinking is their natural way. It is therefore part of their natural constitution, but for man it is corruption, so the old nature is otherwise known as his animal, or brute nature[603], or in other places as the lower nature. The message of Jeremiah 17:9 reveals all:

'The heart is deceitful above all things and beyond cure. Who can understand it?' (Jer 17:9)

As the selfish nature of man deceives even itself, the man builds up what has come to be called the 'ego', which is a kind of wishful personal persona that is projected towards all others in order for it to achieve its best self-interest.

Of course selfish beings do form cooperatives such that they commit to the interests of others in a group. However this is still done at core in the interests of self. Even demons form this type of unholy union. Their gatherings are sometimes legion, but their cooperation should not in any way be mistaken for selflessness. What is seen on the surface in group

---

[602] John 3:19
[603] Ps 73:22

and social behaviour can therefore have complex undertones of selfishness that are concealed and generally denied. For this reason Jesus said:

'if you being evil know how to give good gifts to your children, how much more does God know how to give good gifts to those that ask him' (Matt 7:11)

The fact that fallen man does good things does not diminish the fact that he has become inwardly selfish and evil. Within the fallen spirit we therefore see the full expression of the partisan spirit that is so common in this world[604]. This in turn has the effect of promoting its competitive inclinations on a corporate level, leading to a party/partisan mindedness.

Cooperatives

As we have said: the fact that people form social groups, or cooperatives of any kind where they appear to manifest selfless behaviour, does not diminish the fact that they may still be selfish individuals at root. The demons form these same cooperatives and alliances.

In the gospels we read of Jesus meeting a man that was possessed by a legion of demons[605]. Within this legion there would have been all the hierarchy and structure we see in all worldly organisations, including laws, codes, agreements, and discipline that made it possible for them to maintain their cooperative of completely selfish beings.

Their actual occupation and possession of a man would have given them considerable status and standing in the wider demonic realm. It is something that many of them aspire to because man is made in the image of God.

When the man was driven to Jesus, these demons were terrified that they were about to be plunged into the Abyss[606], which would be a much harsher environment, with its furious power struggles and cruel disciplines, where their little cooperative would disintegrate, and they would be thrust to the bottom of a much larger status ladder, becoming an object to be dominated and cruelly enslaved by all they encountered there.

---

[604] 1 Cor 3:3-4
[605] Mark 5:1-21 Luke 8:26-39
[606] Rev 9:1-11

Instead they suggested their own punishment; that they be banished from possession of the man to possess a herd of swine.

This suggestion was itself an act of self-interested humility brought on by terror. To move from possessing a man to possessing swine would have severely impacted their status and standing in the demonic realm. A man is made in the image of God, and as such demons seek and aspire to that kind of status. On the other hand, pigs in that culture were regarded as unclean beasts, which is a far truer reflection of demons as fallen beings. Jesus accepted this suggestion knowing that it was a radical and humiliating condescension for them, but they preferred this to the abyss.

He gave the legion of demons leave to go, and immediately, as they entered the pigs, the whole herd rushed down the banks and destroyed themselves in the lake. This would have released the demons into their usual disembodied state that is like an arid desert[607]. They clearly preferred this to the humiliation of occupying pigs, after so long holding an esteemed position in the demonic realm by occupying a man. Even the fact that they had occupied pigs for even a moment may well have dented their pride and status, and may have threatened to incur the wrath and discipline of the dark principalities and powers to which they were subject, so they were unwilling to maintain that condition for any longer than they had to, and they destroyed the pigs at the first opportunity.

Cooperatives are therefore part of both the worldly and demonic system, as societies of selfish beings.

By contrast, the kingdom of God is in complete unity under the purpose of love. Within the church all disunity is therefore either the result of misunderstanding and/or disagreement regarding how the purpose of love is best served. Otherwise it is an expression of the old selfish nature, which will generally manifests itself in the form of religion in some way.

Religion

This is a term that in the modern day has different meanings to different people. However in the context of fallen man; it is easy to see how the various expressions of the world system can take a religious form in vanity and pride – the lust of the eyes, and the pride of life. This was the condition of the Pharisees who were supremely religious.

---

[607] Matt 12:43

CHAPTER 16: The Fallen Condition of Man

Over history the other category of the worldly expression; of the lust of the flesh, has also entered into religion on a large scale through lewd images and idols, though generally in modern religions such things are repressed and denied beneath claims of morality. However, although modern religions have repressed these things, it has not proved able to overcome them, they are simply pushed beneath the surface[608].

A general description of worldly religion is man's independent attempt to reach God and God's standard. This in itself is an expression of independence and self-belief, and therefore an expression of the fallen corrupt nature. The competitive pursuit of self-esteem is the basis of much religious practice, which can even descend to a level where it becomes predatory, where one man bolsters his religious self-belief by comparisons with others[609]. The outward forms of religion may not reveal all, but underneath the values on which it operates are as worldly as any secular expression of worldliness.

We should be clear that not all that is called religion in the world is of the world. All that seeks God in faith, humility, and honesty is something entirely different[610]. This is clearly an expression of dependence on God, rather than an expression of self-belief and independence. This state of complete dependence is the state of the true church, the bride of Christ, expressed when all are consistently living in the Spirit.

The old nature is frequently found expressing itself in religious form. In fact all worldly religion, as we have defined it, comes from the sinful nature.

It is ironic that the sinful nature should make such efforts to prove itself to be good. This effort mainly comes from the intrinsic faculty of conscience that judges all men's actions against the standard of love[611]. The old nature also seeks to validate itself through the approval of others, often through apparently selfless acts, but these things can be as geared to self-interest as any other form of self-expression. Of course in such a system there must be denial of the true underlying state, so deception and hypocrisy are unavoidable parts of it.

---

[608] Matt 23:25 Col 2:23
[609] Luke 5:30
[610] Jam 1:27
[611] Rom 2:15

The world itself often places some value on religion because it is seen by many individuals in the world to serve their interest, and as such they see it as an expression of goodness. However if the expression is not based on faith and dependence on God, but is really a form of self-belief, then in eternal terms it is entirely worthless.

The values of heaven

The values of heaven are love – the total commitment of one's heart, mind, soul, and strength to the purpose of the highest good of all things, including God and all creation, and including oneself, but without prejudice or precedence to oneself[612].

The result is that the strong serve, protect, and value the weak. All are servant hearted, humble, and selfless, considering all others of equal value and preferring others to oneself[613]. All live in perfect freedom[614]. There is no domination or exploitation. There is only cooperation in the same cause and purpose of love – the highest good.

This contrasts with the worldly system where, at root, each is committed to a different cause – self. Heaven is a place of fellowship. The world is divided absolutely by its selfish root, or only relates in mutual self-interest. In heaven all are permanently self-sacrificing for the good of the whole. Conversely, in the world all sacrifices are made on the basis of selfish returns.

Faith and the World

As the apostle John points out in the same letter as the categorisation of the worldly expression: it is our faith that overcomes the world[615]. Faith is the place of complete dependence on God, both generally and in the details of life. By stepping away from all independence, and becoming dependent on God as our source in all things by faith, we find that we become able to overcome the world, breaking its dominance over our lives.

---

[612] Gal 5:14
[613] Phil 2:3
[614] 2 Cor 3:17 Jam 1:25
[615] 1 John 5:4

CHAPTER 16: The Fallen Condition of Man

The dynamics of how this works, and how we move into the freedom that love and faith brings, is the progressive work that is built upon the initial foundation of spiritual rebirth.

The scripture tells us that in terms of heaven *'the only thing that counts is faith expressing itself through love'*[616]. In the end this is all that matters.

This leads us to explore this journey into faith, and how the progressive reform actually takes place.

---

[616] Gal 5:6

CHAPTER 17: The Progressive Reform of Man

Why does sin persist?
Rebirth is a real and distinct spiritual experience. It is the complete replacement of the corrupt spirit of man with the Spirit of Christ. This replacement spirit is perfect and completely holy[617]. The big question therefore arises: Why do Christians experience an ongoing problem with sin after rebirth? It is clear that after rebirth, sooner or later, a battle ensues. The Bible describes this in terms of two natures that war against each other, each with its own desires and agenda[618].

Our first task must be to define what a nature actually is, and how it relates to our spirit.

What is a nature?
Man is a three part being of spirit, soul, and body[619]. The nature and the spirit of a man are almost synonymous terms, except that the spirit is part of the three-part being of man, and the nature is that which flows from the spirit.

Some would define the nature as a thing of the soul and its constituent parts – mind, will and emotion. In truth the expression of the soul is just an interpretation of the flow that comes to it from the spirit. The mind interprets the nature into thoughts, words, and deeds but fundamentally the nature is none of these. It is a deeper expression of the character of the spirit[620].

Every spirit has a nature. God is the spirit of Love[621]. All the expressions of God's Spirit are expressions of love as they are seen clearly described in the famous chapter on love – 1 Corinthians 13. We can therefore rightly say that the nature of God is love. If the nature of Love is

---

[617] Col 1:22 Heb 10:10
[618] Rom 8:5-11 Gal 5:16-17
[619] 1 Thes 5:23
[620] Matt 15:18
[621] John 4:24 1 John 4:8,16

in control of the mind, then the nature of love is interpreted by the mind into loving thoughts, words, and deeds.

Equally the old corrupt spirit has a nature of selfishness. So, if the old nature is in control of the mind, then its selfish nature is interpreted into selfish thoughts, words, and deeds.

The scriptures make clear that only one nature/spirit can be in control of the mind at any one instant. There is never a moment when both are in control at the same time[622]. ***The key issue for controlling behaviour therefore simply becomes an issue of which spirit/nature is in control of the mind.***

Warning to Leaders – Too often this key fact is not realised, ignored, or fudged in the doctrines of men. Many such doctrines come down, in the final analysis, to self-help philosophies that believe the power of change exists in man's efforts, and as such they seek improvement rather than fundamental reform. In the end these doctrines lead only to religion because they end up handing control back to the old nature that remains unidentified.

Those that step up and offer themselves as teachers and leaders should be aware that the true gospel is a noble doctrine based entirely on grace through faith from first to last, and it requires noble characters who understand this to teach it if they are to promote such nobility[623]. Those who step forward in this way should be aware that they and their work will be judged for its worth against this standard. They must understand the key truth: *that man must be reformed by learning primarily and fundamentally to live consistently in the Spirit, and to overcome the encroachment of the old nature by faith alone. And conversely that apart from this, any form of self-improvement is futile.*

Any that have failed to realise, and focus on this key fact, will in the end be seen to have promulgated religion, and the result of that will be nothing more than wood, hay, and straw, that will be consumed upon judgment.

---

[622] Gal 5:17 Rom 8:6
[623] 1 Tim 3:1 2 Tim 2:20-22 Heb 13:7-9

The complexity of redeemed man – two natures

The study of the nature of fallen man is much simpler than the study of the born again, regenerate man. The reason for this is that in the born again man, who is still in his temporal earthly body, and has not yet received his spiritual body, there are two natures at work. We therefore have to understand the dynamics of how these two natures interact with each other, and with the rest of the man's being.

Ironically, in some ways the study of regenerate man is more complex than even the study of God, because God is absolute love with no complications. In him there are no shifting shadows, and therefore there is something profoundly straightforward and uncomplicated about him[624]. Of course the infinite extents of his being, his love, and the immensity of his creative expression as the creator, means that he is infinite mystery, and there will always be more of him to explore throughout the ages, but we can be sure that he is love and goodness throughout.

On the other hand, in redeemed man we see evidence of a huge struggle where two natures are in conflict with each other. This is more complex, so we need to have a good understanding of the constitution and the dynamics of these two natures to progress towards an understanding of how man is to be reformed in God's plan of redemption. We can then go on to see what part the cross of Christ played in the process, and how that works.

How can the old spirit persist?

Once rebirth has happened, the old corrupt spirit of man is expelled from the internal union with the soul and body that make up the rest of the man's being, and the spirit of Christ steps in to form that central union with them. The old spirit is therefore now external to the being and constitution of the man, and ceases to have any legitimate claim on him[625].

However, the old spirit is not annihilated, it continues to exist. Though it has lost its connection to the soul of the man, it still has a connection to the mind in that it can still communicate with the mind in exactly the same way that any spirit can seek to communicate with us from their external position.

---

[624] Jam 1:17 Heb 13:8
[625] 2 Cor 5:17 Rom 6:8

The problem is that the old spirit has an advantage over other spirits; that it once had a union with our soul, and as such it appears to have a stronger claim over us[626]. The old spirit is already a master of deception, and it continues to stake its claim on the mind, claiming to be the true centre of the being of the man. After rebirth this is a false claim, but nevertheless a very persuasive one.

The issue of control of the mind now comes down to which of these two spirits one recognises as ones true identity. If the mind submits to the claim of the old nature, then control of the mind is thereby handed over to the old spirit, even though it now occupies an external position in terms of the constitution of his being. As, by the complicity of the man, the old spirit is allowed to successfully wrest control of the mind from the Spirit of God, who is the man's true centre, then God's spirit is no longer in control of the man, despite its union with his soul, until some successful appeal is made by God's Spirit to persuade the mind back into voluntary recognition that he (Christ within) is in fact the true state and centre of his being[627]. In other words the man must rediscover his true identity to recover his walk in the Spirit, and the Spirit of God is constantly sending the needed word for him to make that recovery.

One may ask: If Christ within is the reality, what difference does it make whether this is recognised or not? The answer to this is that it makes all the difference to outward behaviour, because when the mind acknowledges (believes in) another identity, it enslaves itself to the control of the spirit that offered it – such is the impact of faith.

God has given man authority over his own being, and therefore the complicity of the man concerning his recognition of his true identity is the determining factor in regard to which spirit controls his mind – the old nature or the Spirit of God.

The mind is the control centre of the behaviour. We therefore find that wherever the mind has submitted to the claim of the old spirit as its true centre, then that person may manifest all the kinds of behaviour we discussed in the section on the fallen spirit of man[628]. Sin therefore once again becomes the controlling factor[629], albeit from an external position.

---

[626] Rom 7:1-6
[627] Rom 6:11
[628] 1 John 2:16
[629] Rom 8:8

CHAPTER 17: The Progressive Reform of Man 275

Conversely, for as long as the Spirit of God controls the mind of the man he finds himself *unable* to gratify the desires of the old sinful nature, and he finds himself naturally living the life of Christ as an experiential reality[630]. To live in this way is to discover one's true centre.

How does Sin control the mind?

As we have said: for the old nature to gain control of the mind, it must bring the mind into agreement with itself, and with the false idea that it is still its true centre. To do that it must make a persuasive claim, so that the mind is led to believe the claim, and submit to it as truth. The belief of the mind determines which spirit is in control of it. We therefore see the principle of faith in operation as the defining principle of all behaviour[631].

Within the mind of man, after rebirth, there are numerous untransformed areas of worldly thinking that were established by the old fallen spirit over years of control[632]. Generally these are the access points that the old spirit/nature uses to stake its claim, coupled with associated areas of emotional damage that often come with them. The attack will normally come in the form of some kind of accusation. The old spirit will use something current to suggest a link between a perfectly good reaction, and an old sinful behaviour pattern[633].

For example a man may legitimately react to something with a measure of emotion or passion. At this point the old nature uses the reaction in the form of accusation to draw a parallel with an old sinful behaviour pattern, perhaps of anger. The old nature therefore suggests a new and plausible identity, perhaps of thug or abuser, or some other word that has been used in the past to define the nature of the person whilst formerly under the control of the sinful nature. If at this point the accusation is accepted and admitted by the mind, the old spirit has managed to turn an incident into a whole identity, thereby gaining control of the mind through a challenge to his faith in who and what he really is[634]. In other words, the man now has faith that his true identity is that of a thug or abuser. If he is spiritually reborn this claim is false. His true nature and

---

[630] Gal 5:16
[631] Acts 15:9 Rom 1:17 Gal 2:20 1 Thes 1:3-4 Jam 2:24
[632] Rom 12:2
[633] Rom 8:13 Col 3:5
[634] 2 Cor 13:5 Eph 3:17

identity is entirely Christlike, but his mind has been challenged to accept a falsehood that if believed, delivers his whole behaviour control system of the mind over to the old sinful nature.

When speaking of the mind, there is a difference between the intellect and the mind of the soul. The intellect works by reason, and is of the physical body, whereas the mind of the soul is a repository of values and beliefs – the value/belief system. These together make up the mind.

In a person that is spiritually reborn, the soul has a firmly established belief in its identity as a child of God[635]. The Holy Spirit within him maintains this in the soul by constantly bearing witness to it[636], so it is not easy for the old nature to break this state of saving faith. However the old nature is still able to gain control over the intellectual mind by imposing some false identity; usually through accusation. It thereby gains control of the behaviour system, which will then reflect the false identity in experience[637].

The Galatian church was in exactly such a battle of faith. Having been challenged by men who had come in and sought to re-impose the law[638], they were experiencing the inevitable weakness and misery of those principles[639]. Paul was battling for them in the letter, and said he was *'again in the pains of childbirth until Christ is formed in you'*,[640] clearly showing that this was a critical time for them where they had to decide where their faith would ultimately rest.

Often the initial point of attack will be some form of temptation. Temptation is not sin. Often it is simply an expression of natural desires. However it is at that instant that the old spirit jumps in with the suggestion of a whole past sinful identity, or even with a whole new identity. It is at this split second point that the controlling factor is decided. If the false identity is admitted, then the sinful nature takes control of the mind, and the temptation may well progress into sin.

For a man that begins with his mind and faith firmly stayed on Christ as his true identity, the accusation always comes at the point of

---

[635] Rom 8:15-16
[636] Gal 4:6
[637] Rom 8:6
[638] Gal 3:1-5, 1:6-9
[639] Gal 4:9
[640] Gal 4:19

legitimate temptation when no sin is present. It is only the acceptance of the accusation that allows the old nature to quickly capitalise on the temptation and turn it into the sinful behaviour of thoughts, words, or deeds. A mature believer will be secure in their identity in Christ, and will hold steady with that identity while the temptation passes. This can be far different from simply trying to resist by self-effort because a man may resist the sinful behaviour, and at the same time accept the accusation of 'sinner' in some form that it is being thrown at him. This is not his new identity in Christ, and as such it is a lie. Always when Paul speaks of the sinful identity, it is in the context of the past tense, and never the present.

Even if a man is tripped by a temptation and led into sin, the real problem still comes after the failure when the sinful nature attempts to use it to offer the man a whole identity, and define him by his sin. As a born again believer this sin does not define the truth of who he is, but the old nature will put forward an aggressive argument to try to persuade him that it is, by citing all the physical evidence.

Of course once a man is tripped, and then led into a new identity, he needs to return once again to see the truth of who and what he really is, which is what the process of repentance is. This is something that is not always very well understood.

The process of repentance

The general understanding of repentance is simply to say sorry for something we have done, and perhaps commit ourselves not to do it again. Unfortunately this idea can completely miss the point.

Sin is caused by the controlling factor of the old nature wresting control of the mind by persuading it to accept a false identity. This old spirit/nature is otherwise known by the name 'Sin' – a noun. When we repent of our sin correctly, we repent of accepting this false claim of Sin as our true identity. We admit to any act of sin, but most importantly we must reject any claim of 'Sinner' as our true identity. Instead we uphold the claim to a new identity in Christ despite the present failure of sin.

A new believer simply does this for the first time by hearing and accepting God's revelation to them of their need for it[641]. Often this is done by identifying those sins that are most prominent to their mind, and by them asking forgiveness for these things, but these sins will only be a

---

[641] Rom 10:17,13

minor fraction of the total sins actually committed up to this point. If it were essential to name them all then none would find salvation and complete forgiveness. However what is really needed, and what is taking place as a sinner repents, is repentance from; or rejection of, the principal of Sin within – the sinful nature. This will bring the person back into recognition of complete forgiveness through the transplantation and transformation of a new nature when they were born again[642].

Christian religion often sees the title of 'sinner' as a permanent claim based on some idea of humility, but for the born again believer it is really a falsehood in terms of our current true identity, notwithstanding the fact that we may have failed by an act of sin. Instead we seek to re-establish the truth that it is no longer I that live, but Christ that lives in me[643]. We repent of believing a lie, and choose again to believe the truth. With our minds we accept him as the centre of our being again, and at the same time reject 'Sin' as our centre, confirming its claim to be false[644]. This is true repentance. The deed itself should be admitted, but it is almost secondary to this process of repentance where we repent of admitting the old nature, with its false identity, and reaffirm the new.

From this understanding of repentance, we can see how it is perfectly possible to say sorry for the sinful thought, word, or deed, commit ourselves never to do it again, and yet walk away from the confession still holding to the belief in a sinful identity. Ironically we walk away with the sinful nature/spirit still in complete and utter control of our mind and behaviour[645], thereby setting us up to fail in the same way again.

Historical examples – There are many historical examples of Christian people who have run into this problem. Among them are Martin Luther, and Joan of Arc. At times they could not even exit the church door after confession before remembering more that they must confess, never finding relief from their inner suffering.

Condemnation is a permanent feature of such a life. However the truth is that there is really no condemnation for those that are spiritually reborn. The condemnation is an imposition of a sinful and false nature, so

---

[642] 2 Cor 5:17 Eph 2:15 Ti 3:5
[643] Gal 2:20
[644] Rom 7:20, 6:7,11 8:2
[645] Rom 8:6

CHAPTER 17: The Progressive Reform of Man

that it can maintain its control of the mind. The sinful nature is in fact condemned, but it is not the true nature of the believer, it is an imposter.

This condition is often the result of legalism, where some form of law is used as the controlling principle of behaviour[646]. Methods of law, as a means to righteousness, appeal to our core belief in our independence, and as such only strengthen and entrench the sinful nature. By contrast such battles with sin are only won by an act of faith[647] where we begin to recognise our true identity, even against the onslaught of contrary evidence. In God's scheme of things, faith always comes before experience.

Luther finally overcame his early problems as he was impacted by the revelation that he was saved and justified before God by grace through faith alone[648]. This was only the beginning, as it is for all who discover it.

Practicing the presence

In my early experience, like Martin Luther, I had come to understand the truth of justification by faith alone. Fortunately this truth has been well established and carried forward by the modern church since the reformation. However the realisation that this is how the whole of the Christian life is lived from beginning to end, was something I had yet to realise. One of my early steps into this came through a remarkable book called *The Healing Presence* by Leanne Payne. It is a book that profoundly ministers to those that struggle with the spiritual problems of the mind. An active mind is both a great asset, and a real vulnerability to spiritual attack.

The problem is our tendency to lean on the understanding as an act of independence of God[649], rather than surrendering our mind to God and living primarily from listening to the Spirit of God within. I had yet to come into a full understanding of what this meant, but through this book I was led into a kind of preliminary exercise that opened me up to it.

A struggle of the mind – Immediately prior to the discovery of the teaching in this book, I was working in the British coal mines as an

---

[646] 1 Cor 15:56 Rom 3;20, 7:5, 8:7
[647] Gal 3:11 Phil 3:9 2 Thes 1:11
[648] Rom 3:28,24 Eph 2:8,9
[649] Prov 3;5

engineering manager. As such after deploying men through the mine, I would have to go underground as part of my duties, usually to some trouble spot. Often my preliminary work would delay me enough to make me miss the transport. I would then have to walk up to seven miles underground along an unlit roadway tunnel to my destination. I was a fairly young Christian at the time, and often plagued by spiritual battles in my mind. On one occasion, whilst down the mine, I remember reaching a point where I was over half a mile below ground, and more than four miles out from the mine shaft, walking along a pitch black roadway tunnel, in the middle of an inner spiritual battle of the mind. At that point I tried in some desperation to sense God, but had no sense whatsoever of his presence. The experience was indescribably dark and bleak.

In her book Leanne Payne refers to another book from several centuries ago called 'Practising the Presence' by a monk known as Brother Lawrence. The teaching of this little book, in summary, was that Christ is always with us[650], our renewed spirit knows it, but our minds are often unaware of it. We therefore actively align our minds with this truth by faith alone without reference to feelings or senses. We draw on the inner resource of the spirit and allow him to enlighten us with deep conviction to the truth by faith alone[651].

I took this lesson on board, and experienced a profound release of peace and joy in my life as I began to practise the presence of Jesus with me at all times, by faith. Even when there was no sense or feeling, I could still come into a deep inner conviction that Jesus was right there with me. From this point on I became aware of Jesus as my constant companion. He is my counsellor and friend. When I need him he is there. I sometimes neglect him but he never neglects me. He is with me now, looking over my shoulder as I write this, and smiling. I think he likes it!

This was, and is, a first great lesson in living spiritually. I moved forward from here, even coming to the point where I preferred not to have the sense, because feelings are so fickle and limited that they can in fact hold us back from spiritual discernment and vision.

Those that have a less active emotional constitution should see their advantage here.

---

[650] Heb 13:5 Jam 4:8 John 14:16
[651] 2 Cor 5:7

I began to worship God from that same place, not allowing the senses to dominate, but only allowing them to follow the lead that my spirit gave. Through doing this I have sensed God in more profound ways than I believe I ever would have if had I relied on my senses. At times I have known the hair on my body stand up in anticipation of his presence before a meeting, yet at all times keeping my focus on the Spirit and not reverting to the senses. The life of faith is spiritual and profoundly real. Sometimes we cling to shadows rather than the realities that made them[652].

C. S. Lewis put it well when he said: 'some days I wake up and feel as if there is no God. Mind you, when I was an atheist some days I would wake up and feel as if there was a God.' Feelings are fickle. Faith is solid. God is always present. Listen to your heart and just believe it.

Feelings can act as a kick-start, but we should always quickly switch to be moved and powered by the Spirit in all we do. Relying on feelings is like trying to travel in a gas fuelled car on the energy of the battery; it soon runs down. The battery can get us started, but the real power only kicks in when the engine starts, and then we can just keep going regardless of whether the senses keep up or not.

Dependence – the hallmark of God's way

We read in the Apostle Paul's letter to the Ephesians, that we are saved by grace through faith, and that it is a gift of God so no man can boast[653]. Salvation clearly eliminates all possibility of self-effort and of self-dependence. It is a totally undeserved gift of God. This is the hallmark of all that God does. This is how it starts, and this is how it continues[654]. Self-effort and self-achievement belong to religion[655]. All that comes to us from God is by undeserved grace through faith. There is no room in it to boast. If we cannot credit God with our every success, we should be suspicious of it[656]. God's priority in his dealings with us is to lead us into a place where we recognise our complete dependence on him. Faith is therefore the key issue, and the means of God in all he does with us because this is an expression of dependence, not in any way based on merit.

---

[652] Col 2:17
[653] Eph 2:8-9
[654] Rom 1:17
[655] Heb 4:2 Rom 10:3 Phil 3:8-9
[656] 1 Cor 15:10 Rev 4:10-11

When asked by some: 'What they must do to do the works of God?' Jesus told them *'The work of God is this: to believe in the one he has sent.'*[657] – They must simply believe. This is often more difficult than it would seem because our temptation to believe in ourselves, rather than God, is often strong. We believe we can handle some things alone. However for anything we do to have a positive eternal impact, it is most important that we focus on believing and trusting in God in all things. Nothing else will fulfil the purpose of love[658].

In the book of Hebrews we are told to labour to enter his rest[659]; which is one of those remarkable biblical paradoxes. The rest is the rest of faith. Our efforts should be aimed primarily at believing, and thereby doing all that we do on his resources and enabling, rather than through our own.

Watchman Nee wrote a famous book entitled *'Sit, Walk, Stand'* that expounded this very principle: that one must learn to sit and rest in faith before we can walk effectively. Then beyond that we must go on to defend our position of rest – to stand.

He also followed this book with another called *'The Breaking of the Outer Man and the Release of the Spirit'* that showed how essential it is that God does the work in us, and all we can do is to surrender to it, thus highlighting the degree to which we are in fact dependent on God as his workmanship[660] – as clay to the potter.

God often has to wait for us to lose heart and hope in any possibility that we can mould ourselves, before we submit to him in the way we must to see his design for us emerge.

Dividing true & false doctrines

This leads us to a major principle by which we are able to discern spiritual truth from error – true doctrines from false ones.

There are many books in the world expounding principles for successful living, but in the final analysis many of these turn out to be doctrines of this world, and of no real spiritual value. The major test for the validity of any such book, or doctrine, is whether it depends on man's

---

[657] John 6:28-29
[658] John 15;5
[659] Heb 4:11
[660] Eph 2:10

CHAPTER 17: The Progressive Reform of Man 283

natural ability, or on God's enabling. In the former, the overall message generally comes down in some form to – try harder – you can do it – self-improvement principles. In the latter the underlying message is generally – you can't do it, you must access God.

As always the bigger problem comes when a book has a mixed message. In such a book one may often find many a paragraph that is in some way, by itself, spiritually helpful. The problem however is that false doctrine is like yeast; it works its way through the whole dough. Often it is as hard to separate and divide such a book as it would be to remove the yeast from bread.

I recently came across just such a book, which is fairly highly acclaimed. The book and the author will remain nameless because it would not be fair to single out one instance, but in this case I decided to examine the author's life and background because I was interested to see if there were indicators of the final outcome of such doctrine in terms of fruit, especially since the author had written about a major fall in his early ministry into adultery.

It seemed to me that though there were many good thoughts in the book, the underlying philosophy was based on self-effort, and would lead to failure. What I found was that after this major fall, the author had found their way back into ministry by political manoeuvring, and a clever handling of their situation. Though there was almost certainly genuine remorse and repentance on exposure of this problem, there were things in the story that led me to strongly doubt whether this author, having fallen in such a way, had taken time to seriously examine their doctrine to see if it was at fault in any way. Instead they seemed to have played the system and worked it to their 'advantage', carrying with them the same ideas that led to their fall into sin.

Of course anybody can find themselves under this kind of temptation, but when it comes the only real defence must come from God. To find oneself in this situation, with only the philosophies of self-effort to combat it, is an extremely precarious situation. I will share some of my own experiences and trials on this issue later, but in these times it is only leaning hard on the grace and help of God that brought me through it.

As I examined this person in their later life, what I found was that their main message had eventually become one of – expect failure. They were openly recognising that though their lifetime of teaching and sermonising had captured and enthralled audiences, the outcome of it all, in terms of spiritual fruit, was a disappointing failure. Their main message in their later years, especially to fellow ministers, was one of – to doubt that cleverness and skills in public speaking and writing would produce anything of value.

In this way this person has come to agree with the point we are making here, but sadly so far only to emphasise the negatives rather than the positives. They have discovered the truth of *'apart from me you can do nothing'*[661], but have not yet discovered the truth of *'I can do everything through him who gives me strength'*[662]. Fortunately there is still time for this one, and given the encouraging signs of honesty, perhaps in their later years, as for many, they will still come through to a full realisation of it.

It is therefore vitally important that we learn this basic lesson as quickly as possible if we want to be fruitful in life. All that is ultimately of spiritual value is that which depends entirely on God[663], which is why Paul instructed Timothy to *'Watch your life and doctrine closely'*[664]. Why? Because if you do *'you will save both yourself and your hearers'*.

Self-denial

There are times when we discover that we have misunderstood a Bible word, and the actual understanding has a significant impact on what we thought it said and meant. Occasionally we find a word, or interpretation of scripture, that totally reverses the accepted meaning. This should not be too surprising because although the Spirit of God speaks to us from the scriptures, the deceitful old nature also utilises the Bible, through misinterpretation, to back its arguments as it seeks to establish control of the mind. It seems that for almost every important doctrine in the Bible, there is a counter doctrine of the flesh designed to serve its own purpose.

Probably the foremost and most important misunderstanding of scripture, in my view, is the interpretation that is commonly placed on the instructions of Jesus that we must *'deny our self'* and then *'take up our cross and follow him'*[665].

---

[661] John 5:15
[662]
[663] John 3:21
[664] 1 Tim 4:16
[665] Matt 16;24 Mark 8:4 Luke 9:23

CHAPTER 17: The Progressive Reform of Man

Self-denial has come to mean something in the English vernacular that is far different to what Jesus is saying in this verse, and far even from the original meaning of the English word. The wrong interpretation of it has come to mean *self-deprivation* – to deprive oneself. However the real meaning of deny is not to deprive, but to affirm something to be false. We deny that something is true. We declare it to be false.

Yes, the word is now used in common English as a replacement for deprive, but this comes down to the battle that is sometimes fought to distort the Bible into something it is not. Just as more recently the word 'wicked' came to mean something good. Or further back the word 'awful' meant 'awesome', so the word 'awesome' had to be invented to replace it. In this way the English language has adapted, as it does, to allow the use of the word 'deny' to mean 'deprive', but in the original Greek text this is not what it means. So what is Jesus really saying?

To deny myself really means to deny that I am my old self. To declare that the self I was before rebirth I am no longer[666]. It is to refuse to be identified as that old self. It is to consign the old self to where it belongs; nailed to the cross[667], where I am dead to its influence. This is what it means to take up the cross. It is an act of faith that acknowledges who I really am – I am Christ in me. It affirms that what Christ surrendered on the cross I now am[668], and what I was before is now on the cross and rendered powerless. Its claim over me is totally nullified. It can no longer claim to be me. I am a new creation. This is both a denial and a confession in one. I deny myself and I take up my claim to what Jesus surrendered for me on the cross – his life.

Both the idea of denial as deprivation, and the interpretation of taking up the cross as some kind of embracing of suffering, are errors! One thing that reveals the error is that it has been taken up by religion and turned into an expression of self-achievement. Some Eastern religions carry self-deprivation to the limit, with some real demonic forms; such as a man who lived up a pole for decades, or another that raised an arm until it withered. These acts of religion have no relevance to the purpose of love – the highest good. They are men seeking to prove themselves to be special, or worthy, or holy by their own efforts according to the ideas and

---

[666] Gal 2:20
[667] Rom 6:6 Gal 2:20, 5:24, 6:14
[668] Rom 6:5,8,11

rules of men. C. S. Lewis remarks that among the Fakir's of the east there are some that deprive themselves to the limit by fasting, but among them one can find immense pride, clearly as they and others come to believe in their own shows of self-worthiness.

We should recognise that this misinterpretation of the words of Jesus would push us into our own attempts to validate ourselves through religious observance and performance, and as such it is of the old nature.

On the other hand, the true interpretation has the hallmark of the Spirit of God in that it leads us into total dependence on God, by grace through faith alone. It is not accomplished through self-effort and leaves no room for boasting, but through laying down our self-belief and embracing a full dependence on God to work through us, we experience victory by grace through faith alone.

Self-deprivation

Having said that self-denial does not mean self-deprivation, we must ask whether self-deprivation has any valid part in the Christian doctrine, or does this mean that it reprieves us of any such demand? Are we to simply enjoy ourselves whenever we feel the urge? If we accept such an idea faith would seem to be the soft option, and the doctrine would even suggest that we can even be hedonistic.

However the truth of self-denial as an act of faith, rather than self-deprivation, does not mean that we are never to engage in self-deprivation. In fact faith will often lead us to deprive ourselves at many times and in many ways: by fasting; temporary or permanent abstentions; change of habits etc., but there is a profound difference between self-deprivation that comes from faith in God, and that which comes without it.

As we will see later: those who tried to use the law directly as a means to produce righteousness failed and stumbled[669]. Though the law holds out a high and righteous standard, it does not contain within it the power or means by which men may keep it[670]. The only way the law can be kept in truth is by combining it with some relevant area of faith. It is then the faith that produces the righteousness[671].

---

[669] Rom 9:32
[670] Rom 7:11-14 1 Tim 1:8-11
[671] Heb 4:2

CHAPTER 17: The Progressive Reform of Man

Though this is not explicitly taught in the Old Testament, it is implicit to many parts of it. For example, we see this most clearly in the teachings of David in the Psalms, where he extols the virtues and value of the word of God – the law[672]. However, what is implied here in David's enthusiasm for the law, is his faith in the law as a way of life. It is the faith that produces the righteousness, not merely the direct application of the law, and faith is only possible to the heart that is reborn[673]. A direct application of the law that is not based on faith, would invariably be an expression of self-effort and self-dependence, which is something that goes to the root of the sinful condition as the Pharisees showed. However faith comes from God through revelation of truth, and any response of righteous living that comes from faith is therefore something that stems from dependence on God, and not from self-effort. This means that the direct application of law, and the application of the law through faith, are fundamentally different things. One is an expression of the sinful nature that is entirely self-dependent, the other of the new nature that is entirely God dependent.

Similarly, to teach self-deprivation directly, apart from faith, will stimulate expressions of self-effort that are independent of God. However to teach some aspect of faith in God will often naturally lead to self-deprivation indirectly as a means to fulfil that faith. For example, we may come to see the value of fasting as a means to gain greater sensitivity to God, which will lead to a season of fasting. We may therefore be led to deprive ourselves through fasting, but only indirectly, based on a revelation of its value for something of worth that has been revealed to us by faith. Through this God given faith we then find the strength to sustain the fast.

In all of this we must remember that it is only the new nature that can receive faith in God. The old nature is incapable of such, and is entrenched in self-belief. If we choose to fast in response to faith, then once we come under the full impact of the self-affliction, that is an inevitable part of fasting, then it is the continued revelation of God, and the faith that comes through it, that will sustain us in the fast. However under this affliction the nature of flesh will come to question the value of what we are doing, and if the old nature is in control, will ultimately

---

[672] Ps 119
[673] John 5:24, 8:47

abandon the cause, seeing insufficient value of it to self. In fasting it is therefore essential to remain in a walk of the Spirit, which is generally sustained by faith in our true identity in Christ. This need to remain in a walk of the Spirit, where the new nature is in control, is essential whenever we engage in any activity where the old and new natures differ in their estimate of the value of what we are doing.

The power of the flesh

We have discussed that there are two kinds of faith: one belonging to the new nature, which is faith in God; and the other belonging to the old nature that is faith in self – self-belief. We also discussed the three categories of worldly expression that belong to the old nature of flesh: it believes that it can find satisfaction through the lust of the flesh; and it is committed to its own image (lust of the eyes); and its own abilities to live entirely from its own resources (pride of life)[674].

These three categories are in tension, such that the old nature finds itself unable to satisfy them all at once. For example, if it pursues the path of self-gratification through the lust of the flesh, then the conscience ensures it loses in the department of self-image. Given such self-indulgence, which tends to have a momentum of its own, it is also likely to lose control of its passions, depleting itself in the self-belief of the pride of life.

On the other hand, if the old nature deprives itself in the area of the lust of the flesh, then it may find itself able to boost itself in the area of self-image (the lust of the eyes), and the pride of life (pride of self-control).

Generally the old nature is forced into making such trade-offs.

By contrast, the new nature has no such dilemma because all of its fulfilments are mutually compatible. Often the old nature is able to make impressive changes by switching from one form of worldly expression to another. The world is often impressed by these revolutions, but in real spiritual terms, these are simply trading one form of corruption for another.

If the lust of the flesh is not dominating the person, then the pride of life (self-belief), and the lust of the eyes (vanity, image, status) generally are. The only way to truly overcome is to change the whole

---

[674] 1 John 2:15-17

agenda, which can only be done by living from the new nature and denying the old.

Mortify the old nature

Having denied that I am the old nature, and affirmed that it is Christ who is my life by faith alone, I am able to walk by the Spirit, controlled by the new nature[675]. We are then instructed not to *deprive* the sinful nature, but to kill it – to mortify it – to die to it[676]. Once again some would interpret this to mean deprivation, but once again the same thing applies. This is not an act of deprivation, but an act of faith[677]. By faith I affirm that old habit, or sinful behaviour pattern, to be an expression of my old nature, and not of the truth of who I now am. I don't deny it happens, but just that it is an imposter and that my new nature actually behaves as Christ in every aspect. We must hold to this confession of faith even through seasons of failure, until we see that aspect of sinful expression overcome and mortified – dead, in our actual experience by faith and faith alone. Holding on to faith is a very different thing to directly trying to suppress the behaviour.

This is far from the try harder message of self-effort. It is the walk of the Spirit by faith that is righteousness itself, and by the Spirit we put to death all that belongs to the sinful nature[678].

As we have discussed: this does not mean that we will never deprive ourselves of anything. What it means is that we are launched into a natural life of living by the Spirit of God, where we do the right thing naturally as an act of our new nature. Once the new nature is in control, we are free to live naturally, which is a wholly different thing to trying to be righteous while still under the control of the sinful nature.

Living naturally by the Spirit

If the Spirit of God is in control of our minds, then to live righteously we can simply live naturally[679].

---

[675] Rom 6:8-12
[676] Rom 8:13
[677] Acts 26:18, 15:9
[678] Rom 8:2,13 Gal 5:4-6
[679] Gal 5:16

As a youth I had a fascination with birds of prey, and for a time I kept owls and falcons. In recent years I visited a falconry show that I found really enjoyable, mainly because of the quality of the commentary. The highlight of the show came when the falconer produced a Black Kite. We have Red Kites in England that were recently reintroduced. At one time, more than a century ago, Red Kites occupied every city in the country, feeding on the pigeon population, but were wiped out through fear that they may attack chickens which most people kept back then.

As the Black Kite was brought out, the commentator explained that this was a much bolder bird than its cousin the Red Kite, and relatively fearless in its whole attitude to life. As he released the bird, it hardly flapped a wing, but it just flew and glided through the trees and among the crowds with hardly a hint of effort.

The commentator explained that here this bird was doing exactly what it was designed to do – to fly. This was what it was made for, and this is what it was most happy doing. As I watched I heard God whisper to me 'this is how it is to walk by the Spirit'.

For those that are born again, living by the principle of love is a natural walk for which we are perfectly adapted and suited when we are controlled by the Spirit.

Though this bird was awesome and powerful in its flight, no-one would have dreamed of describing its actions in terms of striving or effort. Had the bird been made to swim or walk, rather than do its natural thing of flying, the story may have been very different.

Equally, when the old nature tries to walk in the way that the Spirit does naturally, it is an extremely stressful and frustrating experience, because it is striving against its true nature[680]. In contrast to the bird, the old nature is like a burrowing animal that is earthly/worldly by nature. It prefers to be hidden in the darkness, concealing its true self[681]. It digs its way through life with great effort. Flight is against its nature and impossible for it, but it nevertheless seeks to prove its claim on life by seeking to make the same progress by its own effort and will.

This is the extreme contrast between living in the old nature, and living in the Spirit. If the Spirit is in control, then striving does not come into the equation.

---

[680] Rom 7:7-25
[681] John 3:19-21

CHAPTER 17: The Progressive Reform of Man

Does this mean that when we live in the Spirit we make no effort? Is living by the Spirit the soft option? On the contrary, the new nature is naturally devoted to the purpose of love; as the old nature is to its underlying purpose of self[682]. To the cause of love, the new nature commits all of its heart, soul, mind, and strength, and when called upon it may go to the limits of its capability to serve the purpose of love. However its actions are always its natural and normal expression.

Finney uses the example of a babysitter. Normally they would not babysit with all of their strength as no such exertion is needed. But if the house caught fire they would immediately spring into action to protect the little ones in their care, putting forth all the strength and effort they have available to secure them.

Of course in many cases, including this one, the actions of both natures are aligned because the full expression of love is aligned with that of self-interest. There would certainly be a considerable cost to self in this case in deciding to do otherwise. But the difference comes when the two purposes diverge, which is something that often occurs at the point where love demands self-sacrifice.

Living by Conscience

Living by conscience is not necessarily the same as living by the Spirit. It can translate into either living by law, or living by love.

When a person fails to live according to their conscience, the conscience passes judgement on them by measuring their actions against the purpose of love[683]. That judgment then impacts the person by exacting condemnation when they deliberately deviate from the purpose of love. The impact is powerful and it challenges their very self-worth, based on the principle that those that do not serve the purpose of love are not worthy of life. This may seem a harsh judgement, but if the *'author of life'*[684] is himself committed absolutely to the purpose of love, and he made his creatures to be the same, then to lose that basic standard value is to become entirely useless for the purpose for which they were made. The selfish nature will often therefore seek to conform to conscience to avoid this impact, which is in effect a cost to self. However this should not be

---

[682] Matt 22:37
[683] Rom 2:15
[684] Acts 3:15

mistaken as love. It is rather a response to the principle of law, implemented through the conscience, which is designed to control the selfish nature.

However, the new nature naturally lives by the principle of love rather than by conscience, but since they are both working to the same standard it means that they always conform indirectly to the demands of the conscience[685]. The aspects of judgment and condemnation in the conscience are therefore redundant as far as the new nature of the Spirit is concerned.

God himself does not live under the control of a conscience; he simply lives by his nature. Those who live by the Spirit do the same. There is therefore no condemnation to those that live by the Spirit[686], first because the conscience does not condemn them, but also because the Spirit is not living under it as its controlling principle. In fact there is no condemnation to those that are in Christ Jesus – those that are spiritually reborn, because their true identity is the Spirit. On the other hand their sinful nature is irreversibly condemned[687] regardless of the good it tries to do, or its attempts to justify itself, but this does not reflect on the true person because the sinful nature has ceased to be their true identity. While the sinful nature is in control of the mind, they may feel the effects of its condemnation acutely, but this is a lie that comes from an imposter that is temporarily keeping their mind captive by its false claim to be their true identity.

Therefore conscience, as for law, is something that is designed to only relate to the sinful nature, and not to the new nature of the Spirit. Just as law is something that was added to the covenant that God made with Israel, so conscience, with its aspect of judgement and condemnation, is something that is added to man for a time to intrinsically impose the principle and judgement of law on his sinful nature[688]. On the other hand, the new nature is designed to live in liberty because it lives by the law naturally, so the judgements and dictates of conscience are redundant to it as a guiding principle.

---

[685] Rom 13:10
[686] Rom 8:1
[687] Rom 7:18 John 3:18
[688] Gal 3:19

CHAPTER 17: The Progressive Reform of Man

Personal struggles with sin

I have shared the story of how God led me into the experience of spiritual rebirth. I would have been delighted to say at this point my troubles were all over, but that would be far from the truth.

I had unquestionably been radically born again, and I was now spiritually alive and awake, but I had a problem that is very common: I was in a legalistic church. At the time I had no idea what legalism was. I was new to the faith and was just trying to keep up with what I was taught. For seven years I trod the treadmill of extremely legalistic doctrine that had a basic philosophy of try harder, and do more, as it does for all systems of law. At the same time, despite the inner hardship, I was growing spiritually through the inner counsel of the Holy Spirit, and the parts of the church diet that had some spiritual value. However the main problem is that the teaching of legalism is like yeast; if spreads into everything.

After seven years I had worked my heart out, and I crashed under inner and outer pressures of study, work, and the demands of church and religion. And also with a fairly serious illness that led to a partial lung collapse. As a youth I was quite a competitive character, having a reasonable frame and good strength, but here I was weakened in every way, not least of which was the failure of my Christian walk to produce the kind of fruit I had been expecting – love, joy, peace etc. It was at this all-time low point I finally gave up trying. I immediately felt the burden I had been carrying for years, to achieve spiritual success, lift from me, and I was released to simply believe and receive by grace through faith alone. This was a first great turning point for me since my spiritual rebirth. Over the next three years those truths grew and developed in me until I was able to break away from the legalistic control completely. At this point my life and faith went through a belated honeymoon period with God that lasted several years. I had discovered grace, and I lived on it daily. For the first time in a long time I had found some real inner peace.

Once again I would have been glad to stop there and say I lived happily ever after. However the truth was that although I had some remarkable times, and I lived in relative freedom and happiness, I had a growing concern that I still did not seem to be developing the fruit I had hoped for. I began to look at my walk with some disappointment, and eventually came to a new crisis where I laid my disappointment on the line to God. The following day God sent somebody across my path that just happened to drop me another huge key, and I nearly missed it.

We were talking about the way they approached each day, and how they overcame the sinful nature and saw God move for them in their life. The simple comment was casually dropped out: 'oh I just reckon myself dead to sin'[689]. Of course I knew this scripture, but it was a kind of abstract concept that didn't really have significance or meaning, and which after a while you just learned to read over. What I realised that day was that this person was experiencing success, not only without trying harder, but they were hardly even trying. They had discovered a secret of living an entirely natural life in the Spirit by faith.

For myself my walk was maintained to some degree by spiritual activity, but here I saw something that was much easier. My attention was immediately called back to my early breakthrough and I suddenly had what was for me, something of an epiphany – which was the revelation that this is how it all worked. I had long since got the message of salvation and justification by faith. I had also discovered the truth of *'by grace through faith'*. What I had missed is that sanctification – the change in our behaviour and experience – comes in exactly the same way.

For the next three months I began to exercise faith that aligned my thinking about myself with what the scripture said about me. I realised that at heart I am Christlike in every detail. All I had to do was to discover it and believe it. Over this three month period I found myself in a fresh battle, but not this time a battle to directly generate fruit, or live a successful spiritual life. It was simply a battle to believe the truth about myself. I experienced failure in many ways, more than I had for a long time, but I realised that this was simply a battle to define me in ways that neither God nor the scriptures did as a born again believer. Temptation came thick and fast, but there was a deep conviction within me that this was all lies. As these three months came to an end, my enemy gave up, and fled[690]. I have never looked back since. There have been problems since, sometimes more than ever, but the outcomes are totally different. Victory comes by faith. If you are prepared to believe the outward evidences you will be defeated. Faith is of the heart[691]. I have learnt the

---

[689] Rom 6:11
[690] Jam 4:7
[691] Eph 3:17 Rom 10:8

wiles of the enemy[692], and how he is sometimes able to withhold and delay the truth with his scheming and lying. What I now know is it is by faith from first to last, and I have learnt to listen to my spirit, and then simply believe until I see the truth of it emerge in my experience.

I now spend my life in Romans chapter 8. Romans chapter 7 was tough, but it now seems a long time ago. I have come to understand that God's main agenda is to develop faith, so I welcome those challenges. As faith has expanded, so has ministry. We see God regularly moving among us with miracles on the streets of the city of Nottingham England in which we serve. I am excited daily that God is boundless, and I continue to chart a course into the fullness of the life he has for me in all areas of my living, always wondering what comes next. I am ready for heaven, and no doubt the wait will not be too long, but meanwhile I intend to carry on enjoying and proving God in all things – by faith.

Having had several epiphany moments in my Christian walk that showed me I was only living in part of the truth, I now remain open minded and ready for another such revelation. I have whisperings of further discoveries yet to be had. I hope it is so. But while I remain open and seeking, I leave these things to God who is able to lead me into them when the time is right[693].

Overcoming – the lie of spiritual compromise

There are various methods the old sinful nature has of gaining control of the mind. One of them is to lead us away from realising that there are two possible, and distinctly different, controlling entities over the mind, including itself. If we don't recognise this, we will look at ourselves and the two natures as one being, and own all of our successes and failures together. The effect of this is the same as putting black and white together; we end up with nothing but grey.

The truth about the Spirit, from which comes the new nature, is that it is entirely perfect and holy. It is Christ in me through and through to perfection. On the other hand, the sinful nature is a fallen and dead spirit, and is completely corrupt. There is absolutely nothing good in it, even though it claims to be good[694]. In each case the nature that controls the mind seeks to extend its expression to the whole of the mind and soul.

---

[692] Eph 6:11
[693] Heb 12:2 Phil 2:13

To live a good life while controlled by the old spirit is a falsehood, and it is the very essence of religion, as seen and regarded in all its ugliness by the world. The issue of which of the two spirits has control of our mind is a completely black and white affair. The scriptures affirm that if the new nature is in control, then we *cannot* gratify the desires of the sinful nature[695]. It is a deception to allow these two things to be meshed together in our understanding. The effect is like the fly in the ointment; it contaminates the whole thing. To think in anything but black and white terms about ourselves and our nature, is to play directly into the hands of the sinful nature, giving it complete control. We should never fail to acknowledge when we have fallen into sinful behaviour, but we must always understand that the sinful nature gets control through our letting go of faith in our true identity, and allowing the old spirit opportunity to take control by imposing a false identity of its own.

Overcoming – through reckoning

Reckoning is simply a process of affirming the truth in our own mind. It is something that we need to do on a daily basis, like putting on a coat, or like washing our face in the morning[696]. We can do it anywhere and anytime. It can be done in seconds, though it is best to spend additional time meditating more extensively on the truth of it to really affirm it. There are two kinds of reckoning – general and specific.

General reckoning – General reckoning is to acknowledge and affirm two spiritual realities. The first is that '*it is no longer I that live*'. We reckon on the fact that when Christ died on the cross my old sinful nature was crucified in him. I no longer identify that old nature as myself. That old nature is Sin; that is its name, and I am dead to Sin. I am an entirely new being and it is '*Christ who lives in me*' that is my new and true identity. It is him that has formed the new union with my soul to make a whole new being with a wholly righteous and holy nature. This is who I am; the true me. All other claims of sinful identities are false. Though there may be times of failure, nevertheless that nature is an imposter to my mind, and has no right to be there, or to stake any claim on my mind or the

---

[694] Rom 7:18
[695] Gal 5:16-18
[696] Luke 9:23 Rom 6:11

rest of my being. My life is hidden in Christ[697]. Here we have an act of shear faith that is confirmed in us by the voice of the Holy Spirit, who is our true centre.

Specific reckoning – We may identify areas of weakness where the old sinful nature often manages to gain access. Over these areas we once again affirm the truth by faith: Our new nature is entirely Christlike. We therefore reckon that in these areas we are dead to an old sinful behaviour pattern, and that in this area we are Christlike in every way.

The scripture says that the Holy Spirit takes of the things of Christ and makes them known to us. That does not just mean he shows them to us, but he makes them known *in* us.

For example, if we are aware of areas of anxiety we can be sure that this is not Christ manifesting himself in us, but it is something of the old nature. To overcome in this specific area we look to the Holy Spirit to reveal to us the peace that Jesus has, even in the most trying circumstances. We then simply reckon, as an act of faith, that this is the expression of our true nature. In this way, by faith, we overcome in the area of anxiety, and we come to a place of rest in God in this area. We do not need to produce the result; we leave that to God. If the anxiety does not seem to abate, we simply continue to hold on to the conviction that it is not our true nature, knowing that it cannot hold out for long against the truth. In this way we take every thought and make it captive to Christ – by grace through faith alone.

Overcome – resist the devil

It is a common experience to meet resistance when battling to overcome by faith alone. The devil is able at times to hold out against us, even maintaining symptoms after the work is done. We must resist by drawing on the inner conviction of the truth that the Holy Spirit gives us at all times and regarding all things. We affirm the truth of our position, even in the absence of the evidence. We don't deny that the evidence of victory has not arrived yet; we are into the truth not make-believe. But we keep our spiritual eyes wide open to know the truth from our inner conviction of faith on any issue, rather than by natural sight. The devil resists and delays in the hope that we will abandon our faith. If we feel our faith is waning,

---

[697] Col 3:3

we don't try to sustain it ourselves. We recognise that even this is God given, and we rely wholly on God to sustain our faith in challenging and contrary circumstances.

Of course we must all learn to hear the voice of God correctly, and this comes with maturity, but it only comes by exercising our spiritual senses over and above our natural senses. There are times when wishful thinking gets the better of us over true faith, but we will soon learn to recognise these occasions as we relax in God. For many things we have the added affirmation of scripture, and it is in these areas particularly that we should take a stand on the truth.

Is this just positive thinking?

What we are speaking about here is not just positive thinking. It is the alignment of the mind with the truth, and it is the truth that sets us free. Positive thinking can be deception if it is not grounded in the truth. However it so happens that the things of the Spirit are always profoundly positive for those that are called according to the love of God. Why should they not be when God is a God of infinite love, and the work of the cross is complete? Honesty is a key virtue and if there are negativities to face then we have to face them. However we are not simply trying to think positively. In all of this what we want are the real spiritual truths that will be a firm foundation for us, and to overcome the lies of a deceitful nature that would like to mask the truth for its own ends.

In the context of sport, many have discovered that confidence is a key issue for success. The confidence is derived through faith in some form. We therefore have the pre-match team talks that seek to instil in the players the self-belief that will produce the desired performance on the field. Many teams have found themselves on a roll of success for a time, based on this kind of belief – such is the power of faith. However, though such self-belief has a clear impact for a time, in the long run the true underlying quality of the team tends to be the thing that prevails. That is because faith will always naturally gravitate to the truth. It can only be sustained against the truth by considerable effort to cover up the truth.

The sinful nature is on a constant treadmill of seeking to sustain its self-belief by artificially boosting itself against the underlying truth of its state of corruption. We therefore see it perpetually engaging in self-deception in order to maintain an *ego*.

By contrast, the true nature has nothing to hide. It is entirely Christlike in nature and within it is all the power of Christ to overcome. The battle to live in the new nature is therefore almost exactly the opposite of living in the flesh. The struggle of the flesh is to maintain its self-deception against the onslaught of truth, whereas the struggle of the Spirit is to realise the truth, whilst constantly under the attack of an enemy that seeks to suppress it. One is battling to conceal the truth, while the other is battling to reveal it. The old nature therefore has the problem of maintaining positive thinking. However all the new nature needs to do is to realise the truth about itself to think positively.

The fruit of the Spirit

Scripture uses several expressions to describe the state where the Spirit of God is in control of our mind. These include:

- Walk by the Spirit.
- Clothe yourself with Christ.
- Abide/Remain in Christ.

In the last of these Jesus promises that if we abide in him, we will bear much fruit; fruit that lasts. The fruit of the Spirit is everything that anybody who ever desired happiness ever needs to be happy. If we possess spiritual fruit then externals, such as material possessions, become irrelevant. In truth, though they don't realise it, people seek this fruit above all things, but they are led to believe that through the pursuit of *things* – pleasure, image/status, pride – that they can be achieved. However fruit of this kind is an internal thing. It seems that the nature of flesh realises it does not possess them, so it pursues them through external means, which is its only available resource. The result of this is the acts of the sinful nature that have the very opposite effect.

What is the fruit of the Spirit? – We have already discussed that a fairly comprehensive list of the fruit of the Spirit would be: *faith, knowledge, patience, tolerance, forgiveness, self-control, perseverance, humility, sensitivity, truthfulness, protectiveness, goodness, godliness, brotherly kindness, compassion, hopefulness, peace, joy* and *love* that progressively grows and matures into all of its forms. But this is only possible for a mind controlled by the Spirit, and it can never happen through a mind controlled by the old nature of flesh. Faith is the thing that releases us to live by the Spirit. We are therefore drawn right back to faith in God, and in our true identity in Christ as the fundamental means to producing spiritual fruit.

The importance of spiritual fruit? – We discussed earlier how these fruits parallel with the jewels that makes up part of the very fabric of heaven. The fruit we bear are the highlights of heaven, all set in the foundation of the gold of faith.

As we have said: bearing spiritual fruit only happens as we walk in the Spirit. Time spent walking in the old nature of flesh is like time for land spent lying fallow. Of course for all of us there must be some of this as we learn to live better, but any more than really necessary is a complete waste. It is clear that some will spend their whole lives after rebirth walking in the flesh. Ironically this may take the form of religious activity, but it is only walking in the Spirit of love by grace through faith that can bear eternal fruit.

Both here on earth, and in heaven, the fruit that we bear is enjoyed by all. Even here, when we meet someone that has matured in their walk, and is carrying the fruit of the riches of the coming kingdom, we can hardly ever fail to be profoundly impacted by them. Sometimes we meet someone who is clearly ripe and ready to go, and the experience of it is so profound we are eternally enriched just by the very contact.

We should all desire to be fruitful, and be concerned when we are not. At the same time we must realise that our Father is the gardener, and he prunes us with a view to maximising our fruit. When we realise this it helps us to bear the times of dryness and fruitlessness with patience in expectation of a greater harvest to come. The fruit we produce is eternal, and all other creatures will forever enjoy it in us, as we will enjoy the same in them. Thank God that he is in overall control, but at the same time remember we have been called to walk by the Spirit by grace through faith, and never to treat this as if it were an optional extra.

One thing I have learnt is that the sinful nature never improves. In fact over time it degenerates even further, and though it is often suppressed, underneath there is more and more expression of its corruption.

There is a story about Abraham Lincoln who once said about someone *'I don't like the man's face'*. When challenged on his attitude with the defence that *'He can't be held responsible for his face'*, his famous retort was *'Every man over 40 is responsible for his face'*.

Recently research has discovered, by studying people with different areas of brain damage, that we have a part of our physical brain devoted to object recognition, but an entirely different part developed for face recognition. As a result, through this highly specialised faculty, we are able to see and interpret every minor variation of a facial expression. This part of our brain is finely tuned and devoted to the purpose. The message here is that there is no place to hide. Probably as a result of this, I recently heard a training session to salesmen expounding the latest philosophy, which is that a very high percentage of our communication is body language; therefore the best policy is to tell the truth because we can't easily hide it. Not quite the moral revolution we would have wished for in the salesman community, but undoubtedly a step in the right direction.

In earlier years I had a recurring dream in which I saw a contrasting picture. First of a very smooth clean surface; something like very finely sanded pine that then switched to something I would describe as grotty. The scene would then switch back and forth from smoother to grottier, and the contrast would get wider and wider. When I finally realised the dream had meaning, I asked God to reveal it to me, and I came to understand that what God was saying to me is that there is no middle ground. The good of the new nature is completely good, and the bad of the sinful nature is completely bad. The more we move on in life, the more this fact shows through. The remarkable thing about this dream is that without me ever sharing it, two of my children that have a similar temperament to me, described having exactly the same dream.

The longer we choose to live in the flesh, the more the true state of its nature starts to show in the product of our life. It is clear that some will reach heaven having only the foundation of faith in Christ, but nothing built on it that is of any value. These will suffer the sense of loss as they see what could have been. It is they that show us the cost of living out our lives from the position of the sinful nature, and it serves as a warning that we must treat the whole issue of finding the true Way of living by the Spirit with the care and deliberation it deserves.

Pruning – Jesus made it clear to us that the Father is the one that seeks to maximise our fruitfulness. What he seeks from us is compliance by remaining/abiding in Christ. When we go through times of real fruitfulness, life is invariably good, but God sees our potential for even greater.

Also during these times, the flesh is sometimes able to capitalise on our success, claiming it for itself. This claim is false, but the old nature is deceitful and does not concern itself too much with what is true or false, but just with whatever will serve its own purpose.

The flesh may therefore come to boast in our success derived from living in the Spirit, as if it were its own. If we embrace this claim we may find ourselves launching out again into self-belief, rather than realising that all that has been done has been done through God[698]. This is like the growth on the tree that supports the fruit that the gardener must prune back if it is not to hinder further growth. The pruning process is therefore often a period of dryness and apparent fruitlessness, where God leads us to relinquish our self-belief. These times may be marked by a level of dissatisfaction or even failure. In such times we are forced to lean hard again on grace and mercy, which re-establishes us in a place where our faith is fully resting on God. We return to wholesale dependence on him for all things, and we become ready for yet another season of fruit bearing.

During times of pruning it is helpful to remember that the fruit we bear is fruit that lasts – eternally. Though we may be deprived of its benefit for a time in this age, we are assured that it is like treasure, stored up in heaven. God is already gathering and storing a harvest for us that will only be fully realised in eternity[699].

The responsibility of fruit – As we have repeatedly said: the fruit of the Spirit are pictured as jewels in the ages to come. This dual image of fruit and jewels expresses their beauty, permanence, and the enjoyment that will be eternally derived from them. We previously discussed the fall of Lucifer, and that part of the purpose, position, and calling of redeemed man is to replace him among the angelic beings, known as the morning stars[700].

At this point we should note that the fall of Lucifer came about through pride on account of his great beauty[701], and he is revealed to have

---

[698] John 3:21
[699] 2 Cor 4:7, Matt 6:20
[700] Rev 2:28, Job 38:7

been adorned with every jewel[702]. He became absorbed in his own beauty and engaged in self-worship, thereby becoming the first selfish being, having lost sight of God.

We can speculate that among the angels the morning stars may be the most beautiful, and that Lucifer was probably the most beautiful of them. Even the other morning stars probably admired him as an exquisite work of God. Had he had another to look up to, he probably would not have thought himself in a position to compare himself with God[703].

This leads us to reflect on the fact that if God has purposed us to fill the vacancy left by Lucifer, then his plan is to make our beauty comparable with his before he fell, or even greater. Given, as we have repeatedly said, that God intends to make eternity secure from another fall through the events of this age, it is clear that God's purposes with us must be to make us able to carry such beauty without leaving us vulnerable to the same kind of fall that took place with Lucifer. We therefore see once again how incredibly important it is that we learn true humility in this age, and know and believe in our total dependence on God, while at the same time we are fitted to carry his glory, and are similarly adorned with every heavenly jewel.

The fact that we are fallen and redeemed, and have experienced such depravity, is something that is therefore vitally important to the security of that place of humility. The permanent reminders we have of these things, not least of which is in the Lamb that was slain, are designed by God to eternally maintain it.

It is those that overcome that are promised the morning star, which is something that is only achieved through faith[704]. We therefore see how important it is that the values of the world which we have called *'the lust of the eyes'* – vanity and self-image, is overcome. Those that cling to sinful worldly substitutes, even religious ones, will not have a part in this kind of fruit, or this role of the morning star, but will only come through with some measure of the gold – faith, which forms the foundations in which these jewels are set[705].

---

[701] Ezek 28:17
[702] Ezek 28:13
[703] Isaiah 14:112-14
[704] 1 John 5:4
[705] Ezek 28:13

CHAPTER 18: Living by Grace

The attitude to grace
There is a certain attitude to grace that says: 'yes we are saved by the undeserved favour of grace, but now having received it we should not push our luck, and we should now work to justify it'. Some see grace as something to be accessed in the event of sin and failure to obtain forgiveness, but having received it we should then seek to live the kind of life where we don't really need it, otherwise we are just exploiting God's good nature.

This attitude completely misses the point of grace for several reasons. First it limits grace to mercy, which is just one form of grace. Secondly it completely fails to recognise the difference between the two natures and the battle that goes on between them. It fails to see that God intends us to be extravagant with his grace, receiving grace upon grace.

Mercy
It is a major mistake to limit grace to mercy; however mercy is a form of grace that allows us to access the forgiveness of God whenever we need it.

In the book of Lamentations the prophet Jeremiah shares with us the truth that *'the mercies of God are new every morning'*. Through mercy, every day becomes a new start. We often need it because we often falter and fail. In one sense it is true that we should try not to have to access mercy more than we need to, because we should always seek to avoid failure, but the mercy of God is always available for us when we need it – should we want it!

The need for mercy – The Bible actually says that God has bound all men over to disobedience that he may have mercy on them all[706]. He did it because it is a vital thing that man is reformed by being brought back to the place of total dependence on him. To receive grace in the face of deserved punishment of death and banishment from heaven, is something that fits perfectly into this plan of reform, because it is the most radical

---
[706] Rom 11:32

expression of undeserved grace. It has therefore been carefully placed by God as the very first step into a spiritual life. We come to faith by receiving grace in the form of the mercy of forgiveness. For man to take the step of receiving mercy means moving well away from the state of independence, into a place of total and complete dependence on God. As such it is a vital step, and it is only made possible by God's extreme actions in going to the cross.

The mercy of the cross – Receiving mercy is made possible for God by the cross of Christ. Only because of the cross can God give us mercy without compromising the very principle of his nature, which is love. The cross shows us the extremes to which God went to secure mercy for us. He did it simply because it was possible without compromising love. Had it not been possible to offer mercy, and still serve the highest good – love, then there would have been no way back for us, and we would have fallen beyond redemption, as did the fallen angels.

Grace beyond mercy

As we have said: mercy is only the beginning of grace. In truth everything we have that is of any eternal value to us is a gift of grace, even our normal daily provisions. To try not to live by grace is to consign oneself to a spiritually impoverished life. The poor in spirit are intended to find true riches through grace. They must be ready to receive from God what they don't and couldn't possibly ever deserve.

It may seem right from one point of view to only receive what is offered, and not to be pushy and ask for more grace than we should, especially in view of the fact we don't deserve it. But this kind of thinking is worldly, and fails to acknowledge that God is God and we are entirely dependent on him as his creatures. Once again it is the worldly independent view that says I must be self-sustaining. The truth is: when we ask God for something good we advance the cause of love. God is not only happy to give good things, it is against his very nature not to. Haven't we yet got the message of how extreme God is when it comes to the purpose of love?

When I look back to my early Christian walk, there were many times I prayed ambitious prayers that were probably more an expression of my old nature than the new. However I was often aware of receiving an inspiration of the Spirit that led me to almost inadvertently ask for something good that fitted God's plan. The inspiration came in the form of faith rising with a deep inner conviction that what I had asked for was good, and that it was therefore granted. In many of these cases, though God didn't answer immediately, because at the time that would not have been good, he nevertheless immediately set about transforming me and preparing me to receive it. As a result, by the time I came to receive what I had asked for, my whole motivation for wanting it had changed. Through discipline God had brought me to a place where receiving what I had asked for became genuinely good. This is how ready God is to lavish his grace and goodness on us.

Long before we learn to walk consistently in the Spirit, these sparks of inspiration come through to us from the Holy Spirit to sustain us and lead us into the things of God, even though often we may not fully understand what we are asking.

The conditions of grace – Grace has three conditions: The first is that we ask – this is always true where we are seeking for something within our own domain of responsibility. By asking we express dependence on him, and we use our God given authority over ourselves and our environment which is a profoundly good thing, and vital for our development as his sons.

The second condition is that what we ask must be good. If it is not, then true faith will not rise as God confirms in us that our request is granted.

The third is that we must receive it. Again humility is needed to receive because it is an act of dependence where we receive against merit or desert.

Grace upon grace – God intends that we not only receive grace but that we go on receiving grace upon grace[707]. The more we receive what is good, the more the purpose of love is served. When we receive something good, then that often opens us up to new opportunities, where something further is now good to receive to complement or extend what we have already received – to those that have more is given[708]. The question of whether or not we deserve it is not even a relevant question. Grace is

---

[707] John 1:16
[708] Matt 13:12

radical. The only question that matters with God is: Is it good? – The highest good? If it is, he wants us to have it. If we really get hold of this message we begin to approach every day with a kind of God sanctioned audacity that says each day 'I wonder what I can receive today that I don't deserve?', and God truly delights in it.

Why do many miss the truth of grace?

Many churches miss the truth of God's grace and become completely defeated as a result. Their argument against it usually takes some form that suggests that if we teach people to receive undeserved favour, especially in the form of mercy, they will abuse it and use it as an excuse to live a sinful life; which we call license. Fearing the projected consequences, they then develop a doctrine that emphasises responsibility for righteous behaviour, and the teaching of grace is acknowledge but played down as potentially dangerous. Law then becomes the ruling principle once again.

At best this mistake is rooted in a failure to properly understand the truth of the two natures, and the kind of battle they are in. At worst this is a direct expression of the sinful nature in the form of religion, that is adamant it will not become dependent on God, but seeks to establish an independent righteousness of its own. The former is an error, the latter is a sin.

The end result for the church is the encroachment of worldly ideas, followed by worldly doctrines (law), structures (hierarchy/status), and order of operations (ceremony/programmes), that translate into forms of religion. In our day the norm for the church is to accept and operate on these worldly principles, rather than the order and principles on which the early church was established.

Grace and the two natures

We highlighted the error of failing to distinguish between the two natures, and treating the person as if both natures were one. The effect is like a fly in the ointment, or mixing black and white and getting only grey. The final result is that the person identifies themselves as sinful, and by doing so they hand control of their mind over to the old sinful nature, and inevitable defeat.

What we need to understand is that the two natures react entirely differently to the doctrine of grace. To the new nature grace utterly liberates it into an exploration and receiving of all that is good. To the old nature it is the invitation to live a life in license.

The question therefore arises: to which nature are we appealing when we preach grace? Granted to preach grace without also teaching a flock to live by the Spirit can be problematic, but what we find as leaders is that we are pushed into an all-or-nothing situation. If we don't preach grace in an overt and radical way, we will unavoidably develop some system and doctrine of law, because if our doctrine does not give ascendancy to the Spirit, then the old nature will remain in control and must be restrained by repression. Law stimulates the old nature because it appeals to its self-dependence, and what we end up with is religion. By failing to preach grace, we consolidate our listeners in the position of living in the old nature, and then we find that law is necessary to control it; because law is a principle of this world that is designed to repress sinful behaviour. Though such a system may look noble in its outward form, and in the standard it presents, it is actually an ignoble doctrine designed for law breakers. As such it invariably fails to produce real results, and is therefore a false gospel[709].

We therefore find ourselves in a situation where our people are living in a condition where they are religious, yet controlled by the old nature, and we are preaching a doctrine that merely represses sin, but never leads them into victory over it. This describes the sad state of numerous churches that are in a place of total defeat. They are entrenched in a Romans chapter 7 experience; always wanting victory, but never finding it. In effect such an institution is geared wholly to serving the needs of the sinful nature in their people, and it wholly neglects the needs of the new nature – faith.

A mistake that is often made is that grace is preached but then counterbalanced by warnings of the errors of license. However it is always an error to bring 'balance' to black and white issues, and the issue of living in the old or new nature is a strictly black and white affair. To include an addendum to the message of grace that warns against license, is to end a message on a note that speaks directly to the sinful nature. This is exactly what the sinful nature is waiting for, and ready to hear, because it can use it to entrench itself as the dominating factor over the mind, aided and abetted by Satan who is always waiting in the wings to affirm such a

---

[709] Gal 1:6-9, 3:1-3,10

word. If grace is preached, it must be preached absolutely and radically. To mix it with doctrines of the flesh is once again to contaminate the whole thing.

The way out of religion

The way to lead people out of this huge dilemma is to once again recognise the truth of the two natures, and to begin to teach grace, and the message of faith in their true identity. This will enable them to establish themselves in a consistent walk in the Spirit. The message of grace then becomes the very food of life that launches them into unlimited resources for blessing and victory. Firstly by leading them to discover the liberating rest that comes independently of merit, and which becomes a basis for all true works of the kingdom. Then by leading them to discover the power available to them through grace that they can then use to express their new found liberty.

Some churches preach the radical message of grace, but don't necessarily preach the truth of our identity in Christ. These churches tend to fair far better than those that have fallen headlong into a system of law, because generally grace fosters dependence on God, whereas law fosters independence of him. However these churches often feel they don't reach the radical heights of Romans chapter 8; becoming more than conquerors. Without the message of identity they tend to stumble along to some degree, but generally make progress. In view of their partial success with people, leaders are often tempted to revert to a system of law which sometimes encroaches on them without them realising it. For them to find the true spiritual victory they long for in their churches, a much more focused message of their identity in Christ is needed, together with the radical message of grace.

The gospel of the early church

When the early church began its mission to the world, without yet having access to the full scriptures of the New Testament, they went with a powerful message. The primary and central message was not just salvation by faith through grace, though these things were undoubtedly preached as part of it. Only as the full scriptures emerged and were revealed, was a fuller understanding of these things received, and it took a while for the detail of these truths to be absorbed. But the message that went out with them, burning in their hearts, was the truth and reality of *'Christ in me'*. Above and beyond all that they had heard, this is what they had experienced that had so radically changed them, and they were unstoppable in delivering it to the world. It was Christ in them that delivered the message to the world, accompanied by all the power and demonstration that comes with that message. The message of Christ in me, as it has been made possible through the cross, in still the primary and central message. An intellectual message can never replace it. To come under it is shear experience of God.

Someone has said: 'Blessed are they that receive this message from the beginning' – the message of Christ in me – identification with Christ. Among those that were raised on it from spiritual birth are some of the most powerful men and women on the planet.

It seems that for those that come under the doctrine of law from early on in their Christian walk, once they have encountered it they are bound to a long and circuitous path that they must follow through until they are led back to the true Way. On this road their walk is made rough and rugged, even mountainous, strewn with the humbling pain of failure. They have to grow like alpine plants and trees that must tough their way through the rocky bones of the earth to survive.

But for those that are raised from the beginning with this message and truth of 'Christ in me', every hill is brought low, and every valley is raised up. Their path is made smooth by those that disciple them in the Lord. They become like trees planted by the waterside, with their roots going down deep, rapidly growing to maturity and bearing an abundance of fruit in season. These are the ones that the church must now raise as we come to the challenge of the last days. They are those for whom *'Christ in me'* is abundantly evident.

All of this works in God's purpose and plan. God made men individuals, and some are designed to grow slow and tough. Others were always intended to show rapid growth, with the colour and beauty we see in a well-kept garden. Now is the time the church must blossom into full colour as the days grow dark, and this is the message they must carry. This was the key message of the early church, and it will once again be the message of the church of the last days – that I am dead to my old nature that is nailed to the cross, and it is now not I that live but Christ that lives in me.

Grace is radical

Preaching grace seems radical, but this is only the view from the position of the old nature. For the new nature, freedom is all that it needs to thrive, so grace is its natural principle.

It is important that beyond teaching grace, we go on to teach people to identify themselves with the new nature of Christ in them. If we fail to teach grace our only alternative is law, and we will end up developing another worldly system. As C. S. Lewis points out: Christianity can either make you very much better, or very much worse. Living in the old nature is no picnic. People really suffer. Heavy loads are placed on their shoulders that they are unable to carry. They suffer perpetual disappointment, and sometimes real depression.

The doctrine of identification with Christ, together with the truth about grace, is the only thing that will ensure they come out into the life that they expected to find when they first found mercy at the cross of Christ.

Legalism and churches

Over the decades since my conversion, my experience of churches has been similar, on an earthly individual scale, to what I have been describing will happen through the ages of ages to come. In each age we are prepared for the higher values of the next. In this evil age we are being trained in the values of heaven, ready for us to receive the kingdom that God has prepared us for. Only that part of us that is ready for the next will make it through. The rest will be stripped off and discarded like chaff from wheat.

My beginnings were entrenched in a legalistic church, and in this situation I grew spiritually until I outgrew it and even 'overcame' it. The time inevitably came when the Spirit began to lead me out of it, like the transplanting of a plant into a larger pot. Over several decades there have been several such transplants, and as it is for a plant the move is never too easy, but in each case I have eventually found myself among others that were of like mind, and operating to the higher values I had discovered for myself. I am delighted to have eventually found my way to a place that I regard as of more noble character, and operating on more noble values. These are the values and principles of grace.

Ideally in each situation I found myself in, I would have loved to carry the whole body of believers forward with me into those higher

CHAPTER 18: Living by Grace 313

values, and in each case I tried to do so by words and appeals to the leaders. However God's kingdom cannot be established through conflict, and by political manoeuvring as it is seen to operate in this world. Having done my best to avoid some mistakes on that level in the early stages, I felt severely the check of the Spirit not to embrace such methods. In the end one can only pray and speak the truth in the hope that the hearts of those in control will hear something of God in what is said. If they do not respond to that, then there is no other way forward but prayer, and one must continue to show as much grace as one is able, and wait for God to send the same message to them through other channels. For a time such a situation may even stimulate further spiritual growth in a person under such leadership, but eventually, if there is no change, God will move such a person on to higher climes so they can continue to grow and mature in faith.

My observation, as I look back on these moves and leadings of the Spirit, is that at least some people in these congregations continue to grow spiritually. However for the leaders this is not always the case. They often seem to become the ones who are entrenched at that level, and are unable to move forward, or upward. When this happens it usually seems to be due to something more than simply disagreement on ideas. There is usually some clinging to something; perhaps the security of a salary, or power, or honour or position, or some clinging to assets. If the basic value of servanthood is not a firmly held and maintained value in their mind, then invariably there will be some issues of power or pride involved.

Generally these things must be dealt with by frustrated members by closely following the Holy Spirit and doing what he says. However God does not generally force a leader out of such a position, he simply grows the people around him through it. It is a sad fact that serves as a real warning, that ultimately *'many who are first will be last'*[710]. Often, if leaders press themselves forward into leadership before they have had time to spiritually develop into the higher values, they often get out of step in their walk in the Spirit, and become entrenched at the level at which they stepped forward. God will often act to alert them to their problem, but if they remain entrenched then the growth of those they lead may be much tougher, but God will continue to use it in his plan to develop strong believers.

---

[710] Mat 19:30 Mark 10:31

The only time that leaders seem to really spiritually prosper through the step into leadership, is when they step up in response to a clear direction of God, and they have therefore remained in step with the Spirit in entire dependence on him. Then these leaders seem to grow along with their members. Anything else must be grounded in the sinful nature, and be an expression of independence from God based on a desire for self-achievement, or something on the same level. For as long as such independent motivation exists in them, these men will not be able to grow into greater dependence on God, which is the very essence of maturity. And how can such ones possibly teach dependence on God having stepped out of it. God must work despite them, instead of through them, to mature the flock. Their only recourse is therefore to repent, even though their step into leadership may have been given the hearty sanction of men.

In our time we face momentous days ahead, so I feel compelled to issue that call to leaders. Only in this way can we overcome the more pitiful aspects of the organised church in our day. Please examine your hearts and if necessary humble yourself and repent.

Legalism and Leaders

Having opened this can of worms, I feel I must at least tip out all the worms and get the real issues of legalism out on the table. As I have said: doctrines based on the principles of law only have the effect of stimulating the sinful nature, as the apostle Paul made very clear[711]. Any leaders that find themselves in this position are then forced to address the problem of the rampant sinful nature, with all of its self-belief, lust for status and power, and desire for independence of God. This naturally leads to church structures that are designed to repress and control the sinful nature, which inevitably means some system of penalty and/or reward, and therefore to the introduction of status and of the penalty of law; even if they are only social penalties. This path then essentially leads to power structures and hierarchies through which the sinful nature can be ruled. In our day we see these structures as almost the norm in churches, proving that we are still in the dark ages of the church, in terms of its worldly institutions.

Conversely, any church that has promoted and stimulated the new nature of 'Christ in me' has no such issues. The only need in such a place is to maintain that position, and liberate its members to freely express their

---

[711] Rom 7:5

CHAPTER 18: Living by Grace

new nature, and therefore the structure is entirely different. The only thing that can achieve this is to preach radical grace – as grace is. In these places the leaders become true servants of the body, and not lords.

Where leaders readily step forward to take up the hierarchical roles that stem from legalistic doctrines, there is often some ignorance of the fact that these systems are thoroughly worldly in their structure, and of the way it violates the declarations of Jesus that the greatest among you shall be the least. To step into such a role and structure, a leader is thereby taking to themselves a ruling position, and placing themselves first among their brethren. They then traditionally dominate the contributions that others are able to make to serve the body, and in doing so they truly grasp the worldly 'ring of power' that Tolkien so masterfully portrayed to be so dangerous in his novels, with all of its addictive seduction.

How will all this fare in the final judgement. First of all, as we have said, we can expect as Jesus said: *many who are first shall be last*[712]. This statement most emphatically applies to churches more than any other application. How often will God's judgement of this show, that whilst a leader has dominated the ministry to the flock, there have been others among them that have been better equipped by the Lord to serve the real needs of his body, but are given no right or opportunity due to the structure of the church and the domination of their leaders. In every such instance the leader will be judged to have inhibited the kingdom, rather than promoted it[713].

Furthermore, those that step forward as teachers are warned that it is only a task for those of noble character. This nobility correlates precisely to those that have learned to live consistently in the Spirit, and express only Christ within, which in turn implies they have discovered the true principles of grace and identification with Christ by faith. But we would expect those of such nobility to realise that the structures they are stepping into, and thereby advocating and promulgating, are worldly.

To bring this view back into balance we have to recognise that God does not abandon us when we go astray, either individually or with our systems and institutions. Rather he faithfully continues to show up as promised where two or three gather in his name, even when he is forced to take a

---

[712] Matt 19:30 Mark 10:31
[713] 1 Cor 14:26, 30

back seat, or even when he is locked out altogether so that all he can do is knock, as he did for the church of Laodicea. Our church situation can often be paralleled to the days when Israel demanded a king, even though God warned them against it, and foretold the problems that would arise through it[714]. However the people could only think in terms of what they saw around them in the rest of the world, and chose it anyway. The rest is history; the majority of kings went astray, but among them were a few of noble characters that resisted the trappings of power and prestige, and led Israel through a time of real blessing.

Fortunately among those that step forward to lead in these worldly church structures are not just those that desire power, or honour, or precedence, but there are also those that recognise the faults of the system, but still hear and receive a call from God to take up the role, and so step forward as a kind of protector, like Cromwell did to the English parliament, whose declared intention was only to protect the freedom of those they serve from domination, rather than to dominate them themselves. Among them are clearly some that take the role, but eschew the power, in order to facilitate the freedom that should be prevalent in churches. This would surely then be judged a noble act, but even for many of these the worldly status and benefits have proved to be too much of a temptation to resist.

In the end many that have declined to take these positions because they judged them to be against God's order, will be seen to have served the kingdom better than those that opted for the prominence. These should be humbling thoughts for all leaders. And for those that are aware of the dangers, and are grieved by the state of the church; they can continue to look with expectation to the day of restoration of true New Testament church as it was practiced when it began.

Maturity and identity

The message of identification with Christ is a message that it is often only possible for a believer to receive who has a certain level of spiritual maturity in the faith. This varies from person to person because some are more independently minded than others, so it is usually linked to the need for a measure of failure before they begin to abandon their belief in their own self sufficiency, and start to depend on God by faith in a radical way.

---

[714] 1 Sam 8:6-11

In the meantime believers may manifest all the attributes of the sinful nature: pride, self-sufficiency, vanity, desires of the flesh etc. The question arises: How can we best help these people and serve the purposes of love?

How can we help? – When we see the old sinful nature manifesting itself through fellow believers, we may find ourselves tempted to react in a number of ways. These reactions can be a provocation of our own sinful nature that on the one hand may want to expose them, or on the other hand may seek to suppress their behaviour.

Any suppression would invariably be based on some form of law and application of associated authority. As we have discussed: such a reaction may suppress the sinful nature, but it will not overcome it, and as discussed, it is more likely to stimulate it further, entrenching the believer in their walk in the flesh. It is also likely to stimulate our own sinful nature and lead to us walking in the flesh in some way too.

Similarly the desire to expose sinful behaviour is often an attempt to control it using a form of law enforcement, based on social or group pressure. The problem with such exposure is that it tends to affirm the believer in a false identity of the sinful nature, as does any use of shame as a means of control. For example, if we react to expressions of anger in a fellow believer by exposing the person as 'an angry person', this can then become an identity, which only serves to entrench them in this aspect of their nature because they come to identify with it as their true self. In the short term the behaviour may be suppressed, but beyond that it will leave them with a false view of their true self, thereby handing control to the sinful nature and exacerbating the problem.

To really help such a believer to truly overcome their problems with the sinful nature, we must help them to learn to live in the Spirit. Only this will truly work. Everything else is superficial. To do this we must let the Holy Spirit be our guide, and we must treat them in exactly the same way that God does.

When God looks at a believer he sees their true nature; Christ in them, even when their mind is dominated and under the control of the flesh. God may be aware of the sinful nature they are manifesting, but he in no way identifies them with it. Therefore whenever God speaks to them he appeals to their true nature, and never to a false one. This may happen through numerous sources: a preached message; an impression in prayer; a word of another believer etc. As the mind of the believer hears God speak to them in these terms, they once again realise their true identity, and come into a position of living by the Spirit through their restored faith in the truth about themselves.

To help such believers we must align ourselves with the Holy Spirit, and treat them in the same way, regardless of their constant failure. In other words, we never respond to them by speaking to their sinful nature, as if this were their true self. We speak to their true nature. If we are truly going to help them then all of our words and reactions to them must recognise and appeal to their underlying true nature, recognising who they really are, regardless of their ongoing sinful expressions. In this way we give them the best chance of rediscovering the faith they need in themselves to hand control over again to the new nature. If we speak to them directly about their behaviour, it must be done in a way that recognises and affirms their true nature, characterising the sinful behaviour as something that we do not accept to be of their true self. We don't deny the fact of their sinful nature, but we simply refuse to accept it as an expression of their true inner self.

By affirming a fellow believer by grace in this way, we are helping them to carry their burdens with a view to releasing them – we are washing their feet. As a result we are serving them, the Kingdom, and the purpose of love. The chapter on love – 1 Corinthians 13, shows this to be the way of love. It recognises that faith is the key issue.

Serving leaders – As we have said: church leaders are often in a precarious position with their role often offering them great temptations in all areas of the flesh. It is all too easy for them to begin to derive identity from their position in the form of the '*lust of the eyes*' (image), '*pride of life*' (self-righteousness), or even the lust of the flesh where they are given inordinate levels of recognition and admiration. Many churches have met their demise though the encroachment of these things. If and when leaders are led into a walk of the flesh, the problem for the church can be acute. First of all a leader in such a position may stimulate the same in others, either through the development of fleshly doctrines, or just by the shear provocation and reactions to worldly or sinful behaviour and ideas.

In these situations, as a member of such a church, the same principle applies: The only way to help the church to stay on track is for us to stubbornly continue to recognise the underlying new nature of the leader in question, along with any others that are caught up in it. Whilst recognising that a battle with the flesh is in progress, we must continue to appeal to the new nature of this leader in order to recover their walk in the Spirit.

In my early years of encountering these situations, I have my regrets that my words and actions did little to help these situations. Fortunately I eventually learnt the lesson. What is demanded here is not naivety, but simply a realisation of what it really takes to recover such a situation: faith, through affirmation of the true identity of Christ within, and the exercise of real grace and mercy.

The alternative is invariably ugly, where the church breaks down and all end up only stimulating the sinful nature in each other, usually causing a fair amount of emotional damage in the process. This can even happen on a denominational scale.

Sometimes recovery is not possible. This is especially true where biblical values of leadership and authority, including mutual accountability, are not established and in place. In these situations one can only continue to maintain one's own walk in the Spirit, and follow the lead of the Holy Spirit for oneself, doing whatever is for the highest good in that situation. However, whatever happens we must never embrace the methods of the world when it comes to seeking to restore such situations. In these situations worldly political manoeuvring can become the modus operandi, but this can never serve the purposes of the kingdom of God. We must resist the temptation to engage in these ways, and even be prepared to suffer some injustice in the process. The word of God to stimulate faith based on truth, together with prayer, are our chief weapons in these battles, which are not against flesh and blood, but against principalities and powers in high places.

Serving the church – for maturing believers we can help the people along by affirming to them the truth about themselves, and that to overcome spiritually they have to become wholly dependent on God. We must, of course, model these things for them by living by them ourselves. However it will still take some time and growth before they are ready to hear and receive the truth of their identity. In the interim they will fail – frequently. Our response to this must be to constantly assure them of the continuing and unfazed love of God, and lead them to receive the grace of mercy and forgiveness until they realise for themselves that they can and must always depend of God in everything, even in failure. When the message of mercy has done its work they will soon blossom in faith, and become ready for this message of victory through faith in their true identity.

Any reversion to a system of law to try to control their behaviour will only slow them down or stop their progress altogether. We must patiently hold to the principle of grace and mercy until we see them break through into the good things God has for them through faith; all bought and paid for by the cross.

This does not mean we cannot speak into their life out of a place of a loving relationship, but the problems arise when we introduce methods of enforcement that take us out of the place of a servant, and effectively make us a lord. This includes psychological and social pressures that are so often used as a means of control, and as such are subtle forms of law. We must remain their servant, even if we choose to speak directly, so that they only respond in a free and voluntary way, which is the only kind of obedience God wants or accepts. If we speak we must be careful that it is always done in response to a direct leading and guidance of the Spirit. Anything else will only hinder their progress. Often it is simply right to wait for God to speak to them directly.

Our goal is to lead them through the stages of mercy and grace, and then on to full identification with Christ by faith. Once they begin to get the message of victory through the cross by faith alone, it is then that the fun begins, and one day they may thank you for all you did to help them through. On the other hand they may just be blissfully unaware of the trouble and heartache you saved them. Either way God's purpose of love for them is served, and we should be more than satisfied with that.

For many believers in our day that come into the truth of the message of identification with Christ, they come without ever hearing it taught explicitly. As a result they express their revelation of it in a wide diversity of terms, mostly describing the individual path by which God led them to it. Churches and doctrines are often then seen to have hindered them in this journey, rather than helped them as they should. However, as always God prevails in his purpose and these believer come to show the evidence of their discoveries in the whole look and feel of their lives, often over and above those that lead them.

CHAPTER 19: Overcoming the World

By faith
The sinful nature is of the world, with all of its various forms of self-belief and independence of God. The world is overcome by faith; faith in God, which is total dependence on God to an extent that it leaves no room for boasting of self-achievement, or any measure of independence.

We defined the world in the three categories of: the lust of the flesh; the lust of the eyes; and the pride of life. These three are all based on forms of self-belief that are entirely opposed to faith in God. Let's discuss how each of these expressions of the world is overcome by faith.

Overcoming – the lust of the flesh
The lust of the flesh is self-belief based on the belief that one can find satisfaction in life through the gratification of one's own appetites independently of God.

This is a state of faith in self. It is remarkable how in virtually all areas of appetite that self-indulgence can prove to lead to such dissatisfaction and misery for so long, yet the belief that it will bring satisfaction stubbornly persists, based on levels of gratification that are diminishing, and are often no more than fleeting.

As for all the categories of worldly expression, victory over the desires of the flesh is to be had through new faith in God that completely displaces this self-belief. This means two things. First it means losing faith that satisfaction can be derived from self-indulgence in independence of God, and secondly it means a positive faith that the appetites can be wholly satisfied through God's enabling and provision.

This is something different to the belief that satisfaction can be derived from simply sticking within God's guidelines of indulgence; such indulgence can still be based on self-belief and independence of God. It is something more than this. It is the belief that the provision of God for the satisfaction of all natural appetites is explicitly provided by God, and is therefore blessed and accepted by him. As such these provisions are even received as a form of worship[715].

The scripture says God has richly provided all things for our enjoyment[716]. It is coming into a positive place of faith that believes this – that God has made appetites to fully and thoroughly bless us, and that as we seek to satisfy them though his provision in dependence on him for fulfilment, we will be fully and completely satisfied as God intended.

Developing new faith – We have come to understand that to overcome the appetites, new faith is needed which must be faith in God, rather than faith in self. However we must understand this in the context of the two natures.

The old sinful nature is permanently corrupt, so all it is capable of is self-belief. This is why the sinful nature so stubbornly persistent in its belief that it can find satisfaction though its own means. It is only the new nature that can possibly have faith in God and move in total dependence on him. It therefore follows that we cannot simply acquire new faith; we must also have the new nature in control of our minds. We must therefore know our identity in Christ, and regularly affirm it as much as we need to by denying ourselves, and taking up the cross – by faith alone and not by self-effort, as discussed earlier. We can then embrace this article of faith regarding the specific appetite, and use it to control areas of self-indulgence, thereby bringing the appetites under the control of the Spirit.

Natural Appetites – Natural appetites have their purpose, but for many they also represent an arena where a significant physical and psychological battle is fought.

There is a growing problem with obesity in western society that is a cause of great distress to many. Christians are not exempt, and in many cases they have even greater problems as the war of the natures is often fought largely through self-effort, rather than through faith.

As one of the primary natural appetites of the body, we can examine this as a pertinent example of overcoming the world. What is clear is that the satisfaction derived from over indulgence in eating is largely false. Food and drink is only really properly enjoyed by those that have these appetites under proper control. If we want to see victory, how should we overcome in such an area?

---

[715] 1 Cor 10:31
[716] 1 Tim 6:17

CHAPTER 19: Overcoming the World

It is ironic that the obesity problem is most pronounced in the same societies that are promoting and embracing self-image to an unprecedented degree. The media constantly promote the idea of self-belief through self-image. This idea falls into the worldly category of *'the lust of the eyes'*; a form of self-belief based on what one has. To try to use self-image to control self-indulgence is to try to control the flesh with the flesh – in this case the *'lust of the flesh'* with the *'lust of the eyes'*. It is therefore an attempt to control one worldly expression with another. In the world such a trade-off is sometimes successfully made, but satisfaction is rarely derived from it. Instead what generally happens is that the form of dissatisfaction changes, and the self-belief is switched into a different form of expression of the world. Controlling one aspect of the flesh with another is generally to stimulate the flesh – not mortify it, as when we overcome the flesh by the Spirit. The flesh always therefore bounces back with new vigour, sometimes in a new form, but often in the same or all forms.

Through diet we may trade-off self-indulgence for vanity. In many cases those that succeed find that they soon slip back into old habits, and are back to square one, like a game of snakes and ladders, because through it all the overall effect is that the flesh has been stimulated. Others that successfully make the trade-off may find they then slip into an obsession with their image, and begin to derive their identity from it. This is in total contrast to overcoming the flesh by the Spirit though faith, in which case the flesh is genuinely mortified (put to death), dethroned and stripped of its power, leaving a lasting result of freedom with no backlash.

Believers that are still largely controlled by the sinful nature may for a time be sold the lie that flesh can be beaten by flesh, and they get drawn into it. However their real need to overcome is first to learn to walk in the Spirit through identification with Christ by faith, and secondly to receive faith in what will truly satisfy us in this area of appetite. The idea of trying to overcome the world with the world will clearly fail, which is part of the faith/understanding that is needed.

As born again believers, when we believe the worldly message that we must switch from one form of self-belief to another, we are drawn into a war zone where there are three parties engaged in the battle. These are two worldly beliefs that are vying for supremacy, together with the work of the Holy Spirit that is designed to convict us so we can see the folly of it all. Unsurprisingly life is tough for one that is embroiled in such a battle.

The solution is first to hand control over to the Spirit by identification with Christ by faith, then to ask God for new faith in the area of the appetite in question. Once again we would not seek to be our own source of faith; we would wholly depend on God to give it to us freely by grace. Anything else would be another form of independence. This new faith has the effect of convincing us that God's way is the highest good; the path of love, and only this can truly satisfy. We come to see how our appetites can serve us, and God through us, rather than us being their slave. Only God can deliver such faith to us, and it comes purely through asking. We are then able to reckon ourselves dead to the old nature in the area of this specific appetite, seeing it nailed to the cross. As a result we are able to walk as Christ in victory in this area of our life, rendering the sinful nature powerless.

All of this is done through receiving and applying faith, and it is in no way based on our own self effort. We find faith in our true identity; faith in the work of the cross to free us from our sinful nature; faith that only God can satisfy us in an area of appetite; faith that God will freely give us these items of faith. It is faith from first to last. As such the work is accomplished through total dependence on God, leaving us in a place of humility with only thankfulness, and no room for boasting in ourselves.

Having written this whole section I realised that I had accumulated an extra stone in weight during the last year, and that my words were somewhat hypocritical. When I realised my double standard, I was led to take a break in writing for a week and seek God for a word that would generate the faith to help me to overcome my enlarged appetite for food. I asked God to reveal any underlying problem, and got the unexpected response of 'hardness of heart'. On the same day that I received this revelation, a friend mentioned listening online to a teaching by on hardness of heart by *Andrew Wommack*, a teacher I respect. I had an assurance that I would find some revelation of faith there that I needed to overcome. The teaching defined hardness of heart as areas of insensitivity to God caused by living outside of the guidance of the Spirit. It ended by recommending fasting to diminish the voice of the flesh as one way to overcome these areas of hardness that are essentially pockets of unbelief. Through this word I gained real faith in the value of fasting, which was all I needed to put it into action.

There were also one or two other words that I received through this teaching that were essential for me. One of these was that in recent attempts at fasting I had become concerned at the level of reaction I seemed to get from my body – headaches, energy loss etc. that seemed to be much worse than when I had fasted in earlier years. I had developed a faith blocking idea that said now I am older, it would be much more difficult. Through things that were said in this teaching I realised that I had been deceived here, and the reaction of my body was simply from the fact that I had become undisciplined in this area. Basically my body was behaving like a spoiled brat, complaining and winging at the affliction I was imposing on it.

Remarkably the main revelation I received was not geared to losing weight, but to the potential for gaining something I find far more inspiring – the prospect of hearing God more clearly. I am certain that the trial of fasting for a longer period than I had ever done before, was no less difficult than it would be at any time, but the difference was I had the word of faith to carry me through it. Had my only motivation for fasting been to lose weight, I think I may well have caved when the self-affliction started to kick in, but the revelation I received of greater things gave me a much higher motivation that was enough to carry me through.

The way of faith is not a soft option. It faces the problem head on, but with the power and motivation to overcome. I am now a stone lighter, and happier for it, with a new sensitivity to God, particularly in the area of the appetite for food. The point is I didn't approach this problem independently of God through self-effort, as I would have done at one time. I sought to overcome by receiving a word of faith from God, which is the true way to overcome.

Drugs – Drugs are an unnatural indulgence of the lust of the flesh that is often very powerful and overwhelming in terms of the physical and psychological grip they gain over the user. The primary issue for a born again believer that comes into the kingdom with this kind of problem, is first for them to learn to receive mercy by undeserved grace, then to come into identification with Christ by faith.

Generally drug habits have a huge stigma that impose a whole identity on those that have this problem. The drug addict comes to see himself in precisely those terms; he believes that 'addict' is his true identity. As an addict is born again, his real victory can only come through seeing and believing the revelation that his true identity is not now 'drug addict' but it is 'Christ in him'. He learns to deny himself as a drug addict, thereby nailing that old sinful identity to the cross, and by faith he takes on his true identity and life, which is the life of Christ that was made available to him on the cross.

For drug abuse social workers, the last thing a Christian drug addict needs is co-dependent help that only continues to affirm them as an addict. They need to be given faith in the truth of their new identity.

Generally with such cases it is not then necessary to convince an addict that the path of love is to cease his indulgence in the drug habit. His experience will normally have convinced him of that. The walk of the Spirit by faith is therefore the key issue. The addict may have to stand against a prolonged onslaught of accusation that tries for a time to re-impose the old identity, but he will overcome by relying on God for the faith to sustain him in the truth of who he really is, as someone who has Christ within. In this way, by the persistent application of faith, he can come through to a new life where Christ is manifest in victory over his drug problem.

Once again, it will not be accomplished through self-effort, but by grace through faith alone, and when the work is done there will be no room for boasting, just humility and thankfulness to God. This does not mean a person with this kind of addiction will not first go through the typical cycles of trying by self-effort, and failing, but that he must eventually come to see the truth about himself as a new creature, by faith, to really overcome.

Sexual indulgence – As a powerful and primary area of appetite, sexual indulgence must be challenged in the same way. For a believer, failure in the area of sexual appetites generally brings with it huge problems of condemnation, as do the other areas of failure. The condemnation is in itself the expression of an identity, but for the born again believer it is a false one. That is why the apostle Paul says: '*there is no condemnation to those who are in Christ Jesus*'. The reason is because '*in Christ Jesus*' is the true identity of the believer regardless of the failure.

A Christian with these problems must learn first to continually receive undeserved grace in the form of mercy, where there is such failure. They must then overcome the problem by identification with Christ, realising by faith that the sexual habits and failures are not an expression

CHAPTER 19: Overcoming the World 327

of their true identity, but of a former self that now has no valid claim on them. In its place one must ask God for a word of faith; perhaps for a new revelation of the opposite sex that will allow them to see them in the same terms that Jesus saw the women who were his friends. Of course the needed revelation in every case depends on what the real underlying problem is. In these terms the opposite sex may then be seen with complete purity, and valued as important relationships in life that must be cherished, but in no way exploited. We come to understand that by exploitation the possibility for these pure relationships are destroyed, leaving a deep area of need.

Often the deception in this area is the failure to realise that all people need pure relationships with both sexes, however the possibility for this is often destroyed by sexual habits that believe satisfaction can be achieved independently of God. It is only as the value of purity in such relationships is discovered, that the fulfilment of the need for them is discovered. We must ask God to give this revelation of the value and satisfaction of pure relationships with the opposite sex. Such an outlook will then often release even married couples, who are experiencing problems, into the full intimacy that their relationship should have, including the sexual aspects of that relationship. We discover the truth by faith, that sinful sexual indulgences in fact rob us of all satisfaction in relationships with the opposite sex.

Both the whole of the identity of the old nature, and the specific areas of habit and failure can be nailed to the cross by faith, and the true identity of '*Christ in me*' affirmed. Once again the Christian may need to persist with his faith in his true identity, even in the face of repeated failure in this area, to come through into full experiential victory over it. As in all cases, the victory will not be won by self-effort, though many seem to have to try and fail on that path first. It will be won through faith, and all that naturally comes with it, and once accomplished there will again be no room for boasting, only humility and thankfulness to God.

It is particularly important in the area of sexual indulgence that the Christian earnestly asks God for faith to believe that real sexual satisfaction can only come through God's provision, and that God fully intends that he/she finds his provision and enabling. This is true both in the form of a sexual partner in marriage, and in the grace for the necessary abstention that is needed in some measure, both in or out of a marriage relationship. It must be realised that condemnation will only exacerbate the problem, rather than solve it. Condemnation must therefore be refused, because it is not something that comes from God but from the old nature. As such it can only hinder the quest for victory. The grace of mercy is the right way to deal with all failure, while holding on to faith in one's true identity until experiential victory is established.

I recently heard a profound view on sex in marriage – that the marriage bed is a sanctuary! As such it is a special gift of God. To get the right view of faith on marriage is to access this kind of intimacy. Something which God intended for us, and that is made to reflect the very intimacy of Christ and his bride, the true church.

I have already shared some of the details of my personal mistakes, becoming involved in a relationship at a fairly early age. This led to the inevitable problems, but even after this as a married man, and having been a Christian for many years, there were still areas in which I needed to discover real victory. There are occasions when we find ourselves unavoidably assailed by temptation in these areas. How should we handle these times?

In the early years of my Christian walk I developed some defence mechanisms of my own as a kind of self-protection. As I was working in a fairly aggressive male environment in the coal mines, at the time I developed a kind of aggressive defensive stance that I brought home with me, that would keep me out of trouble whenever unwanted attention came my way from the opposite sex. This proved for many years to be enough to ward off such advances. However this was not something of the Spirit, but something of myself; something religious, and as such it had some undesirable side effects of limiting all my relationships to some extent.

Despite this I was growing spiritually, and I remember a time, having come through and out of legalism, where I felt for once that I was spiritually doing quite well; a rare thing in my early walk. I even received some prophetic confirmation that this was so. However, what I didn't realise at the time was that this was a precursor to some real testing times that were about to come upon me, through which God was going to challenge and strip away some of my home made defences.

It came in the form of attention from the opposite sex, but instead of them heeding the warnings of my aggressive posture and demeanour, they came straight through it as though it didn't even exist. Here was opportunity from someone who was attractive, free, and available. The impact of it took me by surprise. My only recourse was to run to God and lean hard on him, continually asking for the faith and revelation I needed to get through this challenge, without falling. In response God constantly gave me insight to see the deceitfulness of what was on offer. I was given revelation to realise the mess and the hurt that would be caused, and the insight to see the inevitable failure that such a step would ever bring me satisfaction in life. I realised the truth; that only by dependence on God could satisfaction be found in my relationships. I had to get as close to God as possible and stay there until the trial passed, which lasted for months. Faith overcame. After the event I was much stronger in this department, and nothing has since come close. The faith I received then is still with me, without my ever falling into the trap of such a devastating mistake. One thing is certain: having come through it I could not claim any credit. The resources to overcome were entirely found in God, otherwise I would have almost certainly failed.

Given the problems that churches have had in recent years in these areas, I count myself fortunate not to have been overcome by these temptations, however I have to reflect on the fact that the church is awash with teachings that in the final analysis come down to 'try harder', 'you can do it' doctrines. The hallmark of these ideas is their self-belief, self-effort, and independence of God, rather than complete dependence on him. As such they appeal only to the sinful nature, and we end up trying to overcome the flesh by the flesh. It is these very ideas that have engineered the epidemic of failure we have seen in churches in recent years. When testing times come, they prove to be totally inadequate to meet the challenge. Though it goes against natural reason, it is only the doctrine of *'by grace through faith'*, in complete dependence on God, that will ultimately overcome.

Overcoming – the lust of the eyes

This is self-belief based of what one has; or vanity. It is naturally competitive, depending on comparisons with others. It is an attempt to assert ones value as a person based on the views and reactions of others. As such it is parasitic.

The truth of our identity in Christ is the very antithesis of this worldly view. When we see the truth of who we really are, we discover our true value as a person in the eyes of God, rather than the eyes of men. We find ourselves affirmed in our own intrinsic value as an individual without reference to the views of others of us. As such the whole competitive element of worldly self-esteem is stripped out of our thinking, which has the effect of liberating us to love and value others without them threatening our security or sense of self-worth in any way.

We come to derive our own sense of value from the very value we place on Christ himself. He is our life, and the more we appreciate him, the more we gain in terms of a sense of our own worth. The cross is a supreme expression of our worth to God, proven by the fact that he was willing to send his valuable Son to save us from an otherwise wretched condition.

The true wretchedness of the sinful condition is much of what the lust of the eyes seeks to cover up. However, as believers, who are in Christ and have Christ in them as their true identity, there is nothing to cover. Only when the sinful nature manages to impose a false identity will we find any compulsion to do so. When we come to believe in our true identity, we find the freedom to live openly and transparently, so the truth of our identity is all that is needed to overcome this form of worldliness.

Overcoming – the pride of life

This is self-belief based on what one does. It includes the fundamental belief of the old nature in its own abilities, and its self-sufficiency. The real problems come when one projects this belief into a religious form, and we come to believe in self-improvement independently of God. True Christian character is only developed in one way, and that is by living by the Spirit and becoming wholly dependent on God.

The film 'Chariots of Fire' presents a fascinating study of two men and their different approaches to winning an Olympic gold medal in the sprint events of the 1924 games in Paris. One was a Christian who discovered his strength and source in God through faith. The other was driven by self-belief, with an overwhelming desire to prove himself.

Both methods yielded success in the form of a gold medal, but we are left to ponder the effect of these successes on the development of the character of these individuals. Clearly the success of the former enhanced his belief in God as his source, and therefore his dependence on him. The success of the latter would only have entrenched him further in self-belief. The problem comes when such success is projected into the development of character. With the achievements of self-belief often comes increasing pride and self-reliance that eventually leads to a fall. Fortunately such athletes often discover their limits and experience a fair amount failure before they come to succeed, which has the effect of humbling them. However there are some definite examples among sportsmen where the corruption of self-belief becomes inflated to a point of self-corruption, or even self-destruction of character, as it has for many that achieve worldly success.

As the Psalmist and other Bible writers observe; some succeed in life in worldly terms, but only to their own destruction. However for a Christian that has destiny, God has to discipline such belief to bring it to the place of wholesale dependence on him as their source. Seasons of failure and weakness often therefore characterise the experience of a Christian, where they are taken to the edge of themselves so that they may come to depend on God and not on themselves[717]. In this way God leads them to overcome the independence of their sinful nature, and they come to wholly depend on God, knowing and believing that they can do nothing of any spiritual value without his enabling.

Once we come into faith that we can do nothing by ourselves, then this faith overcomes our worldly thinking. We are then free to discover the truth that *'I can do all things through Christ who strengthens me'*.

Overcoming – The World, the Flesh and the Devil

When we realise the truth of grace, we escape the trap of living under law, which is a fruitless existence governed by worldly principles. We are then in a position to challenge the flesh and mortify it by the Spirit, through faith. At this point we often meet extraordinary resistance from the devil, who would push us back into the flesh by accusations that attempt to impose false fleshly identities, and undermine our new found faith that it is Christ in us who is our true identity. If he succeeds in this, he will go further and try to re-impose the principles of law that will then keep us in perpetual failure. He seeks to achieve all of this by the only weapon left in his armoury, which is deception.

Why does the Devil fight our progress so aggressively? – Because if we overcome both the world (law), and the flesh, we are then in a position to challenge him directly. Once the flesh is mortified, we are free to engage in the spiritual battle. All it then takes is a further revelation from the Spirit of our authority over the devil, and all his works, for us to become a highly destructive force against the kingdom of darkness.

---

[717] 2 Cor 1:9

Therefore the devil fights our progress tooth and nail with all he has, because he knows that the realisation of who we really are spells his demise in the sphere and domain of our lives, and ultimately the lives of others. However, though this resistance is fierce, we have the assurance and guarantee of victory if we press forward in the Spirit, because *'greater is he that is in you than he that is in the world'*.

We then enter the ranks of the overcomers, with the rewards of the joy of victory both for ourselves and others, together with the inheritance that is promised to all that overcome – which are substantial indeed!

CHAPTER 20: Fire

Overcoming

We have discussed the issues of overcoming the world though faith, and the fact that there is both an instantaneous application, and a progressive application of faith, that together lead to experiential victory over the old spirit and the old nature. This is generally the way by which we overcome the world and move into the blessing God has for us.

However, just as there is the general gift of faith, and there are special gifts of faith for specific times and purposes, so there are also times and ways that God enables us to seasonally surge ahead of our state of growth, and experience victory that is beyond the norm we have grown into. These times are driven and characterised by the fire of God.

The symbol of fire

God made fire – man only discovered it. As with all natural physical things, in the phenomenon of fire there is a spiritual parallel and reflection of a spiritual reality. The symbol of fire is used widely in the Bible, and is often associated with holiness. When Moses saw the burning bush, he was told to remove his sandals because he stood on holy ground.

It appears in the context of the temple and the sacrifices. All the utensils that could withstand fire were cleansed by it. In the book of Hebrews, God himself is described to be a consuming fire. This particularly raises questions, because even as we began we stated another Bible verse that says God is Love. How does fire relate to Love?

A further symbol that sometimes invokes much fear is the symbol of the lake of fire, as found in the book of Revelation. It is declared to be the place of the final demise and destruction of Satan, of all those that are not spiritually reborn, of all evil, and finally of death itself. We read that John the Baptist proclaimed that the baptism of fire is a ministry of Jesus. John said that though he baptised with water, someone was coming after him that would baptise with fire. That someone is Jesus.

Then we see tongues of fire appearing on the day of Pentecost as each of the disciples were filled with the power of the Holy Spirit, and they suddenly step forward with uncharacteristic boldness and power. How do we understand all this?

The lake of fire

The lake of fire in the book of Revelation is a fearful symbol of a real spiritual place, because it is often associated with judgement, and as the place of final destruction of all that is evil. But what is it?

What is clear is that the lake of fire is only a threat to all that is unholy. Fire is associated with cleansing and consecration. In the modern day, where we are familiar with the existence of germs, we know it to be a means through which we can cleanse things, such as metal utensils, that can themselves withstand it.

As something of heaven, the lake of fire is itself holy. As with the New Jerusalem all that is in heaven is of God. The fire is the same in this respect. In fact we can say that the fire is God, who we are told in the book of Hebrews is a consuming fire[718]. It is an expression of the pure holiness of God. As such, all that is holy is completely comfortable with it, and indeed delight in it. This includes the holy angels, and all men that have been spiritually reborn.

For renewed men, their life is the life of Christ in them – the life of God. The old nature is not part of them, though in this world they continue to suffer its false claims, and its persecution in the form of attempts to re-impose deceptive false sinful identities.

The lake of fire therefore holds no threat for all that are holy, but only for the evil and corrupt, including Satan, the fallen angels, and the old nature. The lake is designed for the destruction of all that is unholy. The new spiritual man is holy, and therefore has nothing to fear from the lake of fire; he will know nothing of its destruction. When we swim in the oceans of this world in our present bodies of flesh, our bodies are largely made of the very same thing – water. In the same way, when we encounter the lake of fire with our new and immortal spiritual bodies, there the holy is meeting the holy, so though we may be awed by the sight of it, as we are for the oceans of this world, yet we feel no threat. In fact the last enemy that is thrown into the fire is death itself, so the fire continues to exist even after death has ceased to be possible for those that remain, because all that remains is holy.

---

[718] Heb 12:29

In the book of Hebrews, the priest Melchizedek was one of the appearances of Christ, going out in ancient times. He was declared to have *'the power of an indestructible life'*. This same life is what we now possess as Christ within, and it is equally indestructible.

Were we in our present condition, to encounter the fire of God with our spiritual being, it would have only one effect; that is to drive the old spirit and nature of flesh far from us in terror, otherwise that old nature would be utterly destroyed. This leads to an understanding of the effects of fire when applied to us in this age.

When Satan and all fallen beings are thrown into the fire, including our old nature; that is no longer us and has no valid claim on us, then they will be utterly consumed, leaving only something like a fossilised record – *their worm does not die and their fire is not quenched*. I see it like the vacuum of the void of their being is suddenly purged and filled with holy fire. For them it is like the ultimate retreat into self and non-existence. We are told that at present men will not come into the light and be exposed. The fire forces them out of even the remnants of the dead spiritual existence that they continue to cling to, because they cannot abide even near that which is holy. Their memory will be the only thing of them of value, serving to affirm the faith in all beings that go on into the eternity of ages, that evil is unthinkable, and there is only life in God.

The baptism of fire

John the Baptist proclaimed that Jesus would bring a ministry of the baptism of fire. This is the same fire that we see in the lake of fire in heaven. When we are baptised in it, the effect is to drive the old nature from us.

We have previously discussed at length the experiential victory that is revealed over the old nature by faith, as we progressively grow to live by faith, but the application of fire is something else. It comes to us in the same way as all other things of God; as a gift by grace through faith, as we wait on God and trust him for it by faith.

As it comes it has the effect of overcoming all the power of the old sinful nature that clings to us, driving it away from us. We are thereby launched into an experience of complete victory and liberty over the old nature, before ever growing to the place where faith has totally overcome the old nature directly.

This liberty is experienced for as long as the fire of God persists upon us. If and when the fire ceases, and the old nature finds the confidence to attack us again, we are once again thrown onto the need to overcome the sinful nature directly by the application of faith in all areas.

While fire persists upon us, the experience we have is just like the experience of Jesus in his walk and ministry on the earth. We are empowered to hear God clearly without inhibition, and move in all the gifts of the Spirit, overcoming all the power of the enemy. We trample on snakes and scorpions, applying the fire to them and making them flee in terror.

If we were able to walk consistently in the Spirit, without ever being tripped by the flesh, the power we wield would be exactly the same, but baptism has the effect of releasing us into a foretaste of this experience, even before we have matured and grown to the point of total victory by faith. The flesh and the devil find themselves unable to prevent it. They have to stand aside and let it happen.

Shadrach, Meshach and Abednego

These three contemporaries of the prophet Daniel dared to resist Nebuchadnezzar, the king of Babylon, by refusing to bow down to his golden idol. As a result they faced and defied the king's threat to throw them into the fiery furnace by declaring to him that God was able to deliver them, or even if he didn't they would not bow down and worship his image. In anger, the furnace was stoked to seven times the normal heat, and even those that threw them in fell dead through the heat. The king then saw the three of them walking around in the fire, with the figure of a fourth who looked to the king like *'the son of the gods'*. All that burned was the bonds that tied them, and as the king called them out there was not even the smell of burning on their clothes.

These times in Israel's history are highly symbolic, and this event expresses the truth that the fire is no threat to those that belong to God. The only thing that will happen when we encounter the fire of God, is that we will be completely liberated from the remaining bonds of the old corrupt and sinful nature of flesh. The fire will drive it from us.

The fire of revival

Revivals are characterised by the discovery, or rediscovery, of the fire of God. In these events we see the fire of God unleashed upon individuals that then go out in ministry and impact people in remarkable ways. Often the unsaved experience the overwhelming fear of God, as they have close encounters with a taste of the pending fire of God from the lake, and seeing their depravity and impending destruction, they turn to God in a step of radical repentance, and are reborn. As a result we see radical revivals, with many coming to Christ under the influence of the gift of the fire of the Holy Spirit.

For example, when the revival of the great awakening broke out in the mid-18th century under the preaching of Jonathon Edwards, the Wesley's, and George Whitfield, it was reported that as Jonathon Edwards preached, people clung to the church pillars, fearing that they would there and then slip into hell. Interestingly, he had preached the same sermon before to the same congregation, but it had had little impact on them. The Wesley's and Whitfield witnessed people that were desperate to be saved as they came under the conviction of the fire on them. In the mid-19th century Finney experienced similar things, at one time simply walking into a factory and having people immediately come to repentance under powerful conviction of sin. I very recently heard of similar things happening among women prisoners in the prisons of Argentina, where revival fire has been raging for some time.

What is very interesting about such revival, that is a source of distress to some, is that when a season of fire passes the individuals that led the way in it often revert to former patterns of worldly and sinful behaviour from areas of their lives that have not yet been overcome by the deliberate and direct application of faith. However this is exactly what we would expect by this understanding of the effects of fire.

Some in revivals tend to idolise men as they experience the holiness of God upon them, but the mistake is to fail to realise that this is a gift of grace, and not something that comes to them by merit. It is also no indication that they are mature believers, or have yet found real spiritual victory by faith and developed any level of character. Nor is it an indication that they have a great heavenly reward either before or after the event, because the reward is associated to their development of character – gold, silver, and precious jewels.

Having said that, to come into such an experience is usually evidence of a measure of faith, which means they have experienced some development of character. However they may not have come to develop significantly in the other fruits, or the character of God.

The baptism of fire can happen to any that are open for it. Ironically there are times when the request is made for entirely wrong motives, but God still grants it for reasons of the highest good that only he can know. If such a person comes into an experience of fire, it may for a while mask the issues of faith that person still has, but God will get to work on those things once his purpose is accomplished.

Once the fire is withdrawn, the battle of faith for growth continues, and the sinful nature even seeks to use the revival and the experience of fire against them for its own ends in any way it can. Such experiences can then become another area that they have to come to terms with through faith.

As Finney observed; who is known as America's greatest evangelist. Once a revival is over it will often leave a deeper and lasting work accomplished in a community well after the fire seems to have gone. This is not always appreciated by those that are looking only at the outward signs. Equally, those that were instrumental in it may come through with some character development as a result, provided it does not push them into some sort of independence of God, or evoke in them the kind of self-belief that is prevalent in the world.

Seeing the value of baptism from this point of view, it is a great thing for God to move in this way, and we should desire it for the good it will do. For those that are prominent in such a move, humility and faith based on grace are the best defence against any counter or after moves of the flesh to exploit it.

CHAPTER 21: The Final Chapter

The wisdom of the cross

As the apostle Paul said: the cross is foolishness to this world, but it is in fact the highest wisdom of God. We have seen that the cross is in fact the very pinnacle of the wisdom of the ages. It is the folly of this world to pursue its own vanity and pride, while at the same time charting a course into inner corruption. The more independent of God a man becomes, the more keenly he feel this inner penalty. Happily for some, they come to recognise the emptiness of such a life, and abandon the road, turning to God before they push on to its full consequences. The conclusion of the matter is simple: man needs God, and if they want him they can find him – at the cross.

Faith, hope and love remain

The things that carry through from this age to the next are faith, hope, and love. Faith – the very foundation of heaven and the solid security of the eternal ages of ages. Hope – the ever present expectation that we will continue to move from age to age, always seeing God as higher and greater than we ever anticipated. Love – the eternal nature of God with its numerous forms of expression, including all the fruits of the Spirit that last for all the ages.

The final victory

The apostle Paul understood the effects of the sinful nature; that it acts like a drag anchor on our lives as it tries to slow us up and pull us down. He looked forward to the day that he would hack it loose and sail freely with the wind. That day has come for him; he has reached his eternal home.

For us we should take the same attitude to the old nature as Paul – who will rescue me from this body of death! I thank God through Jesus Christ our Lord[719]. While we are in this world, the sinful nature will always be there hanging around like the ever hopeful opportunist it is. This is a fact of our existence in this age of evil we live in, but we should look

---

[719] Rom 7:24

forward to far better, and something that makes the sufferings here look light and momentary, as Paul said it would.

As it did for Paul, it only takes a glimpse of heaven, and our new and glorious spiritual body that God has prepared for us, to make us yearn and groan for it. It is a mercy that we only see a faint glimpse of it now, or we would find this world much harder to bear. For the time being we should take comfort that God has assured us of victory, and that when the work is complete we will come into the awesome inheritance he has promised us.

Heaven is coming

Heaven is really much nearer than we think. On this earth time is short. We live with the knowledge that we could in fact reach our eternal destination at any moment. The day of our death is something God knows; he has seen it and it is a precious thing to him. We can be sure that as we make our anticipated entrance into that glorious City, there will be the loud and joyful ovation of saints and angels. Not only to welcome us, but as praise to the God who has brought us home, and done all things well.

Every angel in heaven, and every one of our brethren, are set to be our companions for eternity. They long for our fellowship in the intimacy of that place. All will be released from the husk and chaff of this body and the old nature, and in ours and every case they will come forth in perfection and beauty, perfectly fitted to our new and glorious eternal home in heaven – the New Jerusalem; our Mother. In her we will find every comfort and joy that makes the brief sufferings of this world worthwhile. Here we are merely in the preface of the ages. There the real story of God's purposes begins.

Then for the first time we will see the Lord in all his glory. We will know the love and rest that there is in his presence, and like David we will always be satisfied to the very core of our being with seeing his face.

The final word

Having said all I have to say, I must end by saying this. Soon dear reader we will meet in that glorious place, and when we do you may say to me thanks for the book, but I suspect you will be compelled to add – it didn't even come close to the full truth. And I suspect when you say that to me, I will heartily and humbly agree. So remember my fellow believer, we only see these things as a dark shadow and as a faint reflection through our presently dim eyes of the spirit. No matter how far we explore the truth, until we get there it will always be true that – *No eye has seen, no ear has heard what God has prepared for those that love him, but God has revealed it to us by his Spirit*. We must see it now through the eyes of the spirit which is through the sight of faith – it is the only way.

And when we finally come into that place of glory and magnificence beyond anything we have even ever dreamt, then of one thing we can be sure, both now and forever, that amidst all of that glory when we see the Lord Jesus face to face we will always be compelled from the very depths of our being to say to our precious and mighty Lord Jesus 'thank you, thank you, thank you for the cross.'

Maranatha – Come Lord Jesus, Come!

EPILOGUE

In writing this manuscript I was led to mention Job a number of times as probably the primary biblical example of a man who passed through extreme trials of faith, and came through, not just with his faith intact, but eternally enriched by his trials and experience. These are the riches of the Spirit, and they were reflected in the latter season of his life when God not only blessed him by multiplying back to him wealth and honour, but also it seems by even doubling his lifespan – he lived another 140 years at a time when 120 years would have been a full lifespan. I therefore fully expect to see him among the 24 Elders that encircle the throne when I get to the heavenly city of the New Jerusalem, as described in the book of Revelation, along with many ancients whose life has been used in a similar way to teach and enrich us by their knowledge and experience.

We know the details of the outcome for Job because the last chapter of the book ends with what some translators have headed as an Epilogue. Though I would not dare to compare my life and trials with Job, because they seem miniscule by comparison, I decided (not wanting to be left out) to follow suit, and just say a final word about some of my own circumstances at the time of writing this book, especially since I alluded to it in the text without sharing the details.

At the time I began writing I had just got to the end of a business research and development venture, where to proceed further would have meant me finding considerable investment. Just two months before completion of the project the credit crunch hit, and caused unprecedented events in the global financial sector, where many banks and financial institutions around the world came close to bankruptcy, with some actually going under. My natural instinct at this time was to turn back to the software development that had been my main source of work and income before this venture, just to survive. However God had other plans, and I was led to disregard fairly dire circumstances, and do what he was telling me to do – to write the book. The desire to do this had been growing in my heart for some time, and I had expected to come to it when I was financially secure and could afford to take the time. However God's call to get on with it now was clear to my heart, and I found the conviction and faith I needed to hold my nerve and get on with the task.

The book took a few months, and by the time I had completed the first draft my circumstances seemed even worse. At the time I knew of no way through, other than God, but I had no idea of the means he would use to get me through. Then, having completed the task five months after starting, I came to my 50th birthday. I had a pension fund from the first 11 years of my career from when I trained and worked as an engineering manager in the UK coal mining industry. According to my understanding, this fund would not pay up anything until I was at least 55 years old because the government had changed the rules in the last few years. As it turned out I received a pay-out of 25% of the fund on my 50th birthday, because for whatever reason, the rules did not apply to me. I was (perhaps foolishly) completely unaware of this, but what is clear is that God knew, and he used these events to lead me to take steps that have now, once again, caused my faith and trust in him to grow immensely, and it has completely justified the step of faith I took, and my trust in him.

At God's leading, the book has been left to mature for some years, like aging wine, but I am now prompted to release it, while once again under a similar challenge. But I have the same confidence that my circumstances will work out in a similar, but no doubt unique way. I guess my point in all this is simply to say that in this same way God has tailored the very details and trials of your life too, for the development of your faith and all the fruit that is, and will be, built upon it. These things are of supreme and eternal value to you, and to God, despite the challenges you may be facing, and so they are to be received with joy and thanksgiving at all times. His plan is to spiritually enrich you beyond anything you have ever dreamed. Once you get this perspective on your life, you can just learn to rest in it, and enjoy the roller coaster, no matter how extreme the circumstances that you face, because even though it is sometimes scary, if there is anything you can be certain of it is this – you are God's craftsmanship, and he is going to finish the work he has started in you, and when it is done then you are going to stand back with him and say – 'Yes Lord, it is good, very good. It is well with my soul'.

GOD BLESS

www.ingramcontent.com/pod-product-compliance
Lightning Source LLC
Chambersburg PA
CBHW061630040426
42446CB00010B/1348